David Janssen
Our Conversations

The Early Years
(1965-1972)

Michael Phelps

To Darleana Kathryn Janssen, a sensitive, passionate lady, one of David's favorites! Best of everything!

Mike Phelps
April, 2015

DAVID JANSSEN – Our Conversations
Volume One * The Early Years
1965-1972
Copyright © 2014 Michael Phelps

Cover design: Bradleigh S. Stockwell
Editor/Interior Design: Norma Budden

978-0-9887778-2-8
Blue Line Publishing House, Inc.
New York, NY   *   Miami, FL

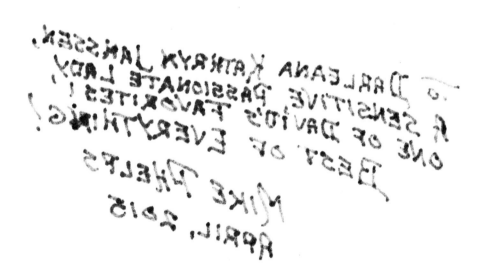

DEDICATION

There are many people who inspired me to write this book.

I would like to thank each of David Janssen's devoted fans, not only fans of *The Fugitive* but fans who appreciate his other works, both in television and film.

My special thanks to award-winning singer/songwriter Carol Connors of Beverly Hills, California for all of her help and contributions.

She and David co-wrote the lyrics of the title song, *My Sensitive, Passionate Man* with Carol Connors and Bill Conti writing the music for the NBC Movie of the Week starring David Janssen and Angie Dickinson. They also collaborated on many other songs.

David wrote the lyrics to a song especially for Carol titled, *If I Could, I Would*. He then asked Carol to write the music. To my knowledge, this is the only song Dave wrote for a lady he truly loved.

Ms. Connors is one woman whom David wanted to marry. Personally, I believe had David lived to obtain his planned divorce from his second wife, he and Carol would have re-connected, married and he would, perhaps, be with us today.

Mrs. Lone Agri of Odense, Denmark - one of David's most devoted fans - has visited David's crypt and other sites and is an annual donor to the McKinley Home in David's memory. My thanks for her inspiration, encouragement and graciously sharing her vast collection of photos and memorabilia.

Mr. Kenneth Huckstep of Kent, England and Naples, Florida - a devoted fan of David's - has my sincere gratitude for his inspiration and unwavering support.

Dr. Richard Peshkin, M.D. and his lovely wife Karen of Boca Raton, Florida: I have no doubt Dave would be humbly grateful for their dedication to him. They have been an inspiration to me throughout this project,

Ms. Pamela Edwards of Luling, Texas for the beautiful and moving tribute videos she has made to David Janssen and posted on YouTube. Link: https://www.youtube.com/watch?v=FSs1arBgAlk

Ms. Diane Quinlivan of Albany, Louisiana: my deepest thanks for her devotion to David and sharing her many videos with me.

Ms. Darlena Katherine Janssen of Concord, California: a single mother whom David helped, quietly, in her time of need. As a very talented poet she has written a book of poems dedicated to David which she has shared with me. It is my hope she will publish her book and share it with all of Dave's fans.

My deepest thanks to the *David Janssen Archives* which provides a wealth of information and trivia about David and his career. Link: http://davidjanssen.net/

Mr. Bobby Nearenberg for his creation of *The Fugitive Views & Reviews* on Yahoo Groups, his excellent reviews of every episode of *The Fugitive* and his forum for David Janssen fans from around the world to exchange their views and remember Dave for all he gave us.

Mr. Moises Raudez of Miami, Florida: my photographer, creative artist and good friend for his support during this long journey with my friend, David Janssen.

Mr. Bradleigh S. Stockwell of Vermont: a devoted fan of David Janssen and a gifted and talented Graphic Artist for his design of the covers for this book. You may e-mail Mr. Stockwell at koloman@pacbell.net.

My sincere gratitude to the many friends and fellow actors with whom I spoke during this project. I thank each for their valuable time and the kind words and glowing praises each had for David.

PREFACE

I first met David and Ellie Janssen at a formal party held in the palatial Bel Air mansion of International Hotelier, Conrad Hilton, in October of 1965. I was part of the private security detail and part of my duty was to wander around the ballroom, yet be inconspicuous.

This was a very formal affair, with the male guests wearing tuxedos and the ladies in designer gowns, wearing what I presumed to be very real and very expensive jewelry.

The security staff was dressed in charcoal grey trousers, white dress shirts, burgundy ties and navy blue blazers. The wait staff wore tuxedo trousers, white dress shirts, black bow ties and white waist jackets with gold-plated buttons, gold-braided shoulder boards and white gloves. The scene was right out of a Hollywood movie. I chuckled to myself.

There were 450 guests on the list for this dinner party. The event was held in the ballroom which was as large as the grand ballroom of the Waldorf Astoria Hotel in New York City, which Mr. Hilton owned. A full orchestra entertained the guests. Cocktails flowed from two bars; aperitifs were passed around on sterling silver platters.

Many of the most famous film and television stars were on the guest list as well as many major business leaders and politicians. I am not one to feel in awe in the presence of celebrities, mainly due to the fact I am not a serious film or television fan. Also, I learned during my Air Force service that every man puts his pants on the same way I do - one leg at a time.

David and Ellie Janssen were among the legendary Hollywood *A* list. Their presence was sought by the highest ranking of the film, television and business leaders in Los Angeles.

I was walking toward the main bar in the northeast corner of the ballroom as they entered. I had seen a few episodes of *The Fugitive* which was now in its third season. I recognized Mr. Janssen instantly.

Being from Indiana, originally, I was familiar with the infamous case of Dr. Sam Sheppard of Cleveland, Ohio. As I knew it, the real Dr. Sheppard was in prison for life.

Observing Mr. and Mrs. Janssen as they walked in, I noted he looked a lot better in his tuxedo, cleaner and more debonair than he did in some of the clothes he wore on the show.

Mrs. Janssen was radiant; she was absolutely beautiful. He was indeed a very lucky man, I thought.

I observed a waiter take their drink order and briskly walk to the bar to fill it. As the waiter returned with their drinks, Mrs. Janssen left David's side and walked over to speak to a small group of other ladies.

Mr. Janssen walked slowly towards the main bar sipping his drink, smiling, nodding and shaking hands with other guests. By the time he arrived at the bar, his glass was empty.

He asked the barman for a scotch and soda, a double. I could not help but notice his demeanor. His eyes darted all around the room. His gaze was intense; he appeared to be physically tired and not really in the mood to be at a party. I was standing less than three feet from him and noted he was taller than he appeared on television.

Perhaps he felt me staring at him because he turned and faced me directly. "I assume you are working," he said.

"Yes, Sir! Security staff," I replied.

"Are you one of the off-duty LAPD officers?"

"No, Sir! Private security, although I am trying to get on the police department. I was Military Police Combat Defense Forces in the Air Force," I answered.

"You look like a cop ... so you have law enforcement in your blood. Anyone in your family cops?"

"No, Sir! My paternal grandfather and an uncle were Circuit Court Judges. I'm the 'black sheep' of the family; I chose to go into law enforcement." I smiled.

"I was in the army and I don't know many guys who wanted to be an MP. Usually they were the most hated guys, at least in the army," he said with a grin.

"Yes, Sir! That is certainly true in the Air Force, too, but I have close friends who are on the police department back home and I asked for it when I enlisted. I was lucky; I became a Canine Handler so it was mostly pretty good duty."

"What kind of dog did you handle?"

"German Shepherd. I had the only female on the base. Of course, she was spayed and the males were neutered."

Our conversation was interrupted by Mrs. Janssen who came to pull him over to a small gathering of ladies.

I wandered around the room carefully observing the actions of all of the *big shots*. As they consumed more and more alcohol, their demeanor would change. Some inhibitions loosened. Soon I was back at the bar, indulged in idle conversation with the head barman.

Mr. Janssen sauntered over to the bar again, sans his wife, and ordered a double scotch and soda. Receiving his drink he walked over to me again. "I didn't introduce myself. I'm Dave Janssen," he said warmly.

"Mike Phelps," I said as we shook hands. "I know who you are; I've seen several episodes of *The Fugitive* and I was a fan of *Richard Diamond-Private Detective* before I joined the Air Force."

I did not know if I would get into trouble chatting with a guest, but that was really of no concern. After all, he is the one who started a conversation with me.

"Do you like the show?" he asked with sincerity.

"Yes. Actually, I think it is one of the best shows on TV and yes, I think you are very believable in your portrayal of *Dr. Kimble*, and I still think the real Dr. Sam Sheppard is innocent."

"Interesting ... you know, so do I. The creator of our show, Roy Huggins, has not admitted the show is based on Sheppard, but the coincidences between the two are too close. Unfortunately, the real doctor didn't have a train wreck to spring him," he said, grinning broadly.

"I have to agree with you ... too many similarities between the two: Dr. Sheppard from Ohio, Dr. Kimble from Indiana; both physicians; ... a wife who had a miscarriage and a wife who was pregnant; both wives brutally bludgeoned to death; a mysterious intruder who escapes; no witnesses ... yes ... too many similarities," I mused.

"Yeah, but I've been on the run a long time," he chuckled.

"This is your third season, isn't it? How long are you going to remain a fugitive?" I asked with a grin.

"Who knows? As long as the writing is solid, the plots remain interesting and we maintain our ratings ... who knows?" he replied with a serious, yet contemplative look.

I noted his voice was the same as it came across on television, very deep and distinct.

"So, how long have you lived in Los Angeles?" he asked.

"I've been here about six months."

"Do you have family here ... married, kids?"

"No, I recently separated from my wife ... no family here, they are all back in Indiana."

"Where do you live? LA is so spread out."

"I live on North Highland, just off Santa Monica Boulevard."

"Oh, that's close to the studio; we'll have to get together for a drink sometime, maybe lunch," he offered sincerely.

"That would be nice. I'd like that," I responded with a smile.

"Ellie and I are not staying for the dinner; I've had a long day so we'll be leaving soon. Let me have your number and I'll give you a call."

I gave him my business card with my home phone number written on the back. He gave me his card and scribbled his private number on the back.

Ellie walked over smiling and planted a warm kiss on his cheek. "Are you ready, sweetheart, or do you want to stay and have another drink?"

"No, if you're ready, we can go ... oh! This is Mike Phelps ... Michael, my wife, Ellie," he said as he introduced us. We shook hands.

"It is a pleasure to meet you, Mrs. Janssen," I said. I noted he had said, *Mike*, and then reverted to the formal *Michael* as he made the introduction.

"So nice to meet you, Michael. Has David been chewing your ear off?" she asked with a beautiful smile.

"No, he hasn't," I replied, smiling back.

It was obvious she had noted from a short distance away that he and I had been involved in a lengthy conversation. I had noticed her looking in our direction several times.

"He likes to talk," she gushed.

David set his empty glass on the bar and we again shook hands, and I with Ellie. They began walking toward the main entrance while stopping to speak and shake hands with the other guests.

That is how I met David Janssen.

* * *

Little did I know that roughly 40 minutes of conversation would evolve into a friendship that would span 15 years. David was 12 years my senior, the same age as my eldest brother, Jack. I had developed maturity beyond my years thanks to my brother Jack and my time in the Air Force.

The age difference between us was not a factor as our friendship developed and grew over the years. Interestingly, I learned much later that Ellie was either nine or 12 years his senior, a fact he did not know until they applied for their marriage license in Las Vegas.

I would learn from David it was 12 years, but Ellie would only admit to a nine year difference. Not that it mattered to David, and she sure as heck didn't look to be older than him. Ironically, Dave was 10 years older than Carol Connors.

I would soon learn that Ellie was never far away from David, except when he was working. When they were out together in public, whether at private parties or restaurants, she kept a close eye on him.

I would only see Ellie Janssen on two other occasions, including a small dinner party at their home before I briefly moved back to my hometown of Indianapolis.

It would only be two weeks before I received my first late night call from David Janssen inviting me to join him for a drink and late snack at The Formosa Café on Santa Monica Boulevard and Formosa Street. It was seven blocks from my apartment.

During the remainder of my time in Los Angeles, this would be the first of many late night calls, drinks and conversations. There would also be a few lunches, a couple of dinners and my best day, a visit to the set of *The Fugitive*.

As we would have our infrequent meetings over drinks, I began to take notice that he was a very 'down-to-earth' man - not what one would normally expect of a mega TV and film star who had instant recognition in public.

I also realized a bond was being formed early on between us. I believe it was based on the fact I had no knowledge of the film or television industry, and no real interest in it. In addition, he knew I liked him as a person, not as a TV and film star.

He seemed to know immediately that whatever he said to me over drinks would not be emblazoned across the tabloids' headlines the next day. He knew without question that what he said to me, no matter how trivial, would be held in the strictest confidence.

I would soon learn how much he valued his privacy. Even when working, it was rare he would socialize with his fellow actors or crew. He would crack jokes with them on his way to or from his dressing room and, later, his mobile dressing room - he dubbed the Silver Bullet - a gift from Mr. Quinn Martin.

He would spend most of his time in his dressing room. He told me when he was not on the set, he enjoyed the down time to read and relax. At the end of the day, he would have drinks with his fellow actors and crew.

As I moved back to Indianapolis, and later to New York City, and years later to Miami, Florida, David and I kept in frequent contact.

Occasionally, we would see each other when he was in New York or Miami. Most of his calls came late at night or in the wee hours of the morning. He knew he had a shoulder to cry on in his times of distress or an interested ear when he was exuberant over a new film role or a new television series.

I was totally shocked on February 13, 1980, while watching the NBC *Today* show and they broke into a commercial with 'Breaking News from Los Angeles.'

The announcement was that David Janssen *died* suddenly from a reported massive heart attack. I was stunned! I could not believe it!

I had spoken with him just four days before and he was excited about starting the filming of a new made-for-television movie, *Father Damien*. He was so exuberant; he sounded as if he was full of energy ... happy. The film was to be shot on the beach, not far from his beach house in Malibu. I knew he was separated again from Dani and she was living in their Century City condominium.

David had told me in our last conversation that he had passed a complete physical a couple of days before, a requirement for the film's insurance carrier.

HOW in the HELL could he pass a physical and die of a massive heart attack a few days later? I was not the only one with that burning question on my mind.

I was at home in Miami when I heard the tragic news. I wanted so badly to jump on the next plane and fly to Los Angeles, if nothing more than to pay my respects. However, business demands prevented me from doing so.

I later realized from the media coverage of his funeral services, I would not have gained access had I been there. I would have been held back with the sea of fans at the cemetery.

Furthermore, I learned years later from Ellie there were attempts to keep her and David's mother from the services; those attempts failed, thanks to David's agent and friend, Mr. Abby Greshler.

* * *

In late October of 1988, I was in the cocktail lounge of the world famous Jockey Club, of which I was then serving on the Board of Governors when Ms. Bobbe Starr, Membership Director, entered with a strikingly beautiful lady.

I watched as they walked around the lounge and exited by the baby grand piano bar and then into the main dining room. I was wracking my brain trying to remember where I had seen this woman before.

The very next evening, again in the cocktail lounge at the Jockey Club, Bobbe Starr and this gorgeous lady returned and sat at a small table before the fireplace.

I was seated at a nearby table with my brother, Bob, discussing the day's business. I felt the lady staring at me, then turned and began to feel self-conscious.

"Mike?"

"Yes ..."

"It's me, Ellie ... Ellie Janssen," she said, flashing her beautiful smile.

"You know each other?" Bobbe asked.

"Why yes, he was a good friend of ours!" Ellie exclaimed to Bobbe, as if *we* were long lost friends.

I stood to walk over and shake her hand and, without standing, she almost pulled me down into her lap as she gave me quite an unexpected hug.

In my opinion, the years had been very kind to her; she was absolutely striking and appeared years younger than what I knew her to be. It did not appear to me that she had any help from the famed Beverly Hills plastic surgeons.

I introduced her to my brother and invited her and Bobbe to join us for dinner and they accepted. We learned Ellie had applied for membership in the Club.

During dinner, of course, the main topic of conversation was

David, although somewhat restrained. The divorce was off limits, not discussed at all. I knew it had been very painful for Ellie. She had never remarried, nor had there been any publicity about any other men in her life, at least to my knowledge.

Our topic of conversation that evening was mostly about his rise to worldwide fame in his role as, *The Fugitive*, and his other series and films. We discussed Dave's tragic, sudden death, his funeral services and the 'good' memories Ellie held so dear. Dani's name was not brought up.

Over the course of the ensuing weeks, Ellie's membership was approved and we would enjoy dinner several times a week, discussing the paths our lives had taken and, of course, David.

She knew David and I had become good friends over the years, that David trusted me and considered me a loyal confidant. She knew we spoke frequently and queried me about what Dave had told me about her, Rosemary and Dani. I politely evaded the questions.

She knew Dave had introduced me to several film and television celebrities but I was not overly impressed and didn't form any kind of friendship with them.

During one of our dinners with my brother Bob and his wife, Cheryl, I asked Ellie why she had not written a book about her life with David, his rise to fame and the role she played in helping him as a faithful *Hollywood wife;* Ellie said she had often thought of writing such a book but did not know where to begin.

I suggested we could find a ghost writer in the area. She indicated she did not have the resources to pay a ghost writer. I suggested I could finance the project and be reimbursed from the royalties. She agreed without hesitation and seemed to sparkle at the opportunity of telling her story.

Within weeks, we located a ghost writer who had written a couple of novels and several award-winning short stories. After about six weeks, Ellie became dissatisfied with the working relationship, with his style of writing and summarily discharged him.

She discovered a lady in Santa Barbara, California, an accomplished and published author and biographer of celebrities. Ellie called her and discussed the project. She expressed great interest and gushed she was one of David's most die-hard fans.

We flew her to Miami and ensconced her in The Jockey Club guest wing. I paid her non-refundable retainer and all expenses, which included five weeks at the Club and working breakfasts, lunches and dinners with Ellie. Once again, in short order, Ellie became disenchanted with her writing style after first feeling they were working well together. Ellie discharged her.

I asked Ellie if I may read what had been collectively written by her and the ghost writers. After reading the less than 100 pages, I exclaimed to Ellie that she and I could write the book ourselves.

At this point, the book had no title. I suggested, *David Janssen – My Fugitive* and Ellie loved it. Thus a six year project began.

Ellie suggested we share ownership of the copyrights and royalties to the book on a 50-50 basis; I agreed. It was incorporated into our contract with the original publisher.

* * *

I was engaged full time as Chief Investigator for a prominent Miami Law firm, specializing in criminal defense. As a result, most of our collaboration was done in the evening hours, nights and weekends.

As I could arrange my schedule, we made trips to Los Angeles, Beverly Hills, Palm Springs, Las Vegas and New York for the purpose of conducting research and hosting interviews with many celebrities who had been close friends with David and Ellie during their marriage.

We interviewed their longtime housekeeper/cook, Beatrice; David's mother, Berniece Janssen; Victor Gentile who had served David as his Secretary/Valet for many years; Suzanne Pleshette; Michelle Lee; Lucille Ball; Jerry Lewis; Raymond Burr; Gregory Peck; Paul and Peggy Burke and many others.

During the initial writing process, Ellie and I had several strong disagreements as she related incidents that occurred with David.

Recalling that David had spoken with me about the same incidents, I would attempt to clarify, to insert David's point of view.

In doing so, I saw first-hand what David had told me about Ellie's wrath: extreme anger. In her home in Las Vegas, as she lounged while drinking a cup of coffee and dictating to me as I typed into my computer, I objected to an incident and, without thinking, said to her, "That is not what Dave told me."

She threw the half-filled cup of coffee across the room and it shattered on the wall above my computer, splashing hot coffee over my face and chest and computer monitor. I was shocked as she screamed; "It's my fucking book! Don't believe every God damn thing David told you!"

There was no doubt she wanted, and demanded, complete control. I learned to keep my mouth shut and write. After all it was her book ... *her* story.

I cleaned up the mess without saying a word. About an hour later, Ellie apologized.

Finally, in early 1994, the manuscript of 350 pages was submitted to our editor and publisher. Included were 12 pages of black and white photos.

Several months later, the editing complete, the book was cut down to 151 pages. *David Janssen – My Fugitive* was published in hardcover by Lifetime Books, Inc. in December of 1994.

Paperback editions followed in 1995, 1996 and 1997. Hardcover and paperback editions combined reportedly sold in excess of 1.2 million copies worldwide.

Both Ellie and I were disappointed the publisher had cut so much of her story, but we were pleased with the reception the book received.

I was, personally, secretly disappointed because I knew it was *her* story as she recalled her life with David - especially his drinking habits, his alleged 'womanizing' and the most difficult period of the protracted divorce proceedings.

It was the period beginning in early 1966, shortly after I met them, when David began sharing with me his feelings about his marriage.

We had many, many serious conversations and he opened up to me about the reasons he felt his marriage was failing; his reasons were in direct conflict with Ellie's recollections of the failure of their marriage. She either could not see it, or she refused to believe it at the time. In her book, she placed all the blame on David.

I took time off from the law firm and accompanied Ellie on a whirlwind book-signing tour, including a guest appearance on *The Geraldo Show* in an episode titled, *Hollywood Wives*, featuring ex-wives of Jerry Lewis, Johnny Carson and Dean Martin.

I was dismayed at the lurid allegations these bitter ex-wives spouted about these great entertainers.

We attended the annual convention of *The Fugitive* fan clubs at The Roosevelt Hotel in Hollywood.

Based on the success of the book and upon early retirement from the law firm, I chose to embark on the challenging career of being an author. However, I promised myself that I would never co-author a book with anyone, especially an ex-wife of a celebrity.

I chose to write about something I know – specifically, police procedurals, detective novels, murder and mayhem, based on actual cases I had worked.

* * *

My debut novel, *The Execution of Justice*, was published by Blue Line Publishing House, Inc. on January 30, 2009. With this novel I created the *Mike Walsh Detective Novels* series.

The novel is based on the murder of a close friend and one-time mentor of mine, Detective Sergeant Jack R. Ohrberg, Robbery & Homicide Unit of the Indianapolis Police Department.

The novel is unlike most detective or crime novels in that I endeavored to give my readers a true and deeply personal insight into the personal, as well as the professional, lives of the dedicated men and women across our nation who serve and protect and all too often pay the ultimate price for their communities.

Detective Sergeant Jack R. Ohrberg was a dedicated police officer. On December 11, 1980, he was brutally murdered by two members of a vicious gang of armed robbery suspects who had previously killed a Brinks guard.

He was killed as he kicked in the door of a house where the gang members were hiding. He lay on a frozen concrete porch as a two and one half hour shoot-out between police and the suspects raged.

Jack died at almost the same hour of the day as David. That was a very bad year for me; I lost two very good friends.

Publicity surrounding the release of *The Execution of Justice* revived interest in *David Janssen - My Fugitive*.

Many of David's fans contacted me wanting to purchase the book. With the cooperation of Blue Line Publishing House, Inc. I released *David Janssen - My Fugitive* Fourth Edition (Hardcover) on July 15, 2010, and at the original 1994 publishing price of $18.95. It is still available at a discounted price of $16.20 through my website (www.michaelphelpsnovels.com) and on Amazon, Barnes & Noble and all Internet book sellers.

The Jockey's Justice, the second title of the *Mike Walsh Detective Novels* series, was published in e-book format and is available through Amazon's Kindle, Barnes & Noble's Nook, Apple iPod, iPad, iPhone, Sony E-Reader, Copia E-Books and Kobo E-books.

The novel is based on the brutal murder of a winning, and highly respected, horse-racing jockey in a small western Kentucky town.

Eight years after his murder, his widow and son-in-law were charged with committing the crime. The law firm I worked for represented them; my assistant and I were dispatched to Kentucky to investigate the case. The novel provides readers with a roller-coaster ride into the sleazy underbelly of the *Sport of Kings*.

Many of David Janssen's fans and a few of his friends have inspired and encouraged me to write this memoir of the private conversations we had over the last 15 years of his life. I was amazed to have been contacted by his devoted fans from Denmark, Germany, France, Spain, England, Italy, Canada, Australia and several in South America.

I am no longer amazed that David Janssen continues to have millions of devoted and caring fans around the world 34 years after his untimely death.

He was the consummate professional, dedicated to his art and devoted to giving each performance his very best. He did not do that to win awards such as Oscars or Emmys. He did it for his *fans*. He was a perfectionist; it was in his genes.

In this memoir, *David Janssen - Our Conversations*, I reveal hundreds of conversations between David and me.

I cover many of the topics we discussed including his marriage, and divorce from, Ellie; his affair with actress Rosemary Forsyth; his relationships with his mother, Berniece, and step-father, Gene Janssen; his half-sisters, Jill and Teri; Ellie's daughters, Kathy and Diane; his alleged womanizing and drinking habits; many of the top Hollywood producers, directors, writers, and stars with whom he worked and his various film and television roles.

Dave's opinion of the Viet Nam War and politics was mentioned as well as his marriage to, and planned divorce from, his second wife, Dani, and, most of all, the two women in his life whom he actually loved and, subsequently, lost - actress Suzanne Pleshette and two-time Oscar-nominated, award-winning singer/songwriter, Carol Connors.

Collaborating with Carol on the theme song for a TV Movie of the Week, *My Sensitive, Passionate Man,* Dave wrote the lyrics and Carol and Bill Conti the music.

A love affair blossomed between Dave and Carol, lasting over two years; at the time, Dave was separated from Dani.

Dave had told me and others he was heading for divorce court again. In retrospect of that time, my opinion now is that Dave was afraid of the outrageous cost of a divorce from Dani and he lost Carol.

I will relate our conversations as close to verbatim as possible. Like David, I have been blessed with an excellent memory. I have not made anything up, nor have I exaggerated. I want to give his fans a true insight into his life as he lived it off screen.

David Janssen was a very intelligent man. He was a voracious reader and quite knowledgeable in history as well as current events of the time. He was also quite opinionated and would stand his ground.

He was also quite funny; he had a quick wit, loved jokes and contrived many practical jokes he would spring on his friends, cast members and crew alike. No one was considered off limits when it came to being the target of one of his jokes.

He also reveled in being the subject of a prank and always took such with a hearty laugh. Sadly, the studios failed to take notice of his comedic talents.

I have tried to concentrate on conversations I believe will give his fans the true picture of the man David Janssen really was.

In looking back over our 15 years of friendship, ending with his sudden death, I cannot comprehend how this man who had it all was so miserable and tormented in his mind.

He had good looks and was multi-talented. He had fame, wealth and millions of devoted and admiring fans.

I was always amazed at how well he hid his anguish from the public. I, personally, place the blame for David's torment on the women he married. By comparison, I had no fame, no wealth, no admiring and devoted fans, no talent like his - yet I was happy.

It is my belief David will not fault me, nor look upon this memoir as a betrayal of his confidence. Actually, I think he will smile down and enjoy a good, hearty laugh or two. That is what I miss most about Dave: his hearty, genuine laugh ... his jokes.

I also miss our sitting in an out of the way bar or lounge, drinking our scotch, almost matching each other drink for drink and sharing quiet, yet intense conversations, and his late night/early morning calls when he needed a friend to talk to.

Now, as I approach the winter season of my life, I seldom imbibe in my favorite J & B Scotch; it just wouldn't be the same without Dave.

David Janssen
Our Conversations

The Early Years
(1965-1972)

Michael Phelps

1

~1965~

I was sound asleep when the phone rang. Clicking on the lamp I looked at my watch ... it was 1:15 in the morning. I picked up the phone and managed a gruff hello.

"Mike? Dave Janssen. Just wanted to know if you'd join me for a drink."

"Uh ... yes, that would be great. Where should I meet you?"

"I'm at The Formosa Café at the corner of Santa Monica and Formosa ... do you know where that is?"

"Yeah ... it's not far from my apartment; I could be there in about 20 minutes."

"Great, see you then." The phone went dead.

I crawled out of bed and pulled on the dress slacks I had worn during the day and a clean shirt. I washed my face, combed my hair and headed for the door. It was now Sunday morning, November 7.

This was a surprise. I arrived at The Formosa Café at 1:40. The Formosa was dimly lit and it took me a few moments to spot Mr. Janssen. He was seated in a booth at the rear of the long narrow bar. As I sat down, he reached across the table and we shook hands. He waved his hand and a waitress appeared.

"What are you drinking?" he asked.

"J & B Scotch, water with a lemon wedge, please," I replied, smiling at the waitress who smiled and headed to the service area of the bar.

"You look like you've had a long day," I said, smiling. I noted he had a fresh drink cupped in both hands and a cigarette between fingers of his left hand. It was obvious it was not his first drink of the evening. I could see, even in the very dim light, that his eyes were bloodshot and his face was drawn, but he did not appear to be drunk.

He was wearing a light blue dress shirt - open at the collar - a navy blue blazer, dark grey slacks and black Gucci loafers. He also wore a Cartier watch with a black leather band on his left wrist and a thin gold bracelet on his right wrist. His hair was a little mussed, probably from the wind outside.

"Yeah ... it was a rough day. We got it done, though ... just wanted to take a little time to unwind before going home. Thought about our talk and wanted to have a drink and talk some more. Thanks for coming."

"I'm honored ... I am," I said.

"Why? What do you mean, 'honored'? No reason for that! Just thought we could have a couple of drinks and get to know each other."

"No, I didn't mean it that way, Mr. Janssen. I mean 'honored' in the sense that you are such a celebrity, you could be sitting here with anyone, so I am honored that you even thought to call me ... actually, that you kept my number," I responded.

"Why? You seem like a helluva nice guy, sharp, intelligent ... but, first of all, don't call me mister. All my friends call me Dave." His grin was sincere.

I was groping for words to say. How could I even have a conversation with a guy who was a big star on television? I knew nothing about the industry and had little time to even watch TV. He was the only celebrity I had met in almost eight months of being in Hollywood. What could we possibly have in common?

"So ... how did your filming go today, *Dave*?" I asked, placing emphasis on his name, and grinned.

"Went well, just long ... put the episode to bed, starts all over again on Monday."

"How many hours a day do you put in ... to actually do an entire episode, I mean? What's this episode about?"

"On the average about 14 or as long as it takes to make the director happy. Most days go between 14 and 16 hours. It takes an entire week, sometimes eight or nine days to do an episode." He added, "Can't tell you the plot; that's top secret. Work is done for the day and that's where it stays. So tell me about being a cop."

"It takes an entire week or more to film a one hour show? I didn't know that. As for being a cop: on uniformed patrol it is mainly a pretty boring job, unless you're proactive and you look for trouble. Routine traffic stops is one way; you never know what you are going to find. Domestic disturbances are another; there you show up, a man and wife are fighting, they see your uniform and they both forget about their fight and turn their anger on you, most of the time. It has its moments of adrenaline rush. It's never the same thing every day, always changing ... always fluid."

"A lot like being an actor ... always changing ... always fluid. Sounds like it would be fun." He smiled.

"I remember you in *Richard Diamond – Private Detective*. That's almost like being a cop, or rather, a detective," I said, then added, "You were damn good in it, too - very believable ... and you always got the girl."

"Thanks for the compliment. I know you mentioned you had seen the show when we first talked. That was a long time ago, but you're right ... it was good writing and I enjoyed it. Actually, it is one of my favorite roles. So, tell me ... how long were you married?"

I recalled telling him I had recently separated from my wife. "Not long. We're still married, just don't know if it will work out. She doesn't want to be married to a cop and she knows that is what I want. That's what I was in the Air Force with her brother and he's a cop now in their hometown."

He signaled the waitress and soon another round of drinks was placed before us. She placed the empty glasses and dirty ashtray on her serving tray and placed a clean ashtray in its place. He smiled at her and she patted his hand, returning his smile. I could not help but notice David was a fast drinker and I was not sure I could keep his pace.

"So, if you don't mind my asking, how many drinks have you had?" I asked.

"I stop counting after the first one ... you think I'm drunk?" he asked with a serious look. "Do you want something to eat? They have really good food here."

"No, thanks. I'm not hungry. As for thinking you are drunk, not at all ... you don't look drunk to me. I'm just concerned about your driving," I said, cautiously. I was thinking I had pissed him off. I did not want him to think I was prying or that I did think he was drunk.

"I'm not driving. I sent my driver home; they'll call me a cab when I'm ready to leave."

"You don't have to do that; I'd be glad to drive you home," I offered.

"No, I live in Trousdale Estates; it'd be way out of your way. You've had a couple of drinks, too... don't want to see you busted for driving drunk," he said with his deep laugh. "So, where'd you say you're from originally?"

"Indianapolis ... it's the capital of Indiana."

"I know where it is ... home of the 500 Mile Race. Have you ever been to the race?"

"Yes, several times. It is quite an exciting event and brings thousands of tourists to Indianapolis and that means a lot of money pumped into the local economy. Have you been there?"

"No, but I plan to ... after all, it is the premier of auto racing. I'm more into horse-racing; I love to watch the ponies."

David signaled our waitress and within minutes she was putting another round of drinks on the table.

"This is our last call, Mr. Janssen," she said with a smile. I glanced at my watch; it was 2:15.

"Well, I guess this will have to be it; you can bring another round and the tab," he said.

We nursed our drinks for about another 30 minutes. The bar had just about cleared of customers. Our waitress brought David the tab. He didn't appear to even look at it; he just signed his name - didn't provide a credit card or anything, and left $50 as a tip.

We walked out into the cold air and I insisted on driving him home. I was right inside the parking garage by The Formosa; he looked at me, shrugged his shoulders, raised both arms as a gesture of surrender and said, "Okay. Sure it's not a problem ... you don't mind?"

"No, I don't mind at all," I said as we both entered my new Thunderbird.

"I used to have one of these ... in 1956."

"Did you like it?" I asked.

"Oh yeah ... it was a fun, sporty car. It was a two-seater."

"Yes, I know. They made them four-seated in 1958."

He gave good directions; it took about 15 minutes to arrive at his home on Loma Vista Drive. It was only about five miles or so from The Formosa Café. I drove very carefully but did not feel the alcohol inhibiting my abilities.

I noted the lights were on in his house and thought to myself: *Mrs. Janssen must be waiting up for him.*

"Here we are, safe and sound ... you're a good driver, thanks ... appreciate it," he said as he exited the car. "We'll have to get together again; it was good talking with you."

"Thanks ... and thank you, for the drinks and conversation. I enjoyed it."

He waved his hand as he turned and walked to his door. I drove down the winding driveway and was back on Loma Vista Drive. It was a short drive home.

As I parked my car I looked at the clock: 3:45. I was really exhausted and glad I didn't have to work in the morning.

I had been in Los Angeles almost eight months and still did not know my way around. It was such a massive, sprawling city; it seemed to take an hour to get anywhere. I had not met anyone with whom to develop friendships other than co-workers, but we did not socialize. I really didn't know anyone.

After this early morning meeting, sharing drinks with David Janssen, I knew I would be comfortable being able to consider him a friend. I was interested in getting to know him as a person, not as a big TV star and celebrity.

I found him interesting, to say the least, and I did feel honored. I felt if he called again and we had drinks together, I would feel I had one friend in Los Angeles; it would make living in the city a little less lonely.

I did not hear from David Janssen for about five weeks and had all but forgotten our late night drinking episode. I had thought maybe that was just a fluke. I knew he was very busy with his work, his wife and all the obligatory social affairs he was required to attend, whether for his position or for his wife.

2

It was again a late night call which awakened me on December 17, 1965.

"Mike? Dave Janssen ... how about a few drinks?" he asked in a gruff voice, almost sounding as if he was coming down with a cold.

I shook the sleep out of my head and managed to answer, "Yeah, okay ... sure, where at?"

"I'm at The Formosa."

"Be there in a few," I replied. It took me almost half an hour to wake up, get dressed and make the few minutes drive to The Formosa. This was a Thursday night; actually, it was 1:30 Friday morning. I had to be at work by seven. *I must be nuts*, I told myself.

Dave was seated in the same booth he had been when I met him five weeks earlier. He had his hands wrapped around a rock glass and seemed to be peering into it, as if searching for something. He was dressed in dark slacks, navy blue or black, a yellow Ralph Lauren dress shirt with French cuffs and a grey Glenn Plaid sports jacket.

"Hey ... good to see ya' ... thanks for coming! Did I wake you again? I feel bad if I did. I just thought it'd be good to have a couple of drinks with a friend," he said as he reached his hand across the table and we shook hands.

I couldn't help but notice his strong, firm handshake; as a young boy, my eldest brother Jack had told me that was a good sign of a man's character. I could tell David Janssen had good character.

"That's okay. I went to bed early tonight. I've already had about two and a half hours sleep. I usually get four hours of sleep a night, so I'm good."

"Damn ... I have to have at least five hours of sleep," he said.

I would learn later, sort of a confession from Dave, that he actually functioned quite well on four hours of sleep. He said he did manage to sleep a little later on weekends but, on the average weeknight, he would average four hours.

"Well, I would think your work is a little more demanding, both physically and mentally, than mine is. In security work, it is pure boredom and no real physical activity. I've seen you work; you're always running, jumping over fences or getting into fist fights," I said smiling. "Do you do all of that yourself or do you have a double?"

"Most of it I do myself. There are some scenes where the director and studio insist using a body double ... see, they don't want to risk me getting hurt," he said with a laugh. "They use a double and then me for the close-up."

"That's interesting, but how do they do that with a fist fight? I've seen you in a couple where it looks like you are really getting a hard right to your jaw, or your gut is getting hammered ... sure looks real on TV," I said.

"There's a secret to that ... now if I tell you, you have to promise you won't leak it."

"My lips are sealed."

"Okay, the way they do it is, with the camera angle set for a long shot, the actors will appear to be right next to each other, but will be a few inches away from each other. It always looks closer on film. Let's say Brian Keith punches me in the stomach but, in reality, he pulls the punch. I bend over clutching my gut with this hellish pain on my face. If the director yells 'Cut', then they speed the film up, and it looks real.

"The reason I use this analogy is that it really happened. In filming our pilot, Brian didn't pull his punch; we were closer than we thought and he hit me hard. I ended up with a couple of broken ribs. Brian is a big guy and I felt his punch.

"Now, on a face shot, the one getting a hard one to the face would throw his head back, director yells 'Cut'; make-up applies a little blood or bruising and director yells 'Action', and cameras roll. In the finished scene, it looks very real. You'll have to come to the set one of these days; you'll see for yourself. Things aren't always what they appear to be ... the magic of television."

"Very interesting. I would like to see how it is done, thanks," I said, adding, "So did Brian Keith apologize? Did it stop the filming?"

The same waitress we had on my previous visit appeared with another round of drinks.

"Yeah, he apologized and, no, we kept filming. That's enough about my work. Tell me more about yourself ... family, parents, brothers, sisters."

"Well, I'm the fifth of six kids; two older brothers, two older sisters, one younger brother. Dad's a labor lawyer, left us when I was about six; my younger brother was just about to be born. He ran off with another woman. Mom went to work in a bank. It was pretty hard for her, strapped with six kids; Dad didn't contribute much in the way of money."

"So your parents are divorced?" he asked.

"No. Mom doesn't believe in divorce. I think she still loves him and believes he'll come back to us eventually. Things got easier for her though. About a year after Dad left, the Korean War broke out so my oldest brother, Jack, joined the Air Force in 1951, and my second oldest brother, Gene, joined the Air Force in '52.

"My oldest sister, Judy, married her high school sweetheart in 1954 and my sister, Janet, married her high school sweetheart in 1956. That left me and my younger brother, Bob, at home so things eased up on Mom as time passed. I joined the Air Force in '59."

"You've got quite a family. I don't have any brothers but I have two sisters. Jill is 11 years younger than me and Teri is 14 years younger. Actually, they're my half-sisters. Mother divorced my father when I was just about two-years-old. She moved us here to Los Angeles when I was about six and a couple of years later married Gene Janssen. He's been like my real father; he wanted to adopt me but I guess my father objected. It doesn't matter. I took his name when I started school and, as far as I'm concerned, he's my dad."

I felt he referred to Gene Janssen with genuine pride. I would learn later that his mother had also divorced Gene Janssen but David kept in close contact with him.

"That's interesting. I didn't know that. What kind of work does your father do?" I asked.

"Which one?" he asked with a grin.

"Okay, you got me there ... both," I answered, smiling.

"I'm told my real father is in banking. My step-father is a trucker."

"Does your mother work?" I asked.

"She was a dancer - in the road shows of the Ziegfeld Follies ... if you know what that was. She also tries to get film roles. I've had her and both of my sisters as extras in a couple of *Fugitive* episodes," he said.

"So, if you don't mind my asking, how'd you get into the movie business?"

"That's easy ... I have a mother who is the classic stage mother. She got me into a couple of bit parts in films when I was young and I thought it was kind of fun."

"How old were you when you got your first role?"

"Hell, I don't know ... just a baby when I won some photo contest or something. Then she got me a small role in a film starring Sonja Henie; that was when I was about 14, then the following year I was in a film with Johnny Weissmuller and Buster Crabbe," he said, smiling.

"What was that like? My sister Janet is a big Tarzan fan. I think she's seen every one of the movies."

"I don't really remember, but it wasn't a Tarzan film. I liked Johnny and learned a lot from him ... mostly to have patience."

"I'll have to tell my sister to look it up; do you remember the name of it?"

"Yes, it was *Swamp Fire*. As I said, it wasn't a Tarzan film; it was a Louisiana Delta film ... not too memorable, I'm afraid. I don't think your sister will find it; I don't think it's playing anywhere anymore."

"So, what would you have been if you were not such a good actor?"

"Actually I wanted to be in sports, professionally. I was pretty good at basketball in high school.

"I was a champion in pole vaulting but I fucked-up my knee showing off one day and that ended my sports career ... any kind of sports," he said with a sad look in his eyes. "Then I found out acting wasn't so bad ... and it paid better than working in a gas station." He smiled.

"You were in the military, weren't you?" I asked and then remembered he had told me at the Hilton party he had served in the Army.

"Yeah, Uncle Sam's Army. Drafted me ... can you believe that?"

"Well, yeah, I can believe it ... Elvis was drafted and, unlike Cassius Clay, like you, he served his time," I said with a smile. "What'd you do? What was your MOS?"

"That's easy. I was under contract with Universal Studios at the time so they stuck me in Special Services, which means I and my company buddies were assigned the tough job of entertaining the rest of the guys with so-called army training films."

"Where were you stationed?"

"Good old Fort Ord ... never left the Golden State of California."

"That doesn't sound too bad; at least you were close to home," I said.

"Not really. It was about a six hour drive to Los Angeles. I got home a few weekends and took leave a couple of times. As for duty, don't get me wrong. I was drafted, so I was willing to do whatever the army said. I sure as hell didn't want to go to Korea, though I would have," he said, grinning broadly.

"Yeah, but Special Services, that's pretty good duty, I would think. I mean, didn't you get to work with the USO, all the Hollywood beauties, Bob Hope?"

"No ... all our entertainment was confined to the post. I never went on any USO tours," he said. "So tell me about the Air Force ... can't believe you actually wanted to be an MP."

"Yeah ... well, the Air Force recruiter couldn't believe it either and my brothers thought I was nuts. I had a couple of close friends, sort of like big brothers to me; they were on the police department back home so I thought that would be cool - be an MP, then go on the police department when I got out of the Air Force."

"Did you really enjoy it?" he asked with a quizzical expression.

"Yeah, I did, especially being a Canine Handler; it was fun for the most part."

We talked a little more about our military service and then I changed the conversation to him - his marriage, specifically.

"So how long have you and Ellie been married?"

"Seven years ... seven long years." He smiled.

"Do you plan on having kids, I mean besides her daughters?"

"No, I would love to have my own, but Ellie can't have any more."

"Oh! Sorry!"

"Well, who knows what the future will bring?" he speculated with a nod of his head.

"Not trying to pry into your personal life, Dave ... but wondering why, after a hard day at work, you don't just go straight home. I mean, if I had a beautiful wife like Ellie, I'd race home!" I said.

"Well, Mike, things are not always what they appear to be. When I finish work, I want to have a couple of drinks, a little to unwind from work, then a few to fortify myself for going home," he said with a serious look on his face and a serious tone in his voice.

I was drawing the conclusion that his was not a happy marriage, as it appeared to be on the surface. I was not about to pry further.

The waitress set another round of drinks before us.

"Dave, after this, I'd better cut myself off. I have to work in a few hours ... and so do you."

"Yeah, it's almost closing time anyway, you are right ... so are you going to drive me home again?" he asked with a big smile.

"Of course! It's not as far from my place as I thought, so no problem," I replied.

I delivered David to his door at 3:15. I noticed lights were still on in the front of his house and assumed Ellie was waiting up for him again.

"If I don't see you before then, you, Ellie and the girls have a happy holiday," I said as he was getting out of the car.

"Yeah ... you do the same ... but we may just squeeze in another drink or two before then," he said, smiling.

"Okay, you have a good tomorrow ... I mean today," I said as I waved.

3

~1966~

Christmas Day came and passed without hearing from Dave. I spent Christmas day working at time and a half pay; I couldn't refuse it. It was just another day to me, being alone in Los Angeles.

The New Year's holidays passed without much fanfare on my part. I had put in for a transfer to New York City to be closer to where my wife was in Greenwich, Connecticut. I had not yet heard if it would be approved but had decided I would relocate there, with or without a job.

Over the next few weeks David would call at least once a week and I would again jump out of bed and go meet him for a round of drinks. The conversations covered a wide range of topics: current events, the burgeoning involvement of the United States in Viet Nam and politics.

I was becoming more and more comfortable and losing the feelings of being guarded around him. I no longer felt I had to wear a jacket and tie when we met at The Formosa; for places I was not familiar with, I would still do so. I was discovering that he really was a well-grounded, 'down-to-earth' guy.

I was amazed at his intelligence, knowing he had not attended college, yet his knowledge of history and current events astounded me. I enjoy American history, World War II and the Korean Conflict. David's knowledge of the subjects was so in-depth; it could easily qualify him to be a college professor in my opinion.

We were at a point we seldom discussed his work, or the series, or my mundane, boring job. I was now watching every episode of *The Fugitive* even if it meant switching shifts with a co-worker. I was also becoming aware that David had an insatiable capacity for scotch.

I was appreciating that he liked me as a person and seemed to enjoy our conversations. Besides, he could always count on me for a ride home. Actually, I'm just kidding about that.

It was on an unusually cold morning in late January of 1966 I received a rude awakening to David's marital woes. In a few of our most recent conversations, he had alluded to, and I had sensed that, his marriage to Ellie was somewhat rocky.

He had called me just before midnight and I went to meet him for drinks at the posh Beverly Hills Hotel's famed Polo Lounge. We had several rounds of drinks and he seemed to be in a very good mood. He told me he had just finished a dinner meeting with Mr. Abner Greshler - his agent - and some studio executives discussing his career.

He told me he had received the nomination for an Emmy as *Outstanding Continued Performance by an Actor in a Leading Role in a Dramatic Series*. That was sure a mouthful, and a very BIG deal and David was excited. He was on a natural high.

As the Polo Lounge was about to close, I could see Dave was showing signs of being exhausted and, yes, I would say he was drunk. This time I motioned for the server and paid the tab, without him even noticing. I suggested I drive him home, as I had far less to drink.

It was just after 2:30 in the morning when I pulled into his driveway. It took him a few minutes to open the door. He used the door as a crutch to raise himself out of the seat and steady his feet on the paved driveway. As he leaned in and was saying goodnight, the front door of his home opened and I could see Ellie's silhouette against the interior lighting.

She took one look at Dave and screamed, "David, where in the hell have you been? Your meeting ended hours ago. I called Abby!"

"Having a drink with my friend, Mike," he said in a soft, firm voice.

With that, I heard the sound of breaking glass as David seemed to duck his head; I then noticed a dark red liquid running down my passenger window. Ellie had apparently thrown a glass of wine and smashed it against my car window.

As he turned and bent down once again to say goodnight, he was smiling. From the car interior lights I saw what appeared to be red wine splashed onto his caramel-colored sports jacket and royal blue shirt.

"Sorry about that ... see you later," he said, surprisingly with a smile. As he closed the car door I could hear Ellie screaming something about him missing a party.

I put the car in gear and drove slowly down their driveway. Driving home I could only think of the scene I had just witnessed. I could not believe his wife had acted in such a manner. She apparently knew he had a business dinner and, still, she expected him to go to some party after a hard day at work? I was totally dumbfounded.

It certainly wasn't the first time he had stayed out late, and I'm sure it was not the first time he missed a party. How could she have reacted that way in front of anyone? I'm certain her screaming at Dave had been heard by at least one or more of their neighbors. I really felt sorry for him.

Here was this major Hollywood star being yelled at by his wife in the driveway of their home at 2:30 in the morning. I just knew she must have awakened at least a few neighbors with her screaming. "Things are not always as they appear to be" went through my mind, as David had said. I knew I would not raise the subject the next time David and I met for drinks.

I was dressing for work when my phone rang at 5:45 that morning; I had only slept about two and a half hours.

"Mike? Dave. Just wanted to apologize for my wife's behavior ... any damage to your car door?"

I had not even bothered to look at my car door. "No, not at all. I guess she was pretty pissed off, huh?"

"Yeah ... seems I forgot we had a party to go to. Actually, I didn't forget; I didn't want to go. I'll give you a call later; maybe we could have dinner ... an early dinner."

"Yeah ... that would be great," I responded, thinking ahead to the evening. I was already tired from the night before and this day was just beginning. I felt he was inviting me to dinner as a way of apologizing for his wife's throwing a glass at my car.

4

True to his word, Dave called me just before seven o'clock. I had just arrived home and was exhausted.

"Mike ... are you still available for dinner?" he asked, sounding fresh and full of energy.

How did he do it? I wondered. *He is older than me, has a far more demanding job, drinks a hell of a lot more booze than me, yet he has all this energy.*

"Yeah ... I just got home and need to take a quick shower. Where shall we meet and what time?"

"Do you know where La Scala Restaurant is?"

"No, sorry! I've never heard of it," I answered.

"It's on Canon Drive, just off Burton Way in Beverly Hills."

"Okay. I can find it."

"Parking is always a problem but they have Valet parking so use it ... say in about 45 minutes?"

"Yes, that would be good."

I arrived and left my car with the valet then entered the restaurant and was greeted by a tuxedo attired Maître D'. I said I was meeting Mr. David Janssen; he smiled and immediately asked that I follow him. I followed him to a small room off of the main dining room as he escorted me to Dave's table. I slipped him $20 hoping David did not notice.

Dave already had a scotch and soda in front of him and was buttering a piece of Italian bread. He smiled as I sat down and told the Maître D' that I would be having a J & B Scotch, water with lemon wedge. He reached over the table and we shook hands.

I noticed he was wearing a deep burgundy sports jacket, a pink Brooks Brothers' dress shirt and caramel-colored slacks and Oxford loafers. I had noticed as I walked through the restaurant that almost every man there was wearing a tie, including me. *Maybe Dave had special dispensation*, I thought in a joking way.

"About last night ... this morning I mean ... Ellie was a little pissed off. She usually doesn't throw her wine glasses at me; she knows how much they cost," he said with a big grin. "Thanks for joining me."

"I understand. I guess she really wanted to go to that party. I really didn't give it another thought ... except I hope your dry cleaners can get the wine out of your cashmere jacket; it's a nice jacket," I said, returning his smile.

"Yeah, I'm sure they can. Is there any damage to your car door?"

"No, actually I think it only hit the window, which is still better than hitting your head, if that is what she was aiming for."

"It wouldn't hurt my head; I have a hard head. She doesn't usually act out like that, especially in front of someone."

"Well, I gotta say, I heard her screaming all the way down your driveway. I hope your neighbors didn't hear her."

"Our neighbors have heard her tirades before; they are used to it by now," he said with a serious face.

I felt he was embarrassed that I would see such an act by his wife even though he had made several innuendos in previous meetings. I now knew his marriage was not as perfect as the tabloids, *TV Guide* and other fan magazines made it appear.

"Maybe I'm better off being separated, although my wife and I have yet to have a real argument ... I mean with yelling, screaming ... throwing things," I mused aloud.

"We've been married just over seven years and things change between people. Trust me! I know," he said.

"Maybe she has the 'Seven Year Itch' ... maybe it will just go away," I said in a joking way, trying to lighten the conversation, letting him know I did not place any real importance to it.

"It isn't that ... she has just become very possessive ... jealous."

"How in the hell can she be jealous of you having a drink with another guy?" I asked.

"It's not that ... it's not you. It's her jealousy of *anyone* I spend any time with. She thinks I should go to work and go straight home and spend all of my time with her ... and *only* her."

"I guess that would be pretty hard to live with," I said, being serious.

"It is, believe me," Dave said with a stern look, as if the mere thought disgusted him.

"It sounds like she doesn't trust you," I said cautiously.

"She doesn't. Then again, I have given her reason not to," he said, his grin back in place.

"Okay ... well, none of my business."

A waiter brought us a fresh round of drinks and menus.

"Do you like Italian food?" Dave asked.

"Love it."

"This is one of the best Italian restaurants in all of California ... Real Italian."

"It's a very nice place ... and very popular as well," I said, having noted the place was almost filled as I entered and was being seated at Dave's table.

"It is one of my favorites. Ellie and I come here a couple of times a month. I think you'll really enjoy the food," he said.

"I'm sure I will," I said as I perused the menu. "One thing is for sure: I could not afford to bring my wife here."

"You are my guest. Have anything you like," he said with a smile.

"What are you having?"

"I'm having the Salmone Affumicato for an appetizer, then a La Scala salad and Salmone Alla Griglia for the main course," he said as if it were his favorite meal. "Have you decided?"

"The Prosciutto and melon, a Caesar salad and the Scaloppine di Vitello Al Limone sounds delicious to me," I said as I set the menu down.

"Excellent choice; you will have a real, authentic taste of Italy tonight," he said just as our waiter approached.

"Good evening, Rafael. Another round of drinks first, and I'll have the Salmone Affumicato, house salad and Salmone Alla Griglia," David said as the waiter scribbled his order, then turned and smiled at me.

"I would like the Prosciutto and melon, Caesar salad and the Scaloppine di Vitello Al Limone," I said.

The waiter smiled at us both and walked briskly toward the bar service area. Within moments a third round of drinks was placed before us, the empty glasses removed and a fresh basket of bread placed in the center of the table.

I could not help but wonder how many drinks Dave had before I arrived. I knew he was drinking doubles, comparing the color of his drink to mine. I decided to slow down, especially since I was driving.

This was the first dinner we had shared and I was determined to be dignified and sober – well, at least, remain mostly sober. I did not know if David had his car or his driver so I didn't know if I would be driving him home. His home was not far from the restaurant so it really would not have mattered.

During dinner, he surprised me with an invitation to the set of *The Fugitive*. "In a couple of weeks we will be shooting the final episode. Maybe you could find time to visit the set," he said.

"Are you kidding! I would love to! What would be the best day for you?" I'm sure the excitement showed in my voice.

"Any day ... Tuesday or Wednesday would be fine."

"I'll see if I can switch with someone. Can I let you know?" I asked.

"Of course you can."

"Wait a minute! You said *final episode*. Does that mean the chase ... the pursuit ends? Does Gerard catch you or do you capture the one-armed man?"

"No ... no ... it's the final episode of this season. I'll still be running with Gerard hot on my heels next year," he laughed.

I was really excited inside but didn't want to cause more trouble for him. "Dave, I don't want to get personal, but I don't want to be the cause of more aggravation for Ellie," I said in a guarded tone.

"Don't worry! I told her I was having dinner with you to apologize for her throwing a glass at me and hitting your car instead," he said with a big grin and a little chuckle.

"Okay. I just do not want to be the cause of more trouble for you," I said. My thoughts were actually of getting to be on the set watching him work. To me it was exciting - the filming, the magic of television.

"You are not the cause of any trouble with Ellie. You mentioned you are separated from your wife; where's she at?" he asked.

"She's at her parents' home in Connecticut," I responded.

"Any chance of a reconciliation?"

"Truthfully, on my part, yes. I do love her but my decision to be a cop has been the major point of tension so I really don't know yet," I answered as I took my wallet and brought out her photo to show him.

"She's a beautiful girl. I hope you can work things out," he said, smiling.

"So do I ... time will tell. What about you and Ellie? I mean, you've been married over seven years. Is she getting the 'seven year itch' a little late?"

"I'm the one with the itch ... joking here but, as I've told you, things aren't always as they appear to be. Ellie has changed a lot over the years and with the success of the series she has started being very jealous of any woman that comes within ten feet of me," he said with a serious look on his face.

I felt he wanted to talk so I pushed a little. "Jealousy is a very dangerous emotion; it tears people apart. To be happy in a relationship, there has to be trust ... doesn't she trust you?"

"Hell, no ... and, truthfully, I've given her reason not to, but she has given me reason to look, too. She has become too damn controlling, trying to dominate me, and that isn't going to work."

"Have you talked about it ... with her, I mean?"

"I can't talk to her. I've tried but she goes berserk. She starts yelling and that ends any chance of a civil conversation. Truthfully, I don't know how much longer I can, or will, put up with it," he confessed as he took another sip of his scotch and lit another cigarette.

"Have you talked with anyone about it? Maybe she needs a therapist."

"I've talked with my agent, told him things were getting unbearable with her. He is pushing me to stay and make it work. He thinks a divorce would be a scandal, hurt the series ... it's all about the series."

"You and Ellie seem so happy together in the interviews I've read. Are you telling me it's all an act?"

"No ... not at all. When we are out in public, she is more concerned with my image than I am. She won't do anything that would even appear she's not the perfect wife," he said with a hint of sarcasm.

"Does Ellie know you aren't happy with how your marriage is going? Do you have fights, I mean real fights at home? Isn't she worried at all that you just may leave her?"

"She doesn't see anything; she thinks everything is perfect, as long as it is all *her* way. She knows I slept with Suzanne; she knows I have strong feelings for her, but she thinks I would not dare divorce her ... it would cost me too much."

"Damn it, Dave! You can't live like this! It's like you're trapped, with no way out!" I exclaimed in an earnest and concerned tone.

"Yeah, you're right, but I can't risk a divorce at this point. Maybe you are right; maybe she does need some professional help. Last couple of years she's had one illness after another and the doctors really can't find anything physically wrong with her. I think she's just trying to play the sympathy card, trying to make me feel guilty for *making* her sick."

"Man, I feel for you ... I sure wish I could offer some advice that could help you."

"Hell, Mike! Just having someone I can trust to gripe about all this bullshit is good so you're helping by letting me bitch about it. I had a brief, very brief, affair with Suzanne Pleshette, one of our guest stars...very discrete. Suzanne broke it off because I'm married," he said and managed the first genuine smile I'd seen since I sat down.

I did not respond because I did not want to know.

We enjoyed a leisurely dinner during which I passed on a refill of my scotch, opting for black coffee instead. The meal was out of this world. It was around 10:15 when we finished and we both passed on dessert. I was surprised that Dave joined me for an after dinner coffee. A busboy cleared our table and brought clean ashtrays.

As the waiter brought our coffee, Dave ordered another round of drinks. I had passed earlier so I accepted this as a final drink of the evening, at least for me.

I noted the dinner had been good for Dave; he looked very satisfied and not the least bit drunk. I scanned the restaurant and was amazed it was still quite full and many of the patrons were easily recognizable.

I felt a change of subject was definitely in order.

"So...comparing Doctors Sam Sheppard of Ohio and Richard Kimble of Indiana, what do you think? By that I mean we know Dr. Sheppard has been convicted and, without the hand of fate sparing him, he is a permanent resident of a seven by eight little cell somewhere in an Ohio prison.

"But Dr. Kimble really seems to be innocent and we all believe that because of his determined search for the phantom one-armed man, crisscrossing the country.

"What's your opinion; is Dr. Kimble innocent? Is there really a one-armed man who killed his wife? Come on, Dave! You can tell me! I'll still watch the chase."

Dave let out a big laugh and broad smile, which I noted attracted the attention of those at nearby tables.

"Well, Mike, personally I think Dr. Sheppard is really innocent and God-willing, someday he will be exonerated. As for Dr. Kimble, the trial seemed to be proper and fair...then the tragic train wreck.

"He was handcuffed to Gerard, who was injured and unconscious. With many other passengers injured - after all he is a doctor - he takes the opportunity to escape...to run...to hide. Does that sound like what an innocent man - a doctor - would do? I just don't see it!

"Personally, from a distance, I would have to say it makes him look *guilty*! I guess we'll just have to wait and see," he said with a mischievous smile. I smiled back.

Dave motioned for the check from the waiter who was a few tables away.

"Do you need a ride home?" I asked.

"No, I have my car. I don't want you to be in Ellie's striking range." He smiled.

We left the restaurant just after eleven o'clock and waited together as the valet retrieved our cars. Mine arrived first so we shook hands and I thanked him for a very nice dinner.

"I'll give you a call," he said as I entered my car and prepared to leave.

The dinner was outstanding and I knew I would one day return to La Scala.

On my drive home I kept thinking how serious Dave looked and talked during dinner. I could tell when his conversation switched from his invitation for me to visit the set to his home situation; he became depressed, like I had never seen. I concluded his marriage was becoming, if not already, a serious burden on his mind.

A couple of weeks later I read in the *Los Angeles Times* that Dave won a Golden Globe Award as the *Most Popular Male Television Personality*. I thought that was great. It affirmed what everyone already knew: *David Janssen was a star*! I could not wait to congratulate him personally.

5

I had known David for just about four months and felt a solid friendship had developed between us. Yes, he drank excessively, yet he seemed to have mastered control over his alcohol consumption.

I had not once seen him so drunk he did not have control over his major faculties. There were times his speech would be a little slurred and his eyes would be bloodshot; however, his mind was always sharp and in the moment.

I had been trying to analyze his personality since the first drinks at The Formosa. I reached the conclusion that David Janssen was a very gifted, talented, intelligent, compassionate, giving man who was dedicated to his work, always seeking to do it 'better than before.'

He liked to joke, mostly good clean jokes, and played a lot of practical jokes on his good friends. He never seemed to get rattled or angry. I never saw him really angry until a couple of years later during his divorce from Ellie, and then the anger was directed towards her battery of lawyers.

However, I could see he was a very unhappy man who was struggling with his main demon, alcohol. I felt, in a sense, he had become very unhappy with Ellie's change over the past couple of years. He felt as though he was 'trapped' in that his agent, publicist and producer, Quinn Martin, were telling him he HAD to stay with Ellie, because of his career.

I determined that, although David enjoyed his success and felt he owed so much to his fans, he was resentful of the fact his fame caused so much disruption in his private life.

He felt such a 'loss' that he could not go to a supermarket, a drug store or a liquor store and shop like everyone else. He had to have other people, like Beatrice or Victor, do his shopping.

He did enjoy going to Sy Devore's clothing store to be fitted for his clothes and he would do that by appointment. I noted he had impeccable taste in clothes and, secretly, wished I could afford the quality.

The majority of Hollywood celebrities of today seem to not care about their private lives. They are frequently seen going out with a platoon of bodyguards - getting stupidly drunk, openly using illicit drugs, getting arrested...it just seems they think they can get away with it because of their celebrity status. To me, it is sad.

The Hollywood stars of David's era such as James Garner, Jack Lord, Telly Savalas, Carol Connors, Suzanne Pleshette, Rock Hudson, Lucille Ball, Carol Burnett, Natalie Wood and Robert Wagner, to name a few, all had 'class.'

As our friendship developed over the months, I would learn just who in the Hollywood elite he considered a friend. I would learn he did not really enjoy socializing but accepted it as a career obligation.

I learned I could get Wednesday, February 9, off and could not wait to ask Dave if that day would be okay for me to visit the set. I did not want to call him for fear of interrupting him so I decided to wait for his next call.

Dave called Saturday night, February 5, and I met him at The Formosa for drinks just after midnight. He had not worked but had attended a party with Ellie at a friend's home and seemed happy the party was over. Ellie was home and he told her the truth: he had 'promised' to meet me for a couple of drinks at The Formosa. Well, that was almost the truth.

"Hello, Mike ... good to see you," he said as I scooted into what I assumed was the *David Janssen booth*. We shook hands as the waitress appeared with my drink. *Now that's service!* I thought to myself, smiling at the waitress and thanking her.

"Congratulations on your Golden Globe! That's one helluva honor ... shows everyone 'you've made it,'" I said, then added, "Dave, I can get Wednesday off ... will it be okay for me to come to the set?"

"Thanks, Mike, and yes, of course, Wednesday will be fine. I'll leave your name with security; they'll give you a pass, a parking permit and directions to the studio. What time do you think you'll get there?"

"Is around eight o'clock too early?"

"Hell, no! We start early; I'm there by five."

"Oh ... I could make it earlier."

"No, eight o'clock is fine. We have a lot to do before then: make-up, wardrobe, places, a bunch of technical stuff you would find boring," he said with a smile.

"Good, eight o'clock it is. I want to thank you. I am really excited about this ... just to watch you - I mean Dr. Kimble - work, I mean run." I smiled back at him.

"That's okay. I am happy you can get the time to come and watch. One thing: no cameras are allowed and you'll have to sit in a certain place and not make a sound ... be as quiet as a church mouse," he said with a grin.

"Not a problem but I'm glad you told me about the camera. I was going to come fully prepared with a full roll of film. I told my sister Judy about meeting you and that you had invited me to the set of *The Fugitive*... she wants a photo."

"Well, we'll have some taken and you can send her one."

"Will you autograph it for her?" I asked.

"Of course, but the autograph costs a hundred bucks," he said.

I must have looked shocked. "I'm sorry. I can't afford that."

"Just kidding, Mike ... for your sister, no charge." He laughed.

"Okay ... you had me going there." I started laughing, too.

I was still trying to analyze his personality, not *Richard Diamond* or *Richard Kimble*, but his real personality; I had already decided it would be a very delicate and complex process.

He came across to me as being a man who wanted to maintain his privacy as much as possible, considering his profession. I even had the thought that he was somewhat lonely, in that he could be in a room full of people and feel alone.

I was wondering what his life at home was really like. I had already determined that he was not content in his marriage or his home.

"Tell me how your day went," he requested.

"Nothing to tell. I went to work ... nothing unusual happened and I went home." We both laughed.

"At least you can laugh about it," he said.

"If I don't laugh, I'll go crazy."

"Well, in my opinion, you have a ways to go before you can call yourself crazy," he said with a hearty laugh.

"I just can't believe that in four days I'll be watching a television show actually being made," I said. I'm sure I was euphoric.

"I'm sure you'll enjoy it ... for all of about 15 minutes. Watching it is really boring; there are so many times they shoot a scene over and over and over ... it gets a little redundant."

"I'm sure I won't be bored!" I exclaimed with a smile.

"Okay ... we'll see," he said with a grin.

Another round of drinks appeared.

"So this will be the last episode of this season? What will it be like next season? How much vacation time will you have?" I asked, feeling like I was bombarding him with questions.

"I have no clue what will happen next season ... don't have any scripts yet, but I know our ratings are good and ABC has signed for another season. I just hope I can do another season. We'll have about three months, but I'll be doing some films, maybe guest appearances, and I've promised Ellie a trip so there really won't be much downtime," he said.

"Man, you really do keep busy. I really don't think I'd like it that way. I consider myself a workaholic, don't really care for vacations, but everyone needs some time to rejuvenate their mind and body."

"You're right, and I do take the time for that."

"So how are things on the home front?" I asked.

"I'm getting her to agree to see a therapist ... she thinks we both need it ... so I'm going along with that, just to get her to go."

"Is it like a marriage counselor where you go together?" I asked.

"No, a real psychiatrist; they can prescribe medications. I think she may need some anti-depressant pills or something."

"I sure hope it helps. I don't know how you can handle the pressure of trying to keep her happy while concentrating on your work."

"It takes a lot of concentration. When I get to the studio, I put Ellie and home out of my mind ... I am Richard Kimble!" he said with a grin.

"So, if you don't mind me asking, what about Ms. Pleshette? I mean, do you think you would be happy with her?"

"No doubt! She's a wonderful girl ... she's in the business so she knows the pressures, how to handle the public ... but we won't be seeing each other. She won't have an affair with me being married."

"Whoa ... that's heavy ... does she think you getting a divorce would hurt your career?"

"That subject didn't come up ... but she told me to call her when I'm free."

"At least that's encouraging ... to know she's there for you," I said.

"Well, I'm willing to see how going to a psychiatrist will help our marriage," he said with a serious expression.

"What about Ellie's daughters ... are you close to them?"

"Yeah, I mean I don't look at them as my kids - their father still communicates with them - but I am close to them ... love them, would do anything for them."

"You don't fight in front of them, do you?"

"Try not to ... but sometimes, with Ellie, it just happens."

"That's sad. I hope they understand."

"Ellie has never really liked the mother role ... that's why the girls were in boarding schools - until I insisted on bringing them home for us to try being a family."

"I remember reading somewhere they were in a boarding school while Ellie was getting her divorce from her first husband, I think in Las Vegas - but I thought I read that she was with Frank Sinatra until she met you."

"That's all true ... but I think she knew there would be no future with Sinatra. Don't get me wrong! When we met, I fell hard for her ... she's a beautiful woman, has great qualities ... it is just ... there has been a change. Since the series took off and she sees me kissing beautiful girls on the show ... she doesn't understand it isn't real, that it's just part of the script. She's like most women, jealous," he said, managing a grin.

It was almost closing time and Dave asked, for the first time, if I would drive him home.

"Sure ... not a problem. Happy to do it," I said.

We arrived at his home just after two o'clock. There were lights on in his home but Ellie did not appear at the door, for which I was thankful.

I drove to my apartment and collapsed in bed. I was really looking forward to the coming Wednesday.

6

Monday and Tuesday passed all too slowly for me, but totally uneventful. Tuesday evening Dave called me just after seven o'clock.

"Hey, Mike! Just wanted to confirm you're coming to the studio tomorrow."

"Oh, hell! YES! I wouldn't miss it for anything," I said, expecting him to ask me to join him for drinks.

"Ellie and I are going to a dinner so I'll see you in the morning."

"Thanks ... you can count on it."

I was hoping that things were getting a little better for him at home with Ellie. I did not know if they had started seeing a doctor, but he sounded like he was in a good mood.

I watched television and couldn't wait for *The Fugitive* to come on at ten o'clock.

That night's episode, announced by the gravelly voice of William Conrad, was *The Shadow of the Swan*.

In the story, Dr. Kimble had just arrived in a little town; the name is not mentioned. In the opening scene he is at a carnival where he wins a goldfish by throwing a ball and knocking over three clay milk jugs. The next scene shows him putting the goldfish in a small lake behind the carnival grounds.

There, a girl approaches him. She is young and attractive. He tells her he had just gotten into town and was looking for a job. She works for the local veterinarian and takes Kimble there where he is hired to replace the former kennel man who had been fired for stealing.

The girl, whom we later learn has some mental problems, is also seen flirting with one of the carnival workers; she had been raised by her uncle since she was 10, when her parents died in some kind of accident.

After his first afternoon as a kennel man, she convinced him to go to the carnival. There, Kimble is separated from her and suddenly hears her screaming. He rushes around, through the crowd, and finds the carnival guy forcing himself on her. Of course, he saves her, but during the fight he suffers a cut on his head.

She takes him to her nearby home where she cleans up the cut and, in the process, introduces him to her uncle. Her uncle is suspicious and questions them both about the assailant but she says she had not seen his face. Kimble says he can't describe the guy; it was too dark.

The episode ends with her uncle finding a Wanted poster for Kimble through his friend, Lieutenant Jacobs. He captures Kimble with his niece beside the same lake. I will only say here that Kimble gets away.

The episode was written by Anthony Lawrence and directed by James Sheldon. I hated to see the show end and I was already forming questions I would ask Dave the next day.

It seemed there were so many people in the show, 'extras' they call them, and just a few central characters.

Andrew Duggan was the guest star, who played guest star Joanna Pettit's uncle who had retired after 20 years as a police officer. Another guest star I recognized was David Sheiner who played Police Lieutenant, Lou Jacobs.

I found the episode to be very interesting, with twists and turns I had not expected. I would have a lot of questions for Dave, but I would wait until after watching the filming the next day.

I had a good night's sleep and was awake at six o'clock, excited for the day ahead.

I arrived at the main gate of the Samuel Goldwyn Studios at 7:45. I gave my name to the guard and explained I was a guest of David Janssen's. He smiled and acknowledged me.

He asked for my driver's license and wrote down the information, including my tag number and car description, then filled out a vehicle pass and a plastic visitor pass which I was to clip on my suit jacket. He gave me directions to the studio building where the filming was taking place.

I found a parking spot marked 'visitor' about 50 yards from the entrance of the building. I was surprised as I drove to the designated studio building; I thought I was back on an Air Force base. There was row after row of what looked like aircraft hangars, large enough to accommodate B-52 bombers.

As I approached the studio building I could see a red flashing light over the door and a uniformed guard at the entrance.

On the wall to the right of the door was a sign which read: 'Closed set – authorized personnel only.' I walked up to the guard and showed my visitor pass, gave my name and said I was there as a guest of David Janssen's.

He smiled and told me it would be a few minutes. "They are shooting now. When the light goes off, I can escort you in." I thanked him. I could not help but think their security was as tight as we had on Air Force bases.

About ten minutes later, the light stopped flashing. The guard smiled, opened the door and motioned me in. He escorted me over to a row of folding chairs and told me to be seated, said he would find Mr. Janssen.

I was like a little kid in a candy store. I looked all around the interior and wondered, *How do they do this*?

I could see what appeared to be a living room (furnished, but no ceiling) and a kitchen, same thing – no ceiling but a bunch of Klieg lights hanging from the ceiling.

Cameras on dollies were all over the place and people were running from place to place. Some were gathered in small groups talking.

Then I noticed another room which was supposed to be the interior of a little restaurant with a bar, serving area and a couple of tables flanked by four chairs each.

It all looked so real yet each room was so small, I wondered how they could fit the actors in them, yet make it look so large when the show aired on television.

A few minutes later, Dave appeared. I stood and we shook hands.

"Right on time. Good to see you," he said.

"WOW ... this is unbelievable ... this is where you do everything?"

"Just about all the interior scenes then over there we have the process screen, and dressing rooms are over there," he said as he pointed to the far end of the studio, and along the side where there were a line of doors, which I assumed were the small dressing rooms.

"I saw the show on TV last night; it was good. I have some questions though, later," I said.

"Okay, we are setting up for a scene now; I'll be in the restaurant with one of our guest stars, Michael Strong. We'll be discussing the waitress' nephew who has recently come to live with her."

"What's it about, this show?"

"Well, I am in upstate New York, where this episode takes place, looking for the one-armed man. I have a job as a bartender in a little Italian restaurant. Lois Nettleton plays a waitress there named Susan Cartwright. Her nephew was sent to her after he was removed from foster care; she is developing an interest in me, and I in her," he said.

"Just like last night ... you always get the girl, don't you?"

"Yeah ... well, I don't write 'em. I just do what I'm told. There has to be a little romance, don't you agree?" He smiled.

"Yeah ... I guess so."

"Well, her nephew happens to be from Stafford, Indiana - my hometown - and he recognizes me."

"Ah-ha ... so you're in trouble."

"Sort of ... we will have a lunch break sometime around one o'clock, depending on the time; we can run over to The Formosa and compare notes," he suggested.

"Good ... I promise I won't make a sound. I'll watch in total silence. What is this show's title?" I asked.

"It's called, *In a Plain Paper Wrapper*." Dave smiled and then went over to a group of people.

Someone called for *places*, a horn sounded, Klieg lights came on and crew members scurried all over the set, making adjustments. It was fascinating to watch, as if watching a well-oiled machine moving with precision.

The scene was of David behind the bar and Michael Strong, playing the role of a guy named Shaw - a Child Welfare worker who seems a little suspicious of Kimble's character, Bob Stoddard.

Shaw begins questioning Stoddard about where he was from, where he tended bar before and begins to ask more and more questions.

Of course, this makes Bob Stoddard nervous and the expression on his face and the quiver in his voice is obvious. Although I was not close enough to see it up close and personal, I could recognize the expression in his voice. I made a mental note to ask Dave over lunch.

The Klieg lights were on, cameras rolling from various angles, microphones on long booms overhead being moved around; it was just amazing to me. Every few minutes, the director would yell, "CUT" and everything would stop.

David, Mr. Strong and a few others would gather around the director, Mr. Donner, and have a short conference. Then everyone would return to their places and Mr. Donner would yell, "ACTION" and everything started all over again.

It seemed to me that it took a little over an hour to film this one scene, which would last no more than a couple of minutes in the finished show.

Just about 1:15, Mr. Donner yelled, "CUT ... LUNCH!"

The Klieg lights clicked off and I assume all cameras and microphones were turned off. The crew scrambled in different directions.

Dave walked over to me. "Give me a few minutes and we'll go to lunch."

"Great," I replied. He returned in about 10 minutes wearing the same slacks but a different shirt and wearing his own (I presumed) sports jacket.

"Let's go to lunch ... can we go in your car?" he asked.

"Yes, I have a good spot close by," I said as we exited the building and walked to my car.

It was less than two minutes to The Formosa. The restaurant was busy and the bar was full; David's table was waiting, as if he had a reservation.

The waitress, one I had not seen before, brought us menus.

"Would you like a scotch?" Dave asked, looking at me.

"Ahh ... yeah, that sounds good," I stammered. "It isn't five o'clock yet, but I can handle it."

He smiled as he looked at his watch. "Right now, it is just after 9:40; people are having after dinner drinks in London." He ordered us both a drink.

"The cheeseburgers are out of this world here ... onion rings are great, too," Dave said.

"That sounds good to me," I answered.

The waitress returned with our drinks. Dave ordered a cheeseburger with a side of onion rings for both of us.

"Well, Mike, what do you think so far?"

"I am in awe. I've never seen this done before, but it seems like you do the same thing, repeatedly ... over and over. Why is that?"

"Any number of things ... could be a camera angle, the sound, the lighting ... anything. You see, the director is watching this on a screen, just as it will appear on television when it is finished, so if there is one minor problem, something he sees that doesn't suit him, we stop. The problem is explained and we do it all over."

"Doesn't that waste time ... film?" I asked.

"Time, yes, but they can re-shoot and record over the film."

"Oh ... but it must be pretty hard for everyone, not just the actors, but all the camera guys, lighting, everyone involved with a scene," I said, then added, "Like last night, everything just seemed to flow in a consistency; it appeared so real, so natural ... but I can see it isn't easy, as I thought."

"I won't argue with you there. It sure as hell isn't as easy as it looks once the show is edited and cut," Dave replied.

"It all sounds so technical to me. I wouldn't know how to do anything when it comes to acting. How in the hell do you remember your lines? It seems so easy on TV, you are right ... now I'm sure it's not."

"I am fortunate. God gave me a good memory and, when I screw up, the director is there to straighten me out. I don't write the lines; the great writers do, and I don't set the scene, the director does ... then there are the costume people, the make-up people, the set decorators ... the camera crews, lighting, electricians ... the film editors ... yeah, it is a complex series of people and events that puts it all together," he summarized.

It was very interesting.

"Now, I couldn't really see your face close enough, but when Shaw started questioning you - sounded like he was interrogating you - your voice sort of quivered, like you were nervous. Is that the way we'll see it on TV?"

"Oh yeah! Stoddard was nervous. Wouldn't you be if a state agent pumped you with questions and you were supposed to be an escaped convicted killer?" he asked with a big grin.

"I guess I would ... and I'd probably be on the next bus out of town. I'd say to myself no woman is worth *me* getting captured," I answered in a joking manner.

"Then we wouldn't have the finished episode now, would we?" he commented with a smile.

"Okay, in last night's show, you got mixed up with a girl who got you a job at her veterinarian's office, where she also worked. A carnival was in town and the girl comes on to you, but she had also come on to a carnival worker.

"Her uncle is a retired cop and things turn out to where we see this girl has some real emotional issues, like she is a little crazy, and she turns you in.

"The thing I don't get is, in the end, she is accidentally shot by her uncle who is holding his gun on you and, when the other cops arrive, you just slip away. I can tell you that was way, way off ... no cop would let that happen!"

"Yeah, you are right. In reality it wouldn't happen but you have to go with the scenes as the writer sets them out ... so Kimble got lucky. You do believe in luck ... don't you?"

"Okay, Dave, but I can tell you any cop watching will see that goof," I said with a laugh.

"I agree ... I'm just glad that any cop that saw last night's show wasn't there. I'd be out of a job and back on 'death row' in Indiana." He laughed.

Our lunch arrived and we thanked the waitress.

"Okay, you'll see more when we get back. It is kind of boring so anytime you feel like taking off, just do it. I'll give you a call and we'll meet for drinks," he said.

"Okay, thanks ... I'll stick around for a couple more hours. It is just so interesting ... so complicated," I said. "I notice there is no music in the background, like when it is shown on TV. Why?"

We began eating our lunch.

"The music is the last piece; it is added once the film is finished."

"Oh ... I guess that makes sense."

"Yeah, it would be a little distracting to the actors and the crew."

"Shows how much I know. I expected to see a full orchestra, wearing tuxedos and all," I said only half-joking. Dave had a good laugh.

I wish he had continued talking. I was gaining a real insight into all that was required to make a television show or a movie come across the screen as being seamless, but I did not want to push him about his work.

I had a feeling from our previous conversations, first at the Hilton party where we met, then at this bar a few times, that he really did not talk about his work after he left the studio - exceptions being when he was being interviewed by media and he had to respond to questions.

"So how is everything?" I asked.

"Fine ... well, it wouldn't do any good for me to complain ... no one would listen." He grinned.

"I would ... of course, I probably couldn't solve your complaints, but maybe it would be good to get it off your chest," I invited, smiling.

He laughed.

We finished lunch and Dave signed the tab and left a cash tip. We were back at the studio by 2:15. My parking place was still available. We walked in and I returned to my spectator chair, which was actually the visitor area.

It took about an hour for the director, the actors who would be appearing in the next scene and the crew to get things in place to meet the director's satisfaction.

Mr. Donner yelled, "ACTION" and everyone and everything started moving with what I thought was absolute precision.

In this scene, the three boys who make the theme of this episode are in a little restaurant eating lunch. I could only assume they received money from their parents, as they had trouble getting shipping and handling fees for the purchase of a rifle and they were commiserating over not having any bullets.

The boys - played by a very young (maybe 14-year-old) Kurt Russell as Eddie; the ringleader, Pat Cardi as Gary (Lois Nettleton's nephew); Michael Shea as Rick and Mark Dymally as Joe - had plans to 'capture' Dr. Richard Kimble (alias Bob Stoddard) with the mail-order rifle.

One of the boys spots an older man called Swanzie, played by Arthur Mallet, who agrees to buy them bullets.

It's funny. I wondered then, as I do now, how believable, how probable this scenario would be in 1966, let alone today. I laughed at the absurdity but told myself it would be a good point of conversation when Dave and I next sat down for drinks.

I watched the filming until about four o'clock. The director called for a break and Dave came over to me.

"Well, Mike, what do you think so far?"

"It is not an easy job you have, my friend," I said earnestly. "I think I'll call it a day. I'm exhausted just watching everyone."

"All right, Mike. We'll talk later," he said, then smiled and we shook hands.

I left shortly after he did another scene, when I saw him walking towards his dressing room.

7

I decided I would go back to my apartment and relax a while, hoping Dave would have the time and we could get together for drinks after he was finished for the day. Dave called me just after eleven o'clock and told me he had to go straight home, but we would get together in the next week or two.

I knew this was the last episode for the season and Dave would have a three month vacation, a 'hiatus' they called it in the 'business.' He had told me he had committed to a film in which he was the star. It was a cop show and he would be playing a detective who shoots and kills a man; it turns out the man is a doctor with an impeccable reputation. The movie was titled, *Warning Shot*.

He would have a few weeks before filming started so he and Ellie would have some private time together, hopefully to rekindle their love for each other. I was hoping things would improve for him in his marriage. I felt he was under tremendous stress from a combination of his work and his marriage to Ellie.

At the time, I did not know if Dave had told Ellie about his affair with Suzanne, or how recent the affair had been, but I could tell it was on his mind.

Dave called me late on Tuesday, February 22, 1966.

"Mike, this is Dave. Do you feel up to having a couple of drinks, maybe a sandwich?"

"Absolutely ... just tell me where."

"I'm at The Formosa, just finished work."

"I'll see you in about 20 minutes. Is that okay?"

"Perfect." He hung up the phone.

I arrived in less than 15 minutes and entered The Formosa. After my eyes adjusted I spotted Dave in his booth. I slid into the booth and we shook hands. A drink was placed before me by the smiling waitress.

"It's almost ten o'clock. You finished work early."

"Yes, finally put the episode in the can." He smiled.

"Is this the same one ... *In A Plain Paper Wrapper*?"

"Yeah. I won't be working for a while so I felt deserving of a few drinks. Do you want something to eat?"

"No, thanks! I had an early dinner ... so how does it feel when it's all over? I mean, does it give you a great feeling or just a feeling of relief?"

"Oh! It is definitely a great feeling, that is if I feel we have good writing, good directions, good actors, good crew and Gerard hasn't caught me yet." He laughed.

"I can say that, what I saw last Wednesday, you had all of that and I can't wait to see it on TV. Will it be next week's show?"

"I don't know. I don't have the air date yet but I'll let you know in time so you won't miss it."

"Thanks ... don't forget! I don't want to miss it."

"Don't worry! I don't forget anything ... I'll be sure to let you know. Now I have a little vacation so Ellie and I will be going down to Palm Springs for a week or two."

"That sounds really nice ... seems like things are improving for you and Ellie."

"Yeah, a little ... at least for Ellie. I am still walking on eggshells," he said with a mischievous grin.

"I hope your little vacation away from here will give Ellie a chance to see she has nothing to worry about, as far as you leaving her."

"I really don't think she is all that worried; she knows I can't afford a scandal ... I think that is why she is so bold and demanding."

"Dave, do you think she still loves you? More important, do you still love her?" I asked.

"Yeah, I think she loves me, but things have changed, for both of us. To answer your question, I don't feel the love for her I once felt and it is making me miserable, but I have to try and get things back to where we were. Now, all we do is fight and, when we go out among people, even friends, she puts on such a phony act; it makes me sick."

We had a couple more rounds of drinks and made small talk about politics. Dave was a registered Democrat but he was steadfast in his voting for the candidate he felt best qualified. He did not like President Johnson at all and felt he was very corrupt. He had been told by a reliable source that JFK knew the Viet Nam War was a giant mistake and was preparing to pull all U.S. forces out before he was assassinated. He knew LBJ was making money off the war.

We left The Formosa just after midnight; it surprised me that Dave did not want to stay until closing, which was his normal routine. I could see that he was feeling physical fatigue but his mind was sharp and clear.

As we said goodbye in the parking garage, I again made him promise to call me when *In a Plain Paper Wrapper* would air.

I would not talk with him until early April. Dave called me April 11, just after midnight. It had been overcast and cool all day and, when I walked out to my car to head to The Formosa to meet him, it felt like we may get some rain.

I arrived at The Formosa just before 12:30. Dave was in his booth and already had a drink waiting for me. He looked as if he had just showered but I could tell he was tired.

"Hey, long time no see! How the hell are you?" I asked.

"Good ... tired, but well. We're shooting *Warning Shot* now; I have good feelings about this film, great script and good crew."

"I remember you telling me a little about it but it hadn't been confirmed back then. What's it about? Who are your co-stars?"

"Stefanie Powers, Lillian Gish, Eleanor Parker, Carroll O'Connor, Joan Collins, Ed Begley, Keenan Wynn and a few others.

"I'm a detective sergeant, 10 years on the force ... I am on a stakeout and I see a suspicious man leaving this apartment building. When I try to stop him, he runs. I catch up to him and he pulls a gun on me. I shoot him ... then my troubles begin."

"What do you mean? You get in trouble!"

"Well, when my backup arrives, no one can find the gun the guy had. What makes matters worse, he is a respected doctor and I get suspended and charged with murder, so I have to clear my name."

"Okay, sounds very interesting ... tell me more."

"No ... I want you to go see it when it comes out."

"Come on, Dave! You know I'm going to see it, anyway. I want to see how good you are at playing a cop."

"No ... you'll see it and think I'm pretty good as a cop!" he said with emphasis and a smile.

I chose not to pursue it because I knew Dave didn't really like to talk about his work-in-progress.

"Then you really haven't had much of a vacation. How was everything in Palm Springs ... with Ellie?" I asked.

"We had about two weeks. We talked about building a home there. Things were smooth and Ellie seems to be a little better and more secure."

"I'm happy to hear that. You do look a little more relaxed than the last time I saw you," I said smiling. "When will this film be released?"

"I have no idea ... but I'll let you know. I'm going to have to make it an early night ... have to be on the set early," he said.

"Okay by me. I have to work tomorrow, too."

Dave ordered our last round of drinks. "Any word on your transfer yet?" he asked.

"No, my boss said he will see what he can do, but nothing looks promising."

"Personally, I wish you'd give LA a little more time; it's really a nice place to live ... and you won't know that, leaving after only a few months."

"I know, Dave ... but, outside of work, you are the only person I know and, to get anywhere in town, it takes hours. Like you told me, LA is so spread out ...but the main reason is to get back, be closer to where my wife is ... maybe things will work out."

"I understand. I hope things will work out for you but, then again, I'll lose my drinking buddy."

"Yeah, well I'll miss that, too - just being able to sit down, talk and have a few drinks with you - but you've seen her picture. She's a lot prettier than you ... no offense intended." I smiled.

"We'll just have to make the best of it ... I do hope it works out the way you want it to ... okay, time to call it a day. I'll give you a call ... don't know when, depends on the shooting schedule," he said.

"That sounds good to me ... I'll look forward to seeing you again; maybe you'll tell me more about the movie," I hinted.

Dave had his car and was perfectly sober to make the drive home.

I would not hear from him again until Friday, May 20, when he called to invite me to The Formosa for drinks; it was just before midnight. I arrived at 12:15.

"Hey! It's good to see you; it's been a while," I said.

"Yeah ... we finished *Warning Shot* and we start filming next season's *Fugitive* on Monday," he said.

"Do you know when the movie will be released yet?"

"No, it will be sometime in the fall. They have a lot of editing, technical stuff, but I'll let you know. You'll probably see it in the newspaper before I know anyway."

"What do you think about it?"

"I liked it ... good plot written by Mann Rubin, based on Whit Masterson's novel. Buzz Kulik directed. I liked working with him; he's very good at setting up scenes."

"I can't wait to see it; sounds like it will be a blockbuster."

"I hope it is ... may lead to other screen roles ... that's what I'd love to be doing. It's a lot better than being on the run every week. A couple months of shooting and you're done; in a series, it just seems to have no end."

"Guess what? I saw *In a Plain Paper Wrapper;* they showed it a week after we last met here," I said with excitement.

"What did you think? In your opinion, was it good?"

"Oh, hell! Yes, those kids were very good actors ... and the girl after you, Lois ..."

"Nettleton," Dave interjected.

"She was really good ... beautiful woman, too. I still don't know how they get it put together with no one seeing all the cameras, microphones, all the changes that are made ... it comes across so real on TV."

"That is all done in the editing room, and they are experts! Enough about me and my work. How are things with you?"

"About the same. No word on any openings in New York so I may just end up on the police department after all."

"So you have definitely decided to leave Los Angeles?"

"Yes, I have. Dave, it is just too far way. I mean, 3,000 miles! I feel it hurts any chance I have at a reconciliation and working towards my goals."

"You have a good point there ... I hope it all works out for you."

"Thanks, Dave. I've decided that, if nothing happens by the end of June, I'm just going to give my notice and jump in my car and do it. I've saved enough money to get an apartment and carry me through and I won't have a problem getting a job so I am excited about it."

"That's good. I know how it is. Once you make a decision, you are removing half the stress ... but I'll be losing my drinking buddy. That sucks!" He grinned.

"Yeah, I feel bad about that ... you've saved me a ton of money I may have spent going to bars around here ... but, hey! We can still keep in touch and you go to New York a few times a year so we'll still have drinks ... IF you can find the time."

We had two more rounds of drinks and decided to call it a night. Dave had been left at The Formosa by his driver so I insisted on driving him home.

"Make sure you give me advance warning before you leave LA," he said.

"Hell, Dave! You are the only real friend I have in Los Angeles. I will surely miss our get-togethers, and not just for the free scotch," I said with a little chuckle.

"Mike, I will miss them, too ... you don't know how difficult it is to meet someone you can really relax with, talk to and trust."

"I guess I don't. When you first called me and we met at The Formosa, I was in awe ... not star-struck. I mean here you are, a real celebrity, a big star ... you could sit down and have drinks with anyone you want ... I really was ... I AM honored."

"Mike, most of the people in this town are a bunch of phonies, including the so-called stars, and it is hard to form real friendships. I am a good judge of people. I study people ... and, when we first met, I knew I wanted to count you as a friend. I made the right choice," he said.

"Thank you, Dave! You make me feel very humble."

"That's good ... I meant what I said. Another lousy thing about LA is people come here looking for a dream and, within a few months ... a year, they leave."

"Here you are, Sir. Home sweet home," I said as we arrived at his driveway.

"Thanks, Mike ... I'll call you next week, okay?"

"I look forward to it ... it is the bright spot of my day!"

8

It would be another two weeks before I heard from Dave and he sounded really depressed. I agreed to meet him at The Formosa, arriving just after eleven on Friday night, June 3, 1966.

"Good evening, Mike. Your drink is on it
s way." He smiled as we shook hands.

"You look beat ... how many hours did you put in today?"

"Just 15, but it was 15 hours of hell. The director wasn't happy with anything or anyone - kept shooting the same scene over and over and over ... nerve-wracking!"

"Yes, I can see. You don't look like you usually do ... relaxed. Who is the director? Have you worked with him before?"

"Yeah, I worked with him before. He's not the problem. We have some supporting actors who keep flubbing their lines and then there were some lighting problems. It was just one of those days where you have one problem after another ... anyway, it's over ... now to relax." He smiled.

"I would say you deserve to relax. You just finished filming the movie and now you're right back into filming *Fugitive*. You only had a couple of weeks of a real vacation ... Ellie must be a little sad. I feel for her, too."

"Yeah, Mike, you're right ... but working keeps me occupied and I don't have much time to really deal with the upheaval at home."

"Is Ellie still giving you problems? I would think that having you all to herself for your vacation, she would be a little more mellow. I mean, after all, she knew your *Fugitive* schedule would start right after the movie. Have you found out when it will be released?"

"Not yet; I'll let you know as soon as I do. Ellie seemed to enjoy our time in Palm Springs but, now that we're back here and the shooting schedule has started, she's not happy," he said.

I could tell that Dave was feeling depressed and I concluded the main reason was Ellie. I could not believe he was in such a situation. Here is this mega-television and film star, handsome, rich, millions of adoring fans, perhaps a few other actors and others involved in the business he could really count as friends; it would lead one to think he had it all! Yet, here he was sitting in a bar having drinks with me, a *nobody*, and he was very depressed.

I was convinced his home life was the reason he was driven to drink. It was apparent to me each time someone in the business walked in, or came by the booth to acknowledge him, Dave's demeanor would change; I could not help but conclude he was putting on an act.

With that thought in mind, and seeing Dave's personality change, I felt good that he could feel really relaxed and not put on any act in *my* presence. I was assured that Dave trusted me and could really be himself when he was with me.

"So what is the new episode about? Do you like the script?" I asked.

"It's called, *In Plain Sight,* and, no, I don't really like the script, don't really like anything about it.

"I catch up to Bill Raisch, the one-armed man. He works in a chemical factory and, when I confront him, he uses a chemical mixture that explodes in my face, blinding me. Personally, I don't like even the thought of being blind - and acting blind is not easy."

"Damn! It sounds interesting but I can see your point about acting like you are blind ... don't think I'd like that either. Hell, I can't even use Visine for my eyes."

"Well, when it airs, you'll have to give me your honest opinion."

"I will and I promise to keep an open mind when I see it," I said with a smile.

"Okay ... I'll hold you to that," he said with a grin.

"I guess you are going to have a pretty busy summer. When this season ends, you should take Ellie and get the hell away from Los Angeles, at least for an entire month. Don't even think about work."

"Yes, I've been thinking exactly that. Maybe I'll take her to Europe; I think we would both enjoy that."

"Yeah, and at least that far from Los Angeles, you could walk the streets, go to restaurants, do some shopping without a bunch of people clamoring all around you to get your autograph."

"Well, I don't know about that; *Fugitive* is shown on TV in England, Germany, Italy ... all over ... so there is a better than 50 percent chance I will still be recognized ... not that I mind, but it would be nice to go somewhere I am not recognized," he said with sincerity and a half-smile.

"Damn it! Believe me, Dave! I would not want to walk in your shoes!" I said with a frown.

Dave laughed out loud for the first time that evening. He caught the waitress' eye and motioned for another round.

"Yeah ... I would not want you to ... sometimes I wonder what I did so wrong in my life that I am now being punished for," he said with a serious expression.

"Yeah, but Dave ... it can't be that bad. I mean you have success, you are rich, have a beautiful wife who really loves you, loads of friends and millions of fans ... I'd be happy with that.

"The only thing I wouldn't like is not being able to go to a drugstore, supermarket, regular restaurant ... not being able to walk down a street without being stared at, accosted by fans wanting to have an autograph."

"Yeah, I hate that part, too ... not being able to be like an ordinary person but, when fans come up to me, I am still flattered, and I try my best to be accommodating to them because they are the reason I have everything I have, and they show me that my work is good ... is appreciated."

"I guess I can finally understand the causation of your stress ... and problems. Even though they may not look like problems, they are, in fact," I said. "Are you and Ellie still seeing that doctor?"

"Yes ... for all the good he does," he replied, sounding dejected.

"You don't think he's helping Ellie?"

"Not really ... she seems to be more possessive than before. She calls me on set, sometimes several times a day. She'll ask what time we'll be wrapping up for the day; it is just a hard thing to deal with."

"Dave, I feel for you ... I don't know how you do it ... I don't think I could handle my wife being like that ... no, I couldn't handle it at all."

"Well, my friend, how about you ... have you spoken with your wife lately?"

"No, I spoke with her mother the other day, but I'm getting the picture that it is over ... so I'm trying to figure out what the hell I will do. We're Catholic so a divorce is not a good thing, especially since we've only been married 23 months and been apart for the past 13. It is eating away at me but I'll take one day at a time ... accept what she wants, and move on."

"Well, sorry to hear that, but your strategy is a good one. You can't force someone to love you; you have to be considerate of what they want. If it happens, you'll survive - that I'm sure of," he said in a reassuring way.

"Thanks, Dave! I appreciate that ... I'll keep you informed."

Another round of drinks was placed before us, the filled ash trays removed along with our empty glasses.

I could tell Dave was, indeed, trapped in his marriage - that his love for Ellie was ebbing away and, from my perspective, Ellie was in fact pushing him away from her. I wondered how much longer he could take such an environment of animosity, jealousy and mistrust.

I wondered about the possible recriminations and impact a divorce would have on *The Fugitive,* how big the scandal would be if he was to take the risk.

I knew Dave had a strong will, but it made me mad as hell to know that he was being so mistreated by his wife. For crying out loud, I felt she should worship the ground he walked on. He had given her everything she could have ever wanted, had even provided a home for her daughters; for that alone she should have been grateful.

"So, Dave, how are Ellie's daughters ... are they aware of any problems with you and Ellie?"

"Oh, hell! Yes, they know. I try to keep it from them, try not to argue with Ellie when they are around but, sometimes, it just can't be helped."

"How do you think it affects them ... your arguments? Do they seem to take sides?"

"No, they don't take sides; they retreat to their rooms until it's over but, you know, Diane (especially) seems to know that I am not the cause of her mother's tirades," he said with a serious expression on his face.

"Weren't they in boarding schools before you and Ellie bought your home?" I asked.

"Yeah, she had them in boarding schools - first in New York when she left her husband, their father. Then, when she moved to Los Angeles, she brought them out here and immediately put them into a boarding school. When we built the Trousdale house, I insisted we bring them home."

"Do they seem happy ... do they think you are a good step-father?"

"Yeah, they seem happy for the most part ... this is the only home they have had since they were very small. As for my being a good step-father, I don't know about that. With my schedule, I'm hardly ever around, but we have a good relationship. They know I would be there for them ... I'd do anything for them."

"That's nice. I'm sure they see the truth about how their mom treats you ... still, no doubt, it's sad for them."

"Yeah, I think you are right. If I could change things, believe me, I would."

"What the hell could be going through Ellie's mind? You have given her everything she could want. It's not your fault you have women swooning all over you, that you have beautiful ladies appearing with you on camera ... I just can't understand her."

"Mike, when I first told her about Suzanne, my taking her to dinner when she appeared as a guest star the first time, I had not broken my vows. I had not slept with her but, then, after her second appearance and the nasty scene Ellie created on the set, I did. I went to bed with Suzanne ... and I loved it ... and we had a short-lived affair and Ellie found out."

"Oh, man! Now I feel a little for Ellie, but what married man doesn't have an affair, at one time or another - present company excluded?" I asked with a lighthearted laugh. "So your affair with Suzanne is over?"

"Yes, she told me that as long as I was married, we could not see each other again ... but for me to call her if I ever got a divorce," he said with a mischievous grin. "If I ever get up the nerve to get a divorce, I'll definitely call her."

"All I can say is Suzanne is one helluva beautiful woman ... and a good actress, too," I responded.

David motioned for another round of drinks.

I glanced at my watch. "Hey! It's almost closing time. Do you have your car?" I asked.

"Yeah, and don't worry. I am capable of driving home, too."

"Okay ... I would have offered you a ride home, that's all."

"Yeah, I have to get a couple of hours sleep. I'm not excited about going to the set this morning but I'll muddle through it. Maybe next week's script will be better ... make up for this wasted week," he said.

I could tell he was not pleased at all with the episode he was now filming but was determined to give his fans the very best performance he could.

We sipped our final round of drinks, Dave seemingly savoring his, as if it would be his last.

"Dave, I have a question. I've seen you drink a lot and then go to work the next morning, early ... yet, when I see the episode on TV, you seem like you are so fresh, so rested. Don't you get a hangover? Aren't you tired when you get to work the next morning?"

"I save my hangovers for Saturday and Sunday. I memorize my lines the night before shooting the next day's scenes. I go to sleep the minute I get home and I feel great after my hot shower before I go to the set," he said.

I wondered if he was joking about his hangovers. I know I had experienced more than a few hangovers after drinking with Dave - and I don't like hangovers. We left The Formosa at about 1:40. I was exhausted and, for once, it appeared Dave was as well.

"Don't leave LA until I call you," he instructed with a smile and a wave as we prepared to get into our cars and head to our homes.

"I won't," I yelled. "I'm sure we can find time for a toast to my departure."

9

I had made the decision to relocate, first to Indianapolis and, then, after a few months there, I would relocate to New York City, just a little more than 30 miles from my wife's hometown. I had told this to Dave in a brief phone call; I also promised I would not leave Los Angeles without having a farewell drink with him.

Dave called me on Friday night, June 24, inviting me to The Formosa; it was just before eleven.

"Hey, Mike! Good to see you ... what's going on with your transfer?"

"No go; my boss said there are no openings in New York, or even close. I gave my notice last week and this is my final week, and then I'll make the drive. I'm going to Indianapolis first ... don't know how that will work out ... if it doesn't, then I'll relocate to New York City."

"Have you ever been to New York City?"

"Yes, my wife and I spent our honeymoon night - and that's all it was, one night - at the Waldorf Astoria Hotel, then we drove to Indianapolis."

"Well, I'll tell you, I spent about nine months there, years ago, trying to get into a Broadway play ... did not work out for me, but I can tell you New York is a very expensive city to live in and it can be very hard ... so be careful and I hope you have better luck working there than I did."

"It sounds like you don't like New York. I would think that you would. After all, next to Los Angeles, it's the entertainment capital of the world ... all the television networks are there, radio, Broadway ... I'm sure you would enjoy it now, especially since you would not have to worry about money," I said with a smile.

"Oh, I do ... now! We've been there several times and it has some of the best restaurants in the world. Ellie feels at home there and, since expenses are not of concern, yes, I love it."

Another round of drinks appeared and I had not seen Dave give a signal to the waitress. I wondered if she was watching his glass.

"So I guess this will be our last time for drinks together," he said with a serious look.

"Yeah. I must say meeting you for drinks form the best memories I'll have of Los Angeles. Hopefully, I'll end up in New York and we'll have a chance to get together when you are there ... if you can find the time."

"Yeah, of course we will. I don't know how often that will be but, when it happens, I'll make certain we meet up for drinks, lunch, maybe even dinner ... it will be interesting to see how you do. Maybe you will be back with your wife," he said, flashing a big grin.

I did not know if he was serious about my reconciliation with my wife. "I don't have much hope as far as my wife is concerned but, if I do go on to New York, I guarantee you I'll make it there," I said with a genuine smile.

"Make sure you call me so I'll have your phone number and we'll stay in touch, okay?"

"Thanks, Dave! I will. So how are things with your wife?" I asked.

"Rocky, for the most part. We do have our good days but her girls are causing her some problems and that doesn't help."

"I'm sorry to hear that. I guess her girls are at the age where they don't want to listen to their mother, but she certainly can't take that out on you."

"I am just trying to keep things together ... concentrate on work. We're filming the new season and it takes a lot of concentration. I really can't afford any distractions. Now you know why I need a little fortification before going home."

"I knew that soon after we started having our little drinking sessions, but I consider myself fortunate, just to have a friend in this town. Los Angeles seems like a city where you have to be a celebrity to get anyone to even notice you ... a very impersonal town."

"Yeah, I know what you mean, Mike. It's too bad you've decided to leave; now, I'll have to find another, dependable drinking buddy," he said with a big grin.

"You won't have any problem doing that. Like I said when we first met, you could be sitting here, anywhere, drinking with anyone you choose." I grinned, then added, "Well, I hate it, but I guess we won't be doing this again anytime soon, unless you visit Indianapolis or New York. I'm going to miss it, I mean you ... and all the free scotch I can drink," I said, feeling a lump rising in my throat.

"Oh! We'll keep in touch and I don't know about getting to Indianapolis but, if you are in New York, we'll see each other again. I don't forget my friends," he said, a serious look in his eye. He ordered another round of drinks.

"I can tell you one thing for sure: I'll be watching *The Fugitive* as long as you keep running ... and any other movies you make, plus I'm sure I'll be reading about you in *TV Guide* and the other magazines."

"That's good to hear. I just hope it's all good." He smiled. "We'll stay in touch by phone so I can give you a heads-up of what's going on, and you can keep me abreast of what you are up to."

"So, you said your mother pushed you into acting when you were younger. Did you like it?" I asked.

"No, not really. I went along with her because she was my mother. The auditions were hell and, if I wasn't selected for a part, my mother would blame me, say I didn't try hard enough."

"That must have been hard ... but you have to admit, she was right. Look at you now."

"When I decided to be serious about acting, it was not easy ... still isn't, but I have worked my ass off, done everything they asked of me. My mother takes all the credit but, believe me, she did not sweat the blood or tears," he said, again with a serious expression.

"From what I've read since knowing you, it seems like she is so proud of you. She seems to dote on you. How does she get along with Ellie and her girls?"

"She gets along with Ellie about as good as oil mixes with water, and vice versa ... but she loves Kathy and Diane," he answered.

"Now, looking back, aren't you glad she was the stage mother she was?"

"Yes, but again, I am the one who did the work. I am the one who earned my success. I paid her back every dime I ever borrowed and much, much more ... and it gets a little annoying to hear that she *made* me a *star*. She's doing the same thing with Teri, my sister."

"Why doesn't she get along with Ellie?" I asked.

"Ellie took me away from her and Ellie has shut her out and Ellie spends and spends - my mother could have a million reasons I'll never know."

I could tell Dave was getting a little depressed talking about his mother and I regretted bringing her up. I changed the subject. "This is the fourth season ... how do you like Mr. Martin?" I asked.

"Quinn is the best in this business. He knows exactly what he wants and how to get it. He hires the best people and he spends what it takes to keep this show on top. I love him like a brother.

"He doesn't come around the set very often anymore; he trusts his associate producers and he has complete faith in the directors. Although, he is still on top of casting - that's about it. We talk every couple of weeks, but he lets us all do our jobs."

"What about the directors? Do they change all the time?" I asked.

"Oh, yeah! It depends on the producer and what director is available and willing to take on the task. We have a new producer this season, a pro named Schiller ... he knows what he's doing; I expect a lot of good things with him.

"Alan Armer was my favorite producer but he did so many episodes, it wore him out. My favorite director has been Walter Grauman, a prince of a guy."

"Who picks your co-stars? There are some beautiful women, well known from movies and TV."

"The casting director and Quinn pick the guest stars. I don't have any say in that - unless they pick someone I really don't like. It's all right with me, as long as they know their lines and how to act the part," he said with another of his mischievous grins.

"Well, what happens if they pick someone you do not like?"

"They get rid of 'em and cast someone I do like." He grinned.

"How do you get along with your nemesis, Lieutenant Gerard?"

"Barry Morse ... he is a terrific guy, great actor ... we get along great. I have a lot of respect for him. He's not in every episode, so we don't get to see each other that often."

"Do you like working with kids, like the ones in *A Plain Paper Wrapper*?" I asked.

"Oh, hell! Yes, most of them are pretty damn good. They know their lines, the director gets the facial expressions ... body movements that set the scene. They do a little rehearsing and come across with realism - and that's what it takes, what we need. Also, sort of reminds me of me ... long ago." He smiled.

"Since you are interested in police work, what do you think of all the so-called cops you run into on the show? Most of them don't come across to me as believable ... the dialogue, mannerisms ... the obvious mistakes."

"I have to agree with you there, my friend, but keep in mind the dialogue is written by a teleplay writer, not a cop ... and the director isn't a cop either. The actors just play the role. You have to admit, it's a good thing ... and they always allow me to escape."

We shared a genuine laugh over that. Another round of drinks arrived.

"So who are some of the actors you don't like?" I asked.

"There are just a few and they know who they are. I don't talk about someone behind their back, unless I have something good to say," he said with a serious tone.

"Hey, I admire that! My mother taught me if I had nothing good to say about someone, then I should not say anything." I smiled. I gained a deeper insight into the kind of man he was just by that statement.

"Well, time is drawing near. They're about to close the place down. I don't know if I'll have a chance to get together again but, if I don't, then call me when you get settled wherever so we can stay in touch. Okay, Mike? If you run into any problems and need help, just call me ... if you don't get me, I'll get the message and call you back," he said.

That almost made me cry. He was so sincere and I felt a real friendship had developed between us. It made me feel good.

We left The Formosa just before two o'clock. I was caught off guard as we waited for our cars; David gave me a tight hug and a firm handshake.

"This isn't goodbye, Mike ... we'll see each other again. I wish you could have adjusted to LA life but you know best."

"Thanks, Dave! You don't know how much I appreciate that ... you're right, we'll get together, maybe in New York ... if you can find the time when you're there."

"I'll make the time ... you be careful!" he said.

I waved as he drove off. I got into my car and headed to my apartment. I felt a sense of loss and had to wipe a tear then take a deep breath. I had not realized how important his friendship was to me.

Yet that was not what impressed me about David Janssen. What impressed me was his being such a grounded man, which made me feel such empathy with him. With all his success, wealth, millions of adoring fans, I felt he had NO real friends with whom he felt close enough to spill his guts about the details of the problems he faced in his private life.

I did not feel in the eight months we had been sharing conversations over drinks that he revealed the demons he was fighting.

He was successful, true – and, to ensure the security of his success, he was living in a marriage which had turned to one of more tension than love and he had to endure the whims and demands of his wife, even put on an act whenever they were together in public.

I left Los Angeles on the morning of June 30 and arrived in Indianapolis on Sunday, July 3. I spent two weeks at my mother's home, visiting family and friends at the Indianapolis Police Department. I made several attempts to call my wife, each attempt in vain.

Finally, I decided to relocate to New York City. I took my family to a nice restaurant on Friday, July 22, and advised them of my plans.

I left Indianapolis for New York on Saturday, July 23, and arrived late that night. I checked into the Holiday Inn Motel at the entrance to the Holland Tunnel, on the Jersey side.

10

I spent Sunday morning perusing the classified ads in *The New York Times*. I was amazed at the size of the newspaper, about the size of the telephone book in Indianapolis. I found some interesting prospects for employment and jotted down those I felt I would have interest in and be qualified for.

My next search was for an apartment in Manhattan. After breakfast and reading the Times, I drove into Manhattan and decided to do some sightseeing since I had never really spent any time there.

First, I drove all around the city - east side, west side, all around the town. I felt like a tourist from the Midwest but I loved the magic of the city; the vibrant life, the magnificent architecture, the skyscrapers, the crowds of people - to me it was exciting.

My first poignant observation was the way the New York City cab drivers manoeuvred the streets, in and out of traffic. I concluded that any one of the cab drivers could enter the Indianapolis 500 Mile Race and win.

I ended up in Greenwich Village and found a metered parking spot on Greenwich Avenue near Sixth Avenue - also known as the Avenue of the Americas. I walked around for about an hour and found a nice little Italian restaurant to have dinner.

It was just after eight o'clock when I finished a leisurely dinner and went back to my car. The lights were just coming on and the city seemed to really come to life. I drove all around Times Square and the Theatre District, which brought Dave to my mind.

It had been about a decade earlier when Dave had pounded these streets seeking a part in a Broadway play. Around 9:30 I finally headed back to the Holland Tunnel to get to the motel. I wanted to be fresh and eager Monday morning to find a job.

I was in Manhattan at 8:30 Monday morning heading to the Pan Am building. First on my list was an executive recruiting firm,

Management Science International. I was introduced to Mr. Norman Fayne, the president of the small firm. After an intensive interview, he offered me a position as a trainee. The salary was very good so I didn't hesitate in accepting.

I mentioned to Mr. Fayne that I would need a few days to find an apartment. To my good fortune, he owned a small apartment at 231 Thompson Street, just off Bleeker Street, in Greenwich Village, close to NYU. He gave me a key and told me to go see it; if I wanted it, I could move in the same day.

I accepted the apartment. I look back on it fondly as *the Dump*. It was a dingy, studio apartment on the second floor, facing Thompson Street, with a fire escape and all. It was extremely noisy, especially on the weekends. I would live there for eight months before I found a more respectable address at 288 West 88th Street, Penthouse A, where I lived for three years.

When New York Telephone installed my home phone, I called Dave in Los Angeles. I should have known I would not connect with him. Instead, Ellie answered the phone. I told her who I was and she was very cordial.

"Of course! I remember you, Michael; you were our guest at a dinner party last April."

She told me Dave was still at the studio and he may not get in until late. I gave her both my home and office telephone numbers. She assured me he would get the message.

Los Angeles was three hours behind us in time so I knew, if Dave got my message, I would most likely get a phone call in the wee hours of the morning; my phone rang at approximately 3:15.

"Mike ... Dave Janssen. I see you are in New York. How are things?"

"Good, Dave! I've taken a job in executive recruiting and I have a nice little studio apartment on Thompson Street in Greenwich Village."

"Hey, that's near an apartment I shared when I was there. I lived at 66 Barrow Street. How do you like the city?" he asked.

"I love it! I just have to adjust to the culture shock and I need three more jobs to be able to afford this place," I said with a little laugh.

"Yeah, I know, and it's probably much more expensive than when I was there, but it's one of my favorite cities. How is your apartment?"

"Well, it isn't really that nice; it's actually a dump! It's on the second floor of a three story walk-up, faces Thompson and it gets kind of loud with all the weekend partying. Of course, I've only been here a week. Maybe it will get better."

"You could have stayed in LA and joined the police department here. Are you going to check out the New York City police force?"

"Yes, but I'm going to give this job a chance. I know already it is a long process to get accepted by NYPD," I replied.

"Any good news regarding your wife?"

"No ... but I've tried contacting her several times ... no luck. Maybe now that I am just 30 miles away, and I'm not on a police department, who knows?"

"Okay, I'm sure I woke you up, so I'll let you get back to sleep ... and we'll stay in touch," he said.

"Okay, great."

"I'm drinking alone now ... and that's no fun," he said with a laugh.

"Sorry ... you know something: I haven't had a drink since the last time with you."

"You're on the wagon ... that is definitely no fun." He laughed. "Okay, we'll talk soon," he said and the phone went dead.

I was happy to know that he received my message from Ellie and felt good that he had called, even if it was in the middle of the night. It was hard getting back to sleep. I had not even asked him how things were going with him, his work and Ellie. He sounded good so perhaps his situation was improving; at least, I hoped it was. I made a mental note to ask him the next time we spoke.

At work I was assigned to handle electronic engineers, computer programmers and analysts and corporate executives in the engineering fields. I am a fast learner and it only took me a few weeks to learn the various terminology and basics of the job descriptions.

I was paid a salary and bonuses based on the starting compensation packages of the individuals hired by companies we represented.

Management Science International was not an employment agency so there was never a charge to the applicant, which I respected.

Norman Fayne was an extraordinary mentor and highly educated man. I would learn a lot from him in the two years I spent in his employ.

My next call from Dave came just before midnight three weeks later, July 29. I was surprised; it was just before nine o'clock in Los Angeles. I had just gone to bed so I was still awake and happy to hear from him.

"Hey, my friend! Do you want to have a couple of drinks?" he asked, then let out a big laugh.

"Hell, yes! Are you in New York?"

"No, I just finished the day. I'm still in my dressing room at the studio, thought I'd give you a call and hope I didn't wake you."

"No, you didn't wake me. So how are things with you ... how's Ellie?"

"Things are good here ... Ellie has calmed down a little ... how's work going for you?"

"It's good, everything is going good here. Any idea when you may be coming to New York?" I asked.

"I'm glad to hear that. I won't be going to New York anytime soon. We're in the middle of filming this season. How are things with your wife?"

"It looks like I may be permanently single soon; her mother told me she wants a divorce. Hell, she won't even get on the phone with me!"

"Sorry to hear that, Mike, but I'm sure you'll survive. Hey! I know New York. There are millions of beautiful women there just looking for a guy like you," he said with a chuckle.

"Well, I hope you're right, but I haven't been doing anything but working. I'm putting in 15 hours or more a day ... like you do every day. I haven't even been to a bar in a month."

"Well, you're going to have to take some time and go out, mingle ... meet some people. That was your problem in LA; you didn't go out and meet people. You have to take time and socialize ... all work and no play isn't good," he said in an admonishing tone.

"I know, you are right ... I'll take your advice after I'm a little more secure at work."

"Well, I have an idea. Since you are no longer here to drink with me, buy yourself a bottle of scotch and, when I call you, fix yourself a drink and we can get drunk together," he said, then laughed.

"I like that idea, Dave ... I'll do it. With the time between calls, the scotch should last me several months," I said, laughing.

"All right ... that sounds like a plan. I'll let you go and call me when you get your bottle," he said.

I felt good. Although I'm sure his idea was tongue-in-cheek, it sounded good to me. Dave sounded as though he was in a good mood, sober and things seemed to be calming down with Ellie.

I made a mental note to ask how the filming was progressing for this new season and when *Warning Shot* would be released in theatres. I very seldom go to movies but this was Dave's movie and I had to see it.

I always thought of things to ask or say after he hung up. The last couple of calls averaged no more than four or five minutes. Although I seldom called Dave, because I knew how busy he was and did not want to interrupt him, I decided when I bought a bottle of scotch, I would call him, but at a more reasonable hour than he usually called me.

I called his number just after eight o'clock, Los Angeles time, and again Ellie answered. I apologized for disturbing her and asked her to tell Dave that he could return my call at his convenience.

Dave's convenience at returning my call was just after four o'clock in the morning, Saturday, August 11, which meant it was just after one o'clock his time.

"Mike, Dave ... I just got your message. Did I wake you?"

"Of course you did, but that's okay ... I'm ready to get up anyway. You told me to call you when I got a bottle of scotch. Well, I have a . 750 litre of J & B so we can have a drink anytime you feel like it," I said in a joking voice.

"That's great ... since you say you don't have time to go out and have some fun, at least you can have a couple of drinks to unwind when you get home," he said with a little laugh.

"Yeah, but I'll probably only drink it when you call ... so it should last me at least a year," I said with a laugh.

"Okay, I have mine. I'll hold while you fix yourself a drink," he said in a serious tone.

"Dave ... it's only four o'clock in the morning here!" I exclaimed.

"Well, it's one o'clock in the morning here and it's ten o'clock in London, so make you a damn drink!" he ordered with a big laugh.

"I'll tell you what ... at five o'clock this afternoon, I'll fix myself a drink and I'll raise a toast to you!"

"Okay, I'll hold you to that," he said..

"So are you at The Formosa or home or ... ?"

"I just got home, late day, needed some exterior night-time scenes."

"Then you put in a hell of a lot of hours today."

"Yeah, but we finished this episode, so I can recharge my batteries over the weekend and do the dance again starting Monday."

"How are things going for you on the home front?" I asked.

"Don't get me started on that! You don't wanna know ... just a bunch of bullshit." I could hear the depression enter his voice.

"Dave, any news about when *Warning Shot* will be released? I've been looking in the papers here but haven't seen anything."

"No, I haven't a clue when they'll release it, but I promise I'll call you when I find out. So how are things with you... work ... your wife?"

"My job is great! I love it! As for my wife ... I guess it is time I face the music ... it's over. I just have to convince myself of that and move on."

"I'm sorry to hear that, Mike ... but think about it. It is better for both of you to realize it now than for you to end up in a marriage like mine ... where you feel trapped, whether it's because of your job or you have kids and you stay in the marriage just for the kids."

"I know ... I know you are right ... I just wished I had not fallen so hard for her ..." I felt my pain seeping into the tone of my voice.

"Okay, I have to go, but I'll call you in a few days. Take it easy in the big city ... go out and have some fun!"

"Thanks, Dave! I will. Keep in touch. I haven't made any friends here yet either," I said with half a laugh.

"Okay ... I will. Now I want you to GO OUT tonight. Get drunk!" he ordered. I think he was serious; I did what he said, but I didn't get too drunk.

11

I had gotten into the habit of reading *TV Guide* and a few of the movie fan magazines and TV sections of the *New York Times*, *Daily News* and *The New York Post* in an attempt to keep up with Dave's career. Articles regarding him were plentiful but didn't reveal much.

I bought *TV Guide* for the week beginning September 3 and was surprised to see an article titled, *What Sort of Women Do Actors Marry?* Lo, and behold, there was a photo of Mrs. David Janssen!

In the article, Ellie was depicted as a housewife, which brought a grin to my face. The article stated she had been married to Dave for 10 years; either she was fibbing or the writer miscalculated.

Ellie was quoted as saying, "My husband works with a lot of people but we, generally, don't get to know them very well. He works with many beautiful women but, if you've ever noticed the number of people that are around on a television set, you know it makes things pretty impersonal. I guess," she adds after a bit of thought, "I wouldn't like it so much if he worked with the same woman for eight months, though."

I had to laugh at her statement since Suzanne Pleshette immediately came to mind. I knew she was extremely angry with David over his telling her about his initial dinner with Ms. Pleshette after her first guest appearance on *The Fugitive*, then her angry and profane telephone conversation with producer, Quinn Martin, when he re-cast Ms. Pleshette for another guest appearance several months later.

She even threatened to bring a gun to the set and shoot Ms. Pleshette. She did show up on the set and created quite a scene and managed to disrupt the filming several times, until Dave ordered her to go home.

I made note to let Dave know I had read the article. I wondered if his publicist had arranged for Ellie to be among the five wives of stars to be interviewed.

I would not have to wait long. I was in my office when my phone rang just after nine o'clock on the morning of Monday, September 19, 1966.

"Mike, Dave ... is it okay for me to call your office?"

"Of course! This is a surprise! Where are you?" I asked.

"I'm at the studio waiting to go into make-up, so thought I would touch base with you."

"Thank you ... I wanted to tell you about an article in *TV Guide* a couple of weeks ago ... had a photo and small interview with Ellie and some other Hollywood wives. Did you see it?"

"Yeah, Liberman set that up and I know what you're thinking and, yeah, she was alluding to Suzanne," he said and laughed. "How is everything with you?"

"Good ... good ... I followed your advice. I've been going out, having a blast ... although I limit it to Friday and Saturday nights ... haven't found a place that can compare with The Formosa, though."

"There is no place like The Formosa, but you're out and about; that's the main thing. Have you made any friends yet?"

"Yeah, mostly bartenders and waitresses, but I'm doing better," I replied. "What about you? Have you found a new drinking buddy to replace me? How is the filming doing? How are things on the home front?"

"Well, no, I have not found a replacement for you, so you may have to come back to LA. Shooting is coming along just fine ... busted up my bad knee a couple of weeks ago. May need some surgery on it but it can wait until we go on hiatus. Things are pretty cold at home; I'm just trying to keep it calm."

"You hurt your knee on the show?" I asked.

"Yeah, but it was my own fault ... lack of co-ordination, I guess. It's not that bad, just a little painful," he said.

"I thought you had a body-double for all the rough stuff ... how could they let that happen?"

"It was just me. You know I like to do my own thing; I just jumped the wrong way and my knee went the right way," he laughed. "I'll have it fixed when we take a break."

"Damn ... I can see it now ... Gerard spots you and you start to run, your knee gives out ... he walks up to you withering in pain, face down on a cold concrete sidewalk and, without a word, he puts a bullet in the back of your head. He claims you resisted and pulled a gun; he had no choice but to shoot you.

"Of course, he drops a toy gun, looks real, but he has problems explaining the bullet in the back of your head - but then we hear Pete Rugolo's music and the gravelly voice of Conrad, 'And so the running has stopped ... Dr. Richard Kimble has been captured ... as the Wanted poster states, *Dead or Alive.* Lieutenant Philip Gerard has captured *The Fugitive.*

"He did it his way; he assured the people of Indiana that justice was served. *The Fugitive* ... Dr. Richard Kimble is DEAD!'" I said jokingly.

"Hell, Mike! Come back to LA and I'll get you a job writing our scripts!" he said and let out a big laugh.

"Really? I don't think Mr. Martin or ABC would like my ending but, then again, we could write it that way and convince Ellie that YOU really died, change your looks a little with plastic surgery and you could be reinvented as *Clark Gable, Jr.* ... no divorce, no property settlement."

"That sounds really good, Mike ... except the Clark Gable Jr. part. I sure as hell don't need that," he said in a joking voice.

"Well, then too, I didn't think but, since you'd be dead, Ellie would get your estate and you'd have to start from scratch. Guess it wouldn't work out for you. Sorry," I said with a laugh.

"Yeah ... and I damn sure don't want her to get it all. I'd hate having to start from scratch. I've already paid my dues, and then some," he laughed. "Okay, Mike, they want me ... gotta go. I'll give you a call later in the week." The phone went dead before I could say a word.

I had a laugh about the conversation and then went back to concentrating on my work. Although I never knew when he would call and, albeit, his calls were infrequent, I felt good knowing he thought of me as his friend who could be trusted.

I also felt that, when he did call, he was feeling some sort of pressure or perhaps depression and I would bet it had to do with his deteriorating marriage.

I would not hear from Dave again until Saturday, October 22; it was almost four o'clock and the phone woke me from an alcohol-induced sleep.

"Hello ..." I muttered.

"Wake up, Mike! Time to smell the roses. It's me, Dave."

"Yeah, I know it's you. Who else would call me at four o'clock in the morning?" I asked. He sounded a little inebriated.

"I know it's early for you but you don't want to sleep your life away. Besides, this time difference between the coasts can be confusing. How the hell are you?" he asked.

"Sleepy ... had a few scotches last night ... falling into your bad habits. I'll be okay after a shower and some Excedrin," I replied, adding, "So how is everything with you ... anything exciting?"

"Not really ... still shooting this season's episodes ... contemplating this will be my last season for *The Fugitive*," he said with a serious tone.

"WHAT? Are you serious? The show is at the top of the ratings; you could go on running another two or three years!"

"No, I can't. You don't understand. Doing a series, the same grind week after week, is physically and mentally like being in a corner of hell; it is not fun, it's damn hard and it has to come to an end sometime," he said. I knew he was serious.

"I guess you've been thinking about this for a while, huh?"

"Yeah ... I've had busted ribs, knots on my head, busted my knee several times ... this *being a fugitive* is tearing me apart."

"You know best. What will you do then? I mean you have millions of fans, literally, around the world. You don't want to be forgotten after all the work you've done to obtain your success ... you've earned it the hard way."

"Oh, no! Don't get me wrong! I won't just stop working. Abby is making inroads at the studios; he'll get me in some major films. Mike, making a movie is a hell of a lot easier. You work two to three months and then you have a month or so to relax and recharge. I really want to make the transition to film; this is my second series and I'm worn out."

"I see what you mean ... I understand, too. I just don't think you're quite ready for the actors' old folks home."

"You're funny. No, I'm not quite over-the-hill and I won't be disappearing from the screen, but it's time for me to make a decision and make some changes ... in several areas of my life."

"I appreciate you telling me all of this. I won't tell a soul, but make sure you tell me when it's done so I won't be pissed off at ABC for cancelling *The Fugitive* ... and let me know what you'll be doing next. How's Ellie?"

"Well, she's going to a battery of doctors ... says she's sick ... so I'm being the perfect, understanding husband. I hope they find out what is wrong with her so we can have it fixed, but things are not as bad as they have been."

"That's good to hear. I've been praying for you ... at least, you feel some relief from the stress."

"Yeah, it's still not the same ... but things are a little calmer now. What about you ... found anyone that you like?"

"No, I'm not really looking for anyone ... a little too soon for me ... but, if it happens, it happens and I'll just take one step at a time."

"Well, I have to go ... so now that you're awake, get up. Go out and have breakfast. Go have some fun in the city ... it's Saturday!"

"Okay, Dave. I'll do just that ... you have a good day, too. Get some sleep!"

12

Dave must have been very busy as I did not hear from him again until November 23, 1966.

"Hey, Mike! Dave ... how are you?"

"Dave, I thought you either forgot about me or were just pissed off at me. I'm fine. How in the hell are you?" I asked.

"Good ... I'm good ... no, I haven't forgotten you and why would I be pissed off? I'm just calling to wish you a Happy Thanksgiving."

"Thank you and the same for you, Ellie and the girls."

"What are your plans for Thanksgiving?" he asked.

"None, really. I'll probably go out to have the traditional dinner but, aside from that, I'll just lie around the apartment and relax. It's pretty cool outside so not really much to do," I said. "What are you guys doing? Is Ellie making a big turkey?"

"Ellie is having the turkey prepared for us. Beatrice is doing everything, then she'll have tomorrow and Friday off and we have temporary help to serve," he said.

"Oh! I'm so sorry, Dave. I forgot that the rich are not like the rest of us peasants," I said in a joking tone.

"Hey, Mike! I'm not rich, just that Ellie is spoiled. By the way, did I tell you about my Thanksgiving in New York?"

"No ... you didn't ... so tell me."

"I was all alone ... it was cold and I was flat broke, not even enough for a cup of coffee - and I was not about to call my mother. One: I was too embarrassed and two: she would charge me interest. Anyway, there were about three friends, also struggling actors, and they were almost as broke as me, but they invited me and we spent a cold Thanksgiving in one of their apartments, with deli sandwiches, pickles and water. I'll never forget that."

"Wow! You really had it rough back then. I guess I have a lot to be thankful for so I will enjoy the day much more, now that you told me your experience."

"Hell, Mike, this time next year you will probably have met a girl and fallen in love and be spending the holidays with her ... so think positive and enjoy what you have." His voice was firm.

"You're right, Dave, and I will. So how is everything else going with you? Have the doctors found anything wrong with Ellie ... that they can treat?"

"Ellie has a condition and they are treating her, and she seems to be responding. Still filming and thinking this will be the last season ... not really decided yet. I know both Quinn and ABC want to go another year, but I'm not sure I can do it, or want to do it. Everything else is fine ... except I still don't have anyone I would enjoy calling to meet me at The Formosa for a few drinks after a long day at work," he said. I was sure he was kidding on the last part.

"Glad to hear that about Ellie. I hope you make the right decision ... for you ... on whether to do another year with *The Fugitive*. You know you could be having drinks at The Formosa with anyone you want, so don't give me that BS. Besides, I bet that does not stop you from stopping there on your way home anyway."

"No, you're right; I stop there every night." He let out a chuckle. "I have slowed down on drinking lately ... a lot ... since Ellie has been sick."

"That's good, Dave ... for you. I'm not saying you have a drinking problem; as a matter of fact I've told you before, you have good control. I've never seen you really drunk that I would worry about you driving, or having control over your faculties."

"Thanks ... but I do have a problem, and I know it and I keep telling myself that I can control it ... but I know I can't. It takes a lot of will power but I'm drinking a helluva lot less than before."

"I still got a full bottle of scotch - only had a couple of drinks during a call with you," I said jokingly.

"Mike, enjoy your scotch ... you don't have to wait for me to call ... just don't go overboard. Thinking about that, I've noticed you have pretty good control over your drinking, too."

"I try. I think I know my limit, but it is hard to keep up with you."

"I've cut down, way down. Okay, Mike ... enjoy your Thanksgiving and we'll talk soon." The phone went dead.

I didn't ask Dave what condition Ellie was being treated for and wondered if it was physical or mental. I knew they were both seeing a psychiatrist and I hoped that was the problem with Ellie. I went back to sleep.

It would be a month before I heard from Dave again. As was his habit, my phone rang just after three o'clock in the morning.

"Good morning, Mike! Dave ... wake up!" His speech sounded slurred and I noted he sounded very tired.

"Good morning, Dave! I'm awake. How are you?"

"Tired ... was sitting here having a few after work and thought I'd give you a call. How's the weather there?"

I knew he did not call for a NYC weather report and I was concerned over the way he sounded.

"It must be somewhere in the twenties ... no snow yet," I answered. "How is it there?"

"Cool ... in the fifties."

"Okay, Dave. I know you didn't call me for a weather check. What's up? You sound a little down."

"Ahh ... just wanted to give you a call. The situation with Ellie is deteriorating; she's driving me crazy with her insane jealousy and, this time, I haven't done anything. I've about had it; I know I can't go on like this."

"I'm sorry to hear that, Dave ... wish I had the answer for you. I agree you can't continue to live like this. I'm starting to believe it is causing you to drink more than you should, and I know you don't enjoy it."

"You're right; I don't enjoy it, but it is the only way I can go through the motions and keep my temper under control."

"How many drinks have you had already?"

"I don't count 'em ... but I know I've had more than one." He let out a little chuckle.

"Do you have your car or a driver?"

"I have my car but you're not here, so I think I'll just take a cab home ... when I decide to go home."

"Well, let's see. It's after midnight there. Why don't you just go home and get some sleep? Are you working today?"

"No, we shut down until after Christmas. Yeah, I guess I need some sleep so I'll follow your advice. I'll go home. I called to wish you a Merry Christmas. What are your plans?"

"I'll go out for dinner, maybe walk around Rockefeller Center, see the displays ... just take it easy. There's not really much to do when you're alone but, then again, it is a good feeling in one respect: I don't feel obligated to be doing anything."

"Yeah, you're right. I miss that freedom; there's so much to do when you have family obligations," he said.

"What are your plans? I mean you and Ellie still have the girls at home to think about. What about *The Fugitive*; have you made a decision on next year's season?" I asked.

"Yeah, I want out. Abby's negotiating with ABC. I've talked with Quinn; he thinks we could do another season but I told him I'm just plain worn out. I think this will be the last and, if it is, we only have about eight or nine more episodes to shoot. Of course, the writers will have to come up with an ending that Quinn likes and that I'll be willing to do."

"Have you told Ellie or anyone else about your decision?"

"I've talked with Ellie about it but she wants me to do, at least, another season; that's her words *at least*," he said.

"Personally, Dave, as a fan I must admit that I will miss it but, then again, you deserve a good, long vacation ... and like you said, Mr. Greshler will be getting you into other roles, films, so it isn't like you will disappear - and your fans will go see whatever movie or TV show you're in."

"Yeah, we haven't had a real vacation in a long time. Weekends in Palm Springs is not a vacation in any sense of the word; we planned to go there to relax but we know so many of the people there, it is always one party after another."

"I can only wish you the best; you know what you're doing. Maybe Ellie will feel better too and things will get back to being good for you both."

"I don't know if that can happen, but I agree we do need a vacation. Who knows what will happen?"

"I think things will work out and you'll be relieved from all the pressure and stress the series causes you ... and, hopefully, Ellie will come to realize that you love her and she has nothing to worry about."

"Mike, I hope you are right, but people change. Love changes and I'm not sure I love her anymore; there's a lot for her to forgive, a lot for me to forgive. You can forgive, but it is hard as hell to forget ... for both of us," he said in a serious tone.

"You know best, my friend."

"Okay, anyway, the movie, *Warning Shot*, is being released next month; I guess you'll have to check the movie listings in the paper to see when it will be in New York."

"Hey! That's great news! I really can't wait to see it!" I exclaimed.

"All right, Mike. I wish you a Merry Christmas and, if we don't talk before, have a very Happy New Year. I'll be in touch."

"You, too, and that goes for Ellie and her girls, too."

Dave ended the call and I was wide awake. I put on a pot of coffee. I analyzed the conversation and, for the first time, I realized how sad I felt for Dave. A guy who, in the eyes of the public, seemed to have everything, inside he was a very miserable man. I was starting to worry about his excessive drinking. I had read in a Hollywood tabloid that it was being rumored that David Janssen had a serious drinking problem.

I drank my coffee and turned on the TV news. At about six o'clock, I showered and dressed for work.

I could not help but worry and think about Dave several times which was distracting, to say the least. For the first time I found that I really was starting to worry about him.

He had told me when he and Ellie started seeing the psychiatrist in San Diego that he was pretending to seek help, but it was his ploy to get Ellie to see the doctor; he felt she was the only one who needed help.

I was beginning to think Dave should take advantage of his sessions and really open up to the doctor, that maybe he would get some good advice. I decided I would bring the subject up during our next conversation.

13

Dave called me just before one o'clock in my office on December 11, 1966.

"Mike, we're flying into New York tonight for a taping of *The Merv Griffin Show* ... wanted to check with you and see if we can get together for a couple of drinks," he said.

"That would be great; it will be good to see you in person again ... not just on TV," I replied with a little laugh.

"Good. We'll be staying at The Carlyle Hotel. Do you know where that is?"

"Yes, on Madison Avenue, around Seventy-Fifth Street."

"Right. Actually, I think it is East Seventy-Sixth Street. Anyway, I'll call you when I get a chance and we can meet, okay?"

"Perfect. I'll be looking forward to it."

Dave called me on Monday afternoon, December 12 and asked if I could meet him in the Bemelmans bar off the lobby around 10:30. I agreed.

I arrived at The Carlyle right on time. David was seated in a small banquette with a drink in hand.

"Great to see you, Dave!" I said as I sat down, reached across the small table and shook his hand.

"Likewise, Mike. You look good ... so you have adjusted to life in the big city."

"Yes, and I love it ... so many things to see and do - the history, the architecture, the people, so many cultures ... oh, and yes, the restaurants," I gushed.

"Well, tell me how everything is with you ... your work, your love life, everything," he said.

A waiter appeared then took my drink order. Dave ordered another.

"Still working with Management Science International ... great boss, I love the work. Sorry to say, no love in my life ... yet ... but there is hope," I said with a smile. "Have you taped the show yet?"

"Yes, we taped it early this afternoon. We're going back to Los Angeles in the morning; I have to be on the set Wednesday."

"Did Ellie come with you?" I asked.

"Oh, yeah! We finished dinner and she isn't feeling well so she went upstairs."

"How are things going with you?" I asked.

"Same ... but I am muddling through ... maybe not always with a smile, but I'm doing it just the same."

"So you have made the decision to end the show; it's final?"

"Definitely! It's really past the time I think we should have ended it, but I will be glad when it is over," he said.

"Will that change your thoughts on your present situation ... with Ellie?" I inquired.

"Yes. I just haven't decided when, or how, to do it. Right now, I am just trying to play the role of a devoted husband."

"How is your drinking ... still tapering off?"

"As a matter of fact, yes. I still have days where I'll have more than my usual ... depending on the circumstances."

I could tell he was tired, though he looked refreshed in a dark blue suit, white shirt with French cuffs and burgundy tie.

"So you are staying here at the hotel?" I asked.

"Yes, it's my favorite place in the city. I've come a long way from the nine months I spent pounding the pavement trying to catch a break on Broadway," he said with a big grin.

"I would say you have ... you've come a long way."

We spoke about the escalating war in Viet Nam, which we were both against. Dave expressed his hatred for the cold, winters of New York, but added he loved the city. We had three drinks each - well, Dave had at least four.

"I guess we should call it a night. I have to work in the morning," I said.

"Yeah, and we have an early morning flight. It was good seeing you again ... still wish you had stayed in LA but we'll see more of each other. After the series ends, I'm sure I'll be coming to New York more often. I hope you have a Merry Christmas and a great New Year. Oh, this is for you," he said as he took a package from beside his seat, in a plain paper wrapper and handed it to me.

"Thanks, Dave, and thank you for the drinks, and taking the time to get together. What is this?"

"It's a book I thought you may like; I have it and think it's well written," he said.

I opened it; it was a hardcover of *The Embezzler* by Louis Auchincloss.

"Thank you, Dave! I certainly didn't expect this. I've heard of this book and, actually, have been intending to get it. Thank you! I'll read it this weekend. I wish you, Ellie and the girls a very Merry Christmas and all the best for the New Year."

With that we shook hands and he headed for the elevator and, me, for my apartment.

I felt a sense of embarrassment that I had not even thought to get a gift or even a Christmas card for Dave and Ellie.

Christmas for me, alone in New York, was without any personal significance. I called my family in Indianapolis and did nothing but read *The Embezzler* and relax.

I did go to Times Square to celebrate the arrival of 1967. It was my first experience witnessing the mass of humanity gathered in such a tight space.

I was amazed at how everyone was so friendly and having such a grand time; there did not seem to be any trouble at all. I was also amazed at the number of police officers present; there were more police officers in Times Square than we had on the entire Indianapolis Police Department.

I took a cab home, arriving just before one o'clock. It was then I noticed I had been the victim of a pick-pocket. I never carry money in my wallet but they got away with three credit cards, my drivers' license, voters registration, Veterans Administration identification card and the photos of my wife.

I called the local precinct and the credit card companies to report the theft. I knew the minute I saw the slit at the bottom of my left rear pocket that I had not lost my wallet. How slick the perpetrator must have been! I did not feel anything. *Welcome to New York City*, I thought to myself. It would be a real hassle to replace all of my cards and identification, but I learned a lesson.

I wondered if that had ever happened to Dave. The rest of my weekend was relaxing. I was off on Monday, January 2, and spent the day roaming around the city after having breakfast at my local diner.

I was startled awake by my phone at 4:45 on Saturday, January 13, 1967.

"Morning, Mike! You awake yet?"

"Hello, Dave ... just about ... yes, now I'm awake," I said as I rubbed the sleep out of my eyes. "What's up? How were your holidays?"

"Good ... peaceful. Ellie, Kathy and Diane were happy and mellow and that's all I could ask for."

"What about your mother and dad, your sisters?" I asked.

"I stopped by and dropped off their gifts. What about you? Did you enjoy the holidays?"

Based on the tone of his response when I mentioned his mother, I did not push the issue. "Yeah, they were fine, except New Year's Eve. I went to Times Square - a mad-house and a sea of people; I discovered when I got home that I had been pick-pocketed. Has that ever happened to you?"

"No, I have been fortunate. How much did they get?"

"They got my driver's license, social security card, voter's registration, three credit cards, veteran's identification card and my photos of my wife. No cash; I never carry cash in my wallet," I said.

"Did you report it ... especially your credit cards?"

"Oh, hell, yes! First thing I did. It took me hours with the credit card companies and then I had to take time the following week to get a new driver's license and the other I.D."

"I'm sorry to hear about that, especially your photos. You gotta watch the city - all kinds of nuts there," he said.

"Yeah, I feel so stupid ... so much for my being a good cop." I laughed.

Dave understood my humor and gave a hearty laugh.

"Hey! I saw this new movie the other night called, *Warning Shot.* The star's a guy named David Janssen ... lots of major stars in supporting roles. Janssen plays a police detective sergeant who stops a suspicious guy and ends up shooting him. When his back-up arrives, he tells them the guy pulled a gun on him, but they can't find the gun. Janssen's character gets arrested, charged with murder.

"Anyway, I can tell you this guy Janssen plays a good cop; he knows the moves, the idiosyncrasies of a cop ... the way he carried himself - very believable performance. I gotta tell you, I think this actor is the next Gregory Peck," I said with a slight laugh.

"No kidding! You saw the movie? Now, tell me what you really think of it," he said earnestly.

"Just what I said. I loved it and will see it again. I honestly think it will lead to many more films for you. It got great reviews here in the New York Post and the Daily News. I clipped them out; I could send them to you if you want me to."

"That's good to hear. I thought it was an excellent script ... glad to hear you say I pulled it off well. You don't have to send the news articles; my publicist gets all that crap."

"So things are getting better between you and Ellie?" I asked.

"Not really, Mike ... the feelings just aren't there anymore. I'm just trying to maintain a status quo."

"If you don't mind my asking, are you still seeing that doctor, the two of you?"

"Yeah, we are, but that won't last forever."

"I know you told me that all you and the doctor really talk about are sports and stuff. Have you thought about telling him your situation with Ellie? Maybe he can give you some advice on how to make things better, maybe get back to normal."

"I have, Mike. He knows the whole story and all of my dirty secrets. Hell, he knows me better than you do ... better than I know myself," he replied, a sincere tone in his voice.

"Well, has he said anything that has actually helped you ... or Ellie?"

"Me, yes ... that's how I've been able to keep my sanity. As for Ellie, yeah, in some ways. After her two hour sessions every week, she's fine for a couple of days, then the same crap starts all over."

"Well, I don't know what to tell you, but you will make it. That I know. Any word on whether there will be a fifth season for your show?" I asked, referring of course to *The Fugitive*.

"Yes, as a matter of fact ... this is it ... no more after this season. Quinn has several writers drafting final scripts; we'll see them in a few weeks and decide which way to go."

"Well, now that you have made a decision, how do you feel about it? Are you relieved?"

"Yeah, Mike, actually I am very relieved. It has been one helluva run and I've got the broken bones and bruises to show for it, not even to mention the marital strife it has caused.

"I think it is time to do other things - movies first. I really don't think I'll be doing another television series. Now, listen, I know this goes without saying, but this is top secret; you're the only one who knows this. Keep it that way," he said.

"Dave, you know - as you said, it goes without saying!" I exclaimed. "You will never have to worry about that."

"I know, Mike. You know I trust you. I didn't mean to say it that way."

"That's all right, Dave. Do you have anything lined up after it ends?"

"Yes, first we're going to take a vacation ... a few weeks, at least."

"Good ... where are you going?"

"I don't know. We haven't decided ... anywhere as long as it is away from Los Angeles and Palm Springs," he said. I detected a slight laugh.

"That's a good idea. I think you deserve it and I think you need it!"

"I'll let you know when I know. I've been trying to convince myself that, with the series over, if Ellie and I go away for a few weeks, maybe things will work out ... at least, I'm willing to give it a shot," he said sincerely.

"I bet Ellie is excited."

"Yes, she really is ... and she has been very mellow since I told her. Maybe things will change; I'm keeping my mind open."

"That is really good to hear. I will pray and hope that everything works out the way YOU want it to. What about when you get back from vacation; has Mr. Greshler lined anything up for you?"

"No, but he will. I am not even worried about that. I don't have any idea what the box office tallies are for *Warning Shot* but, if they turn out to be above average, it will give me box office credibility and that will make it easier for Abby to get me some good film roles."

"How are you doing with your drinking? Sorry! I'm just concerned about you."

"Well, I don't think I'm drinking any more ... don't think I'm drinking any less ... but I'm doing a little diversifying ... trying other mixes," he said with a deep laugh. I knew he was kidding.

"All right, Dave, I deserve that ... but seriously, how are you doing? In case you don't know, I've become a fan of yours. For me, that is way out of character because I look at Hollywood as a make-believe world where no one is real yet, since I've known you, I have this strange habit of grabbing *TV Guide*, *Photoplay* and several other fan magazines ... just to keep track of you. Are you still cutting back on your scotch, really?"

"Yes, I really am ... but I try to make up the difference with a vodka and tonic every now and then," he said with a slight laugh. I did not know if he was being serious or not.

"Okay ... you are a big boy, so far be it for me to tell you what you can and cannot do." I smirked.

"Mike, you sound like my mother!" he said with a quirky laugh. I knew he was serious, but I also felt he appreciated the genuine concern I felt for him.

"So tell me, have you met anyone yet ... anyone that looks promising for you?" he asked.

"No ... not yet ... but I do find my eyes taking stock of what looks to be available, so all is not lost."

"Hell, Mike! You've been there over six months, haven't you? What the hell is taking you so long?"

"Work ... work ... and more work." I laughed.

"Okay, my friend, you know best. I have to go. Call you later."

"Have a good one ... be safe and keep me informed," I said.

The call ended.

14
~1967~

Saturday, January 28, 1967, I was surprised when my phone rang just after nine o'clock in the morning.

"Mike, Dave Janssen. I know I didn't wake you this morning. How the hell are you?"

"Good, Dave! I'm good. Are you just going to bed or just waking up? It's only a little past six there," I said with a slight chuckle.

"Just waking up. I have to go to a meeting at the studio later so wanted to check on you and see how you're doing," he said.

"All is well here. As a matter of fact I am going out to Jersey to buy a German Shepherd puppy in about an hour," I responded.

"Really! That's great ... probably be cheaper than buying a new wife," he said, letting out a laugh. "What gave you that idea?"

"Well, I miss having a German Shepherd and, now that I feel pretty secure in my job, I have gotten a new apartment, with a nice balcony. Since I haven't found a girlfriend yet, I just wanted to have someone to come home to," I answered honestly.

"You moved! Where are you now? What's your address?"

"I found a nice apartment on West Eighty-Eighth Street, just a block east of Riverside Park. It's really a nice apartment, nice terrace, and great views ... two bedrooms. Rent is a little steep but I can park my car on the street, hardly a problem finding a space," I said. "It's 288 West Eighty-Eighth Street, Penthouse A."

"That's nice. Glad to hear you are doing well. Did you see *The Merv Griffin Show*?"

"Yes, I did. You were very good and, finally, people had a chance to see your humor - never see that on *The Fugitive*."

"Mike, you know fugitives find little humor in a position of being constantly on the run, but you're right. Maybe the writers can find something to let Kimble laugh once in a while," he chuckled.

"So how is everything going with you?" I asked.

"Good ... really good. Quinn has several writers drafting the final episode and he'll make a decision in the next few weeks. Ellie and I are going to take about a month's vacation and I will really relax ... first time in years. I've never had a real vacation. Even when the show has been on hiatus, I've always worked. I am really looking forward to it," he said.

"How are things with you and Ellie?" I asked.

"Mike, it's really touch and go. She has her good days and her bad days. Of course, her bad days are always my fault but I've taken your advice. I try not to let it upset me. I smile and try not to respond with anger ... good advice my friend, but very hard to do."

"I know ... but, hey, look on the bright side! Maybe a vacation alone together will bring a spark back into your love life and things will get better for you both."

"I hope you're right ... I know I'm trying."

"What about Kathy and Diane while you're on vacation?"

"Our housekeeper will take care of Diane. Kathy has a job now and Ellie is helping her find an apartment."

"That's good; at least Ellie won't have to worry about them. I am sure it will do you both good, especially you. Do you have any idea where you're going?"

"Maybe somewhere in the Caribbean ... Virgin Islands or Puerto Rico ... somewhere tropical," he said and let out a laugh.

"You will send me a postcard, won't you?" I teased.

"Yeah, of course ... maybe even two." He laughed.

"I hope Lieutenant Gerard doesn't find out you're there. I've been to San Juan, Puerto Rico, but haven't made it to the Virgin Islands yet."

"I've never been to either place yet; how did you like San Juan?"

"It is a great place to relax ... beautiful beaches, great shows, casinos, historic Old San Juan, really nice and fun place. I stayed at the Caribe Hilton, excellent hotel."

"Good, I'll let Ellie know. Okay, I'll let you go and we'll talk later."

"Thanks for calling ... let me know where Ellie decides to take you for your vacation," I said with a chuckle.

"Yeah, I will. You take it easy," he said and ended the call.

I had forgotten to ask him about the episode, *In a Plain Paper Wrapper*. I had not seen it and worried that I had missed it, but I was certain I had not missed the show. Maybe they cancelled it but I made a mental note to ask him the next time we talked.

Another couple of weeks passed before I heard from Dave. February in New York City can be extremely cold and old man winter was showing his force this month, kept us around freezing.

Saturday morning, February 11, just before eleven o'clock, I was debating taking my German Shephard, Baron der Hunter, to the park when my phone rang.

"Hey, Mike! Dave ... not disturbing you, am I?"

"No, Dave, it's good to hear from you. How are you?" I asked.

"I'm fine ... working and working on staying sober," he said with a slight laugh.

"Well, that is really, really good to hear! I bet that is making Ellie happy."

"Ellie finds something else to bitch about so I wonder why I bother to please her. I'm not doing it for her ... cutting back on my favorite pastime; I'm doing it for me," he said firmly.

"Well, that is the best reason ... as I've said many times, you appear to me as being in control. I've never seen you so inebriated that you couldn't think and reason."

"I know, Mike, that is why I'm doing it ... and my doctor says it would be a good idea to give my liver a rest ... for a while."

"Listen to your doctor! You're still a young guy and you have a hell of a lot to give ... anything happens to you and I, along with your millions of other fans, would be very upset. Actually, speaking for myself, I'd really be pissed off at you. When do you and Ellie get to go on your vacation?" I asked, changing the subject.

"It will be around the middle of next month, but we may just go to Palm Springs. I can relax there, play some tennis and really unwind. Ellie is now at a point where she doesn't want to go anywhere ... and that is another thing I have to deal with."

"Dave, it sounds to me like things aren't getting any better with Ellie. Isn't the doctor helping her at all?"

"I don't think any of the doctors are helping her ... and she has a battery of doctors ... just seems like a waste of good money to me," he said.

"I'm really sorry to hear that, Dave, but I know you are trying and you are not one who gives up easily," I said, then added, "Can you really relax in Palm Springs? You are recognized everywhere you go."

"Yeah, I relax there ... there are so many Hollywood people there and no one bothers anyone. Many of our friends are there and we get together for card games, tennis ... I'm even learning to play golf."

"Golf ... you? Wow ... that is a game I don't think I would have the patience for ... do you like it?"

"Yeah, I do. It takes a lot of concentration and I don't take my score seriously, so it is relaxing for me."

"Maybe you can show me someday ... a lot of people in my business here are golfers. I've been invited to play but I don't know anything about the game so I always beg out of the invitations."

"You might want to start watching it on television, the Pro tournaments. Watch guys like Jack Nicklaus or Arnold Palmer; they are the pros and they make the game look easy ... which it's not."

"Okay, I'll do that ... maybe I'll learn something."

"Okay, I have to go now so I'll give you a call later," he said.

"I'll look forward to it ... oh, before you go, have you found out when you will be really ending the series? I don't want to miss it, especially since no one will tell me how it ends."

"I don't know. I'll try and find out and give you a call."

"All right, I'd appreciate it. You take care and I'll talk with you soon," I said, and the call ended.

I bundled myself up in my Air Force parka, flight pants and combat boots then decided to take my puppy to Riverside Park. We had no threat of snow but the wind was biting through the 30 degree temperature so it would not be the usual hour. Baron was now three months old and loved running in the park; he even seemed to love the cold weather.

I had learned my way around Manhattan and found my favorite neighborhood newsstand, diner, deli, dry cleaners, Gristedes' Supermarket and a good barber. That is one thing I loved about the city: no matter what one wanted or needed, it was within a few steps of your door and Manhattan was a 24/7 city.

I decided to stop at the corner newsstand to get *The New York Times* and *Daily News* and scan the Hollywood fan magazines to see if there were any articles about Dave or *The Fugitive*. I had found that with *The Fugitive* in the top five television programs, anything about

David Janssen was news and articles relating to his work - on and off *The Fugitive*, not to mention his home life - was sure to be written about. I did not find anything relating to Dave or the series that week.

15

I had become accustomed to Dave's infrequent calls and to perusing *TV Guide*, *Photoplay*, *Radio & TV Mirror* and other film and television fan magazines as well as *The New York Times*, *The Daily News* and *The New York Post* to catch any articles relating to Dave, *The Fugitive* or any other films, TV appearances or his marital situation. If I found an article, I'd buy the magazine or newspaper; if not, I saved my money.

On Sunday, March 5, Dave called me around four o'clock in the morning. "I know I woke you. Sorry! Just wanted to let you know we will be doing a two hour show for the end of *The Fugitive* starting next week. Quinn has received the script and we'll be going over it tomorrow," he said.

"That's great! I bet you're excited about it ... can you at least tell me if you go back to death row? Do you catch the one-armed man? Does Gerard kill you, or do you kill him? Do you kill the one-armed man?" I asked in rapid order.

"You know I can't tell you that. Actually, I won't know myself until tomorrow and, when I do know, I still can't tell you," he said with a chuckle.

"Yeah, I know, but hell Dave, you know you can trust me. I won't tell a soul..."

"Yeah, I trust you. I know you wouldn't tell anyone but Quinn has put in place a gag order on everyone, including me," he said with a laugh. "If I told you, I'd have to have you killed and you couldn't watch the show."

"The hell I would! I will not miss it for anything! So then you get to have a vacation, a real vacation? How is Ellie doing; is she happy it's almost over?"

"Yeah, but it is still up in the air as to where we'll go or what we'll do. Ellie is really looking forward to the end of the series, but not as much as I am. She's being pretty nice to me lately."

"That's good to hear. Maybe your vacation will revive your feelings for each other."

"I don't know about that; we'll just have to wait and see."

"Do you have anything planned, I mean for after your vacation?"

"Abby has a few feelers out for me with the major film studios ... I'm sure something will come up. I'm not really worried about it. I just want to take a break for a few weeks."

"I sure as hell don't blame you for that ... God knows you've earned it; you sure as hell deserve it!"

"Thanks ... I agree with you. Okay, you can go back to sleep ... sorry again I woke you," he said with another chuckle.

"Wait ... how are you doing with your scotch intake?" I asked in a half-joking manner.

"I'm still not drinking as much as I'd like to, but I do feel a little better ... mentally, I mean."

"Okay ... I am just curious ... don't want to read you've been arrested for a D.U.I.," I said with a laugh.

The call ended and I went back to sleep for a couple of hours.

I was surprised to hear from Dave again on March 13.

"Mike, Dave Janssen. I hope I didn't wake you again. I will be in New York tomorrow. Can you meet me for drinks tomorrow evening?"

"Hell, YES! That's great ... why are you coming to New York?"

"Abby has booked me on *The Merv Griffin Show* again; it will be taped on the 15th," he replied.

"That is great ... everyone will be asking if you're guilty. I mean they'll want to know if Dr. Kimble is really guilty."

"Yeah, I'm sure that will come up," he said with a laugh. "I'll call you when I get in; we can meet at The Carlyle."

"Sure, just let me know the time. Is Ellie coming with you?"

"No ... not this time. She is being seen by her doctors so she's staying home; it will be a real quick trip anyway."

"Is she okay?" I asked.

"Yes but she doesn't think so ... her doctors are running all kinds of tests; so far they can't find anything," he said.

"Well, at least now, I have something to look forward to; it will be great seeing you again."

"All right. I'll call you when I get in," he said, and the phone went dead.

It was just after eight o'clock and I was all ready to go to work. I put in a full day at the office but decided I would pass on my usual happy hour at The Oyster Bar in Grand Central Terminal.

I arrived home just after six o'clock and took Baron for his run in Riverside Park. I returned home and checked my answering machine; no messages. I took a shower and changed into a different suit. I decided to make myself a scotch and water and watch television while waiting for Dave's call.

My phone rang just before nine o'clock; I answered on the second ring.

"Mike, Dave ... have you eaten dinner yet?"

"Actually, no ... what's the plan?"

"If you want to meet me at the Bemelmans Bar in the lobby of The Carlyle, we can have something to eat there. I'll meet you there in about 20 minutes, okay?"

"See you there," I said and hung up the phone.

I was surprised that Dave was back in New York and on *The Merv Griffin Show* again so soon. I knew that Dave had known Merv Griffin for several years and an appearance on his show was great publicity for both Dave and *The Fugitive*.

It only took me 20 minutes to get to the hotel. I had left my car in the parking space on the street near my apartment and opted for a cab. Dave was seated in a banquette facing the door and I spotted him immediately as I entered the bar.

"Hey, Dave! This is an unexpected surprise ... it's really good to see you and you look rested. With your schedule, how is that possible?" I asked as we shook hands.

"I switched booze; the new one gives me more energy," he said with a laugh. "How are things going for you?"

"Good ... everything is good ... brought you a picture of my puppy, Baron der Hunter," I said, pulling Baron's photo from my wallet.

"He is a fine specimen ... look at the size of his head, and those paws ... he is going to be a giant ... how old is he now?"

"Just turned four months and he is smart, really smart. You are right; he's going to be huge when he is fully grown. You'll have to come by and meet him, if you have time," I said.

"Yeah, I'd like that ... maybe I could do it tomorrow, either before or after the taping," he said.

"That would be great. I have my car so I could pick you up. Hell, I can even take you to the airport," I replied.

"No, you don't have to do that; they have a car service for me, but thanks for the offer," he said.

A waiter brought another drink for Dave and took my drink order, leaving menus on the table.

"You said you haven't eaten yet. They have great sandwiches here or, if you prefer, we could go to the main dining room and have a full meal," Dave said.

"No, Dave! A sandwich would be perfect," I said. We perused the menus for a few minutes. The waiter brought my scotch and it was perfect.

"Have you decided?" Dave asked. The waiter was hovering over us.

"Yes, the Angus burger sounds perfect, with onion rings," I said, placing the menu down.

"I'll have the lamb chops with onion rings," Dave said, smiling up at the waiter.

"Thank you, Mr. Janssen," the waiter said, as he turned and smiled at me and left for the kitchen.

"So, Dave, tell me: are you getting ready to film the ending?" I asked.

"We're doing it now; it will be a two hour show, split for airing a week apart next August, after the re-runs have played out."

"Two hours ... split ... you mean everyone is going to be left hanging until the following week?"

"Yes, sir ... they want to milk it and make more money from the sponsors. Can't blame them for that ... makes me more money so I'm all for it," he said.

"So if you are shooting it now, and it won't be shown until August, you have to tell me, Dave. I can't wait that long!"

"If I could tell you, believe me I would. Everyone working on the show has a gag order from Quinn himself ... just about everyone in America wants to know the ending. All I can tell you is it is going be the best and most exciting of all the episodes ... really," Dave said with a big smile.

"All right. I guess I'll just have to wait. So when you're finished with the filming, you and Ellie get to take your vacation?"

"Yes, but she still has not decided where she wants to go, or what she wants to do. I just want to relax and not think about running anymore," he said.

"Well I'm sure she will understand that you need some time to decompress. I just hope you can find some place where your fans won't make it impossible for you to have privacy and enjoy yourselves."

"Can you come to *The Merv Griffin Show* taping tomorrow? I can get you a ticket; it is free for the audience but I can get you a front row seat," he said.

"That is really nice of you, Dave, but I have to drive out to a client on Long Island in the morning, to meet with their VP of Human Resources and tour the plant. It's an important client and I can't mess it up," I said.

"Well, maybe the next time. I have a feeling I'll be back and forth more often, especially after the series is finally put to bed," he said.

"I would really like to see it, to see you with Griffin again; you were pretty funny the last time. Maybe Mr. Greshler can get you into some films like the *Pillow Talk* movies with Doris Day and Rock Hudson," I said.

"Yes, he is trying and I'd like to do comedy. I think it will help in my shaking the stereotype of being a *fugitive*, show people that I'm not so damn serious all the time."

Our food was placed before us and the waiter left to get us another round of drinks.

"Anyone who has seen you on *The Merv Griffin Show*, *Hollywood Palace* or *The Tonight Show* knows you have a sense of humor. Personally, I just don't think your roles give you a chance to really show it, to use it and make people laugh."

"Well, I think once *The Fugitive* is really over, I will be a little more particular in the roles I accept. I enjoy comedy and I like to make people laugh, but I guess it is my voice or my facial expressions; all the producers just look at me for serious roles. I will do my best to change that perception," he said with a smile.

"Rock Hudson plays both serious and comedy, but I think in the *Pillow Talk* films, he is outstanding, and you could sure as hell do that kind of a role," I added.

"Yeah, I agree with you ... but it's not all up to me, and Rock has Doris to work with. We will see what the future brings," he said and laughed.

"Well, I hope you have time to come and meet Baron. I can get off work early after I get back from Long Island, probably be somewhere between two and three o'clock."

"I'll give you a call after the taping. I know my flight back to LA is somewhere around eight so if I can do it, I will," he said.

"That would be great; you can meet Baron and see my apartment," I said.

We finished our meal, had a cup of coffee and Dave ordered us another round of drinks.

"Okay, Mike, I'm going to get some sleep. It has been a long day and it will be a long one tomorrow."

"Thanks a lot for dinner and the drinks and I hope you'll be able to come by the apartment tomorrow."

"I hope so, too. I'd love to meet Baron ... I'll call you for sure."

I took a cab back to my apartment and took Baron out for a late walk.

The next day, Wednesday, I drove out to meet the Vice President of Human Resources at Airborne Instruments Labs.

I toured the plant and received the specifications of 11 electronic and mechanical engineer positions they needed to fill. I was back in the office just before one o'clock.

Dave called me at the office just before four o'clock and said he could meet me at my apartment at five o'clock. I told him that would be perfect and left my office. I wanted to make sure to take Baron out for a quick walk and make certain he had not made a mess or destroyed anything as he had done in the past.

Dave arrived right on time, in a Cadillac stretch limousine. I had already gone down to the door to meet him. I felt kind of awkward as he got out of the limo. I introduced him to our doorman, James.

We went up to the apartment and Baron seemed to like him immediately. Of course, I introduced them and told Dave he had a new fan.

"Do you have time for a drink?" I asked.

"Love one, thanks."

I made us both a scotch, Dave's with soda.

"You have a nice apartment, Mike - a neat little bachelor pad ... good location, too."

"Thanks ... it's comfortable for Baron and me."

"Great view! I hope you enjoy it for a long time to come," he said.

We finished our drinks. Dave said he had to get back to his hotel, pack his bag and head to the airport.

We shook hands and I went down to the lobby with him.

16

I would not hear from Dave again for several weeks. However, I did read several articles relating to the future ending of *The Fugitive*, including the fact the series would be shown in re-runs during the summer months.

I felt we had come to know each other very well over the preceding 18 months and I found him to be a very complex man. I found it incomprehensible to come to terms with the reality of his life. He had worked so hard to achieve the success he had and was adored by millions of fans, both men as well as women.

He was in great demand on the television variety and talk shows and had so many famous people as friends - not just celebrities, but business and political leaders as well. He was a millionaire with no financial worries. Yet, the Dave I knew was not a happy man in his private life. He had lost the love he felt for his wife and I was becoming more convinced that perhaps this was the driving force behind his excessive drinking.

Still, I had great admiration for his ability to control his actions and be able to report for work and perform his role with such perfection. I observed him closely as he conducted himself in public; he knew every move he made would be observed by fans and perhaps those who were not his fans. He handled himself well, protracting dignity while being genuinely humble.

One would think, as I did, that David Janssen had everything any man could ever hope for, yet he was suffering inside and I knew nothing I could say or proffer would, or could, ease his pain.

I had learned a valuable life lesson from my eldest brother, Jack: to be a good friend, one had to be a good listener. If being a good listener - a sounding board for Dave - was of any help to him, I would continue to be just that.

Another thing I learned was not to ask personal, prying questions of anyone. If Dave wanted to tell me something, he would and he knew it would be held in strictest confidence.

It was Saturday, April 22, when Dave called. "Mike, Dave Janssen. How is your weekend going?"

"Great ... just relaxing with Baron. How is everything with you? Where are you ... on vacation?" I responded.

"Yeah, we're on vacation, but we're staying at our place in Palm Springs. We're back in Los Angeles today, though; we have some paperwork to do on selling our house and Ellie is looking at some apartments we may rent here. I just thought I'd call and see how you are getting along."

"That's very nice of you. All is well here, still a little cold, but spring is almost here. I'm still a bachelor but, at least, I'm staying out of trouble," I said with a slight laugh.

"That is good to know."

"How are things going with you and Ellie?"

"Not really as I expected. I thought this little vacation would help us talk and clear up this constant bitching, but it isn't."

"Sorry to hear that ... is that why you're selling your house?" I asked. I had only been inside his home once for a dinner party and it was magnificent. I would not want to sell it if it was mine.

"We decided we would spend more time in Palm Springs and we'll rent an apartment here for when I'm working. Then again, it is better for me to make plans for the future," he said.

"What do you mean by that?"

"Well, Mike, you know I want to get out of this mess with Ellie. It is over, as far as I'm concerned. I can't take much more of it. As soon as the series is over, I'll make plans."

"Does that mean you are going to get a divorce? Do you think it will hurt your career? I mean, you'll be doing films ... major films ... and maybe you'll do another television series. How do you think a divorce will affect you ... your future?"

"It may hurt me ... certainly will hurt financially but, hell, the tabloids are already reporting discord between Ellie and me and, to be honest, if I stay in this marriage, I think it will hurt me more, both mentally and my career."

"It sounds like you've made up your mind. Have you talked with your agent, Mr. Greshler, or anyone else?"

"No ... I will when the time is right. There are a lot of things I have to do: get things in order, talk with Abby, Frank and Fred ... and I will when the time is right."

"Well, Dave, you certainly know what is best for you. I know it isn't going to be easy but I am on your side so if you need someone to yell at, just give me a call ... even at three o'clock in the morning," I said with a little chuckle.

"I know, Mike. I appreciate that. Take some advice from someone who has been through it: before you jump into marriage, make damn sure you have the woman you want to spend the rest of your life with."

"How do you think Ellie will react when you ask for a divorce?"

"Like a wounded tigress; it will be like starting a war and I don't think she's going to let go without one hell of a fight. It's going to be a bloody war ... no doubt about that."

"Is this going to happen anytime soon ... in the next few weeks ... months?"

"I don't know yet ... it will take time for me to get things lined up, so I don't really know."

"Your ninth anniversary is almost here ... think you'll make it to celebrate with Ellie?"

"Who the hell knows ... maybe yes ... maybe no. We'll just have to wait and see," he said, releasing a big laugh.

"Well, at least you can still laugh about it ... so, at least, I know you're still somewhat sane," I said with a slight laugh.

"Yeah ... but for how long my sanity will remain is the sixty-four-thousand dollar question," he said and laughed. "All right, Mike! I'll keep in touch. Have a good weekend."

"You, too, and keep me informed. I don't want to read in *The National Enquirer* that Ellie shot you or something," I said in a joking tone.

"Don't worry! She doesn't know how to use a gun ... I'll let you know."

"Okay, Dave, and thanks for calling," I said. The call ended.

17

In the 18 months I had known Dave, I developed the habit of looking through television and movie fan magazines to see if there were any stories about Dave. Dave had told me that most of the articles about him, or he and Ellie, were carefully arranged by his publicist, Frank Lieberman, and that I should not believe half of what was written.

Knowing that he was not happy in his marriage nearing their ninth anniversary gave me reason not to believe the articles.

A couple of the fan magazines ran articles with color photos showing Dave and Ellie in their home and declaring them as one of Hollywood's happiest married couples. Dave had also told me something I would never forget: *things are not always as they seem.*

I was well aware the fan magazines were full of the Hollywood mystique and most of what they wrote of film and television stars' private lives was just for their fan consumption and to sell magazines.

Having known Dave as a person still had not piqued my interest in the television or film industry. Knowing Dave, and getting to know him as a man, solidified my opinion that those living the glamorous Hollywood lifestyle were people, too, and they had the same feelings as every other human being. However, their lives were not their own.

Being a celebrity of Dave's stature came with a heavy price. Dave, as other television and film actors and actresses with any degree of fame, had to pay the heavy price of sacrificing their *right to privacy*. Everything they did, or said, was fodder for fan magazines, newspaper gossip columnists and the paparazzi. I knew just from observing Dave that I could never live in that type of fishbowl.

Sure it was the same for prominent politicians or leaders of industry but, for Dave and most Hollywood and music celebrities, the inability of living a normal life was a demand their fans hungered for. It did not matter if what was written in the tabloids and fan magazines was based on truth or the figment of a writer's imagination; putting a scintilla of truth with a pound of lies sold magazines and papers.

I had bought some fan magazines with articles relating to the discord between Dave and Ellie having been noticed in public and some private gatherings by their so-called friends, who were never named. This, of course, was reported along with rumors of Dave's excessive drinking and hints of infidelity.

I knew both to be true but I also knew the pressures of his work and the obsessive jealousy and controlling attempts of him by Ellie was a major cause for his drinking. I really felt sorry for him.

On May 3, Dave called me just before midnight.

"Mike, Dave Janssen - just wanted to let you know I'll be out of touch for a while. Ellie and I are going to Europe; I'll be away from phones for a few weeks."

"So, you finally decided to have a real vacation!"

"Yeah, we're going with several friends by ship, sailing from New York. Sorry I won't have time to get together there; we sail soon after our plane lands in New York."

"That is great, Dave ... although I don't know about being stuck in the middle of the ocean for what ... three or four weeks?"

"I'm not certain. I've never been on a ship before, let alone an ocean voyage across the Atlantic, but I'm sure all will go well."

"How are things with Ellie? She must be excited about the trip."

"Yeah, she is ... she has never been to Europe before either, and never been on an ocean voyage, so she is treating me like a king. Who knows? We go from New York to London, spend a few days there, then we fly to Rome and, maybe, we'll make a side trip to Madrid."

"Well, I am certainly happy for you. I know you will enjoy it. I just hope Ellie continues to treat you like a king," I said.

"I'll let you know when we get back so you take care of yourself and we'll talk in a few weeks," he said.

"Okay, Dave, and thanks for letting me know. Now I won't have to read it in the fan magazines or the tabloids," I said.

I would next hear from Dave on Saturday, June 24, just before nine o'clock. I had just walked into the apartment from taking Baron for his morning walk.

"Mike, it's Dave. How is everything with you?"

"Hey, you're back! How was the voyage? How was Europe? How is everything going with you and Ellie?" I asked.

"The voyage was great - very relaxing ... was able to do a little gambling ... great food, it was really nice. London is a magnificent city, as is Rome ... beautiful architecture, friendly people, fantastic food. Ellie and I had a great time; it was almost like we were just married," he said.

"WOW! That is good news ... so now maybe everything will get back to normal for you two."

"I hope so. We are going to the Virgin Islands - just a short vacation alone - so I'll give you a call when we get back from there."

"Good ... again, I hope you have a great time and really relax. I know you need it," I said. "Thanks for calling and letting me in on all the good news."

"You are welcome. I'll give you a call when we're back home," he said. The call ended.

I felt really happy for Dave. I had not heard him sounding this positive and happy in a long time. Perhaps the trip and being with Ellie, with no party demands, no filming schedule and no obligations had worked magic for their marriage. At least that is the impression I got from Dave. The conversation made me feel good for him.

I had bought several fan magazines and noticed the hype for the impending conclusion of *The Fugitive* was really heavy.

There was not a week that went by without a story speculating on how the series would end. There was absolutely no doubt millions of Dave's fans were as eager as I to know how *The Fugitive* would end.

In addition to my eager anticipation of how the series would end, I was wondering what Dave would be doing next. I knew he was hoping to get a good role in a major film, either as the star or at least co-star and was hoping he would land one that he would really enjoy doing. I also hoped the next role would bring him more recognition than he had received in previous major film roles.

On Sunday morning, July 2, Dave called me.

"Good morning, Mike! Dave Janssen ... we're back home; things are great. How's everything with you?"

"Perfect! I've met a girl and we are sort of dating," I replied. "How did you and Ellie like the Virgin Islands?"

"You met a girl? That's great! You have to tell me about her. We went to Saint Thomas, visited with a couple of Ellie's old friends from New York but had to cut it short. Abby has me committed to a new film."

"Great ... what is the name of it?" I asked. "First, let me tell you about Rose Marie. She is Italian, looks like Marlo Thomas, beautiful, fun personality ... now tell me about the movie."

"That's good news! I'm happy for you! Maybe I can meet her the next time I'm in New York. About the movie, it's a war picture ... Viet Nam ... star is John Wayne; it is called *The Green Berets*. Wayne plays a Green Beret colonel; I am the co-star, playing a journalist. Everyone is supposed to hate me, at least the army officers," he said.

"It sounds pretty interesting ... they haven't made any films about Viet Nam, at least none that I've heard of."

"I don't know. I really did not want to do this but Abby thinks it will be a good film and get me more major film parts, so I'm gonna do it."

"Well, I don't think you will be filming in Viet Nam. Where are you going to be doing the filming?"

"We will be at Fort Benning in Georgia for the exterior scenes and then we'll do all the interiors in the studio in Hollywood."

"That's good. Be sure to let me know when it is finished ... when it will be released so I won't miss it."

"Yeah, I will ... but, first, I am off to Africa."

"Africa? What in the hell are you going there for?"

"Abby got me a gig with ABC Sports. I'll be on a Safari, lion hunting."

"Oh man ... how can you do that ... kill a lion? They're just big, overgrown kitty cats."

"Don't know that I will actually kill one. I've never been to Africa, so it will be fun."

"Is Ellie going with you?" I asked.

"Hell, no! They didn't invite her. It will be a good break for me; I know I'll enjoy it."

"Will it be on television?" I asked.

"Yeah, if it's any good, it will probably be one of those *ABC Sports* shows that are shown on Sundays."

"Good ... just let me know ... it sounds like you might be in for a fun trip," I said, then added, "Personally, I don't think I'd like sleeping in a tent in the middle of the African jungle. I'd miss the modern conveniences I have here in New York," I said with a chuckle.

"I'll let you know ... you have a good one. I'll give you a call when I'm back," he said and ended the call.

18

The millions of Dave's and *The Fugitive's* fans, including me, had been treated to a summer of last season's episodes, building up to the climactic grand finale to be aired the last two weeks of August. I must admit the anticipation was nearing the boiling point in me.

I read in *The New York Post* that Dave would be co-starring with John Wayne in *The Green Berets* film that was set to go in production the first week of August. There was also an article about him starring in an *ABC Television Sportsmen* being filmed in Africa. I already knew not to expect a phone call from him anytime soon.

Dave called me on Sunday, August 20, from his motel in Columbus, Georgia, near Fort Benning.

"Good morning, Mike. How is everything?"

"Good, Dave. How are things with you?"

"I'm in Columbus, Georgia; we're filming the movie here at Fort Benning."

"Great ... do you like it?"

"No, it is too damn hot here. I don't like my script; hell, I don't like anything about it," he said in a serious tone.

"Okay ... but here's my advice to you ... not that you asked for it ... but it is free. Remember, you were in the real army. John Wayne never served in the military but he's played generals, admirals ... hell, almost all command ranks, so you just be glad you're playing a civilian and not a major or sergeant that would have to kiss Wayne's ass," I said with a laugh. Dave laughed, too.

"Yeah ... you are right. We'll only be here about another five or six weeks, then back to LA," he said.

"That's good."

"I'm just calling to let you know the first of the last two episodes of *The Fugitive* will air on Tuesday ... don't want you to miss it."

"Don't worry, Dave! I will not miss it! I've been waiting almost a year to see it!" I said. "Is Ellie with you?"

"No, Ellie is home. She was here for a couple of days, now she's back home, visiting her doctors."

"So once you've finished the outside scenes, you do all the rest in the studio back in Los Angeles," I mused aloud.

"Yeah ... just a few more weeks."

"When will the film be released?"

"Hell, I have no idea ... a few months after we're done filming. I'll make sure to let you know," Dave said.

"So is everything still going good with you and Ellie?"

"Not really ... she is slipping back to her domineering ways ... and I'm not going to give in to her. I am not going to let it happen again."

"Damn it, Dave! You do so much for her; how in the hell can she treat you like that? It just boggles my mind."

"Yeah ... I don't even try to figure her out anymore, but now the series has ended. I'll have this film done soon. Abby has another project for me so I'll be pretty busy and I'm not going to let anything stand in my way. I'm taking charge!"

"Personally, I think you have the right attitude. Still, a divorce is going to cost you financially; I'm sure it will cost you plenty, but I don't see any way it will hurt your career. Your fans love *you*, not Ellie ... and everyone you work with knows and respect *you* ... not Ellie," I reiterated.

"Yeah ... thanks! That's what I plan ... don't know when but I will know when it is the right time."

"Well, if you need someone to yell at, you have my number and it doesn't matter what time you call."

"Yeah, I know, Mike and I appreciate it. How are things with your new girl, Rose?"

"Rose Marie ... she's a lot of fun to be with, not too intelligent but not dumb either, but I am taking it slow. I'm not rushing anything."

"That's good ... you're still young, don't rush into anything. Make sure you both want the same thing," Dave counseled.

"So tell me ... how is it working with *The Duke*?" I asked.

"I'll say he lives up to his reputation. He is an extraordinary actor, always prepared and knows his lines as well as the others he is interacting with but, personally, he is rude and arrogant. He comes off as if his shit doesn't stink ... not a guy I'd enjoy having drinks with."

"Wow, Dave! That surprises me. Everything I've read about him, heard about him, is that he is really a nice guy. What is his opinion of you ... does he show you respect?"

"Mike, that's what publicists are for; maybe he is, I don't know. I just gave you my opinion. Remember what I've told you: all is not what it may seem. Yeah, he treats me okay, at least I think he respects my work. I don't see our working together on this film leading to a lasting friendship ... I don't know."

"Well, I'll reserve judgment until I see the movie."

"Yeah. After you see it, I want you to call me and let me know your honest opinion ... no bullshit."

"I will ... and I know better than to try and bullshit you, Dave," I said.

He laughed. "Okay, Mike ... nice talking with you. I'll keep in touch," he said and ended the call.

I knew he was busy and I knew Ellie arrived in Columbus, unannounced to spend their ninth anniversary with Dave. I read that tidbit in *The New York Daily News*.

Dave called me from Las Vegas the day after Ellie had returned to Los Angeles to see her doctors.

"Hey, Mike! How's it going?"

"What a surprise! Everything is good. How about you ... how is the movie going? How is Ellie?"

"I'm in Las Vegas ... just for the weekend. Ellie is here with Peggy ... you know, Paul Burke's wife."

"Is the filming finished?"

"Not yet. Wayne and I had a little disagreement so I walked off ... brought some of the crew to Vegas with me. Ellie was already here so I told her I came to see her because I missed her ... made her feel good."

"That's funny ... what do you mean you had a disagreement with *The Duke*? YOU walked off ... aren't you worried they'll fire you?"

"No, they can't fire me. Wayne was being his arrogant self and treating some people very bad. I stuck my nose into it and we almost came to blows. I just thought it better at the time to walk away. It's the weekend so it won't cause much problem with the shooting schedule."

"Did you know Ellie was in Las Vegas? Was she surprised to see you?"

"Oh, yeah! She was surprised ... but that's okay. I'll be going back to Georgia tomorrow."

"So tell me, are you winning at the tables, the one-armed bandits or just taking in the shows?"

"Well, I'm not winning ... and that's not good, but it happens. Sometimes I win and sometimes I lose," he said with a little laugh.

"Well, I'm glad it's you and not me; at least you can afford it."

"Yeah ... tell that to Ellie. She doesn't like it when I lose but, of course, it's a different story when I win."

"Yeah, but do you feel you are addicted to gambling?" I asked.

"Hell, no! Not in the least ... when I feel like it, I do it. It is a mental challenge and a way to relax at the same time. I don't let it bother me when I lose; I know I'll get it back eventually."

"I'm damn glad I never fell into that addiction; I couldn't afford it. If you enjoy it and can afford it, I say do it."

"That's a good way to look at it," Dave responded.

"So how much longer before the filming on the movie is finished?"

"We'll be wrapping up at Fort Benning in a couple of weeks and then move to LA for the interior scenes ... probably wrap it all up by the end of next month, first part of October."

"Of course, we'll have to wait for the release date, right?" I asked.

"Oh, yeah! They'll have to do the editing, music and all the technical work; it'll take a couple of months for all of that."

"Well, if I don't read or hear about it before, make sure you let me know."

"Mike, with a John Wayne movie, I'm sure you'll hear and read about it long before it is released," he laughed.

"I don't give a damn about it being a John Wayne movie; I don't know him, don't consider him my friend but, since you're in it, I'll spend my five bucks for a ticket. Hell, I'll take Rose Marie and I might even splurge on some popcorn and cokes," I said with a laugh.

"Yeah, I'm sure Rose Marie will enjoy a damn war movie. I'd suggest you take her to a comedy or a romance movie ... take her to *Funny Girl* with Barbara Streisand," Dave recommended.

"Yeah, you're right. I'll go see *The Green Berets* by myself." I laughed.

"Okay, I have to run. I'll give you a call soon ... you take care," Dave said and the line went dead.

I would learn later that Dave had tested with Barbara Streisand for the leading male role but lost out to Omar Sharif. I was disappointed hearing that; it would have been a great film to showcase Dave's comedic abilities.

19

On Tuesday evening, August 22, 1967, I was sitting in my living room at ten o'clock as the gravelly voice of William Conrad and Peter Rugolo's dramatic music commenced rolling across my television screen announcing *The Fugitive* starring *David Janssen.*

I had a fresh scotch and water with lemon wedge and Baron sat on the other end of the sofa. I think in the few months I had him, he had also become a fan of Dave's.

I watched this episode, knowing full well there would only be one more and I would have to wait an entire week to know what would become of my friend, Dr. Richard Kimble.

The hour, minus the minutes dedicated to commercials - which I knew were necessary to pay Dave's salary as well as the entire cast and crew - seemed to fly by with lightning speed. I watched and put my mind into thinking like a cop. I was trying to solve the case of the murder of Mrs. Helen Kimble.

Could Dr. Richard Kimble really be innocent? Was he wrongly convicted? Did the one-armed man actually exist? If the one-armed man was real and Dr. Kimble saw him fleeing his home, why was he never found? Why was Lieutenant Philip Gerard so convinced of Dr. Kimble's guilt?

As the end of *The Judgment, Part One* rolled to its final credits, I was a firm believer that Dr. Richard Kimble would soon be vindicated. After all, Lieutenant Philip Gerard had seen the one-armed man in the flesh, had interrogated him at the Los Angeles Police Headquarters. Still, the question remained ... how will it end? I knew my friend's running would stop on Tuesday evening, August 29, 1967, at 10:58; I just did not know how.

I could not help but wonder how many television sets were tuned to ABC that hour. I would get the answer in the Wednesday edition of The New York Daily News. I also could not wait to again hear from

Dave. I wanted to commend him for an outstanding performance, viewed by millions in less than one hour, yet I knew it took him approximately eight days of working between 12 and 16 hours each day to get it perfect.

The week passed all too slowly to suit me. Although work kept me busy, I caught my mind wandering to what Dave was doing at Fort Benning, Georgia. Was he glad to be free of Dr. Richard Kimble, that he was no longer running ... crisscrossing the country?

I made a note to ask Dave if he liked his character, George Beckworth. He had told me he did not like his script but, maybe after having a few weeks of walking in a journalist's shoes, he may have come to like him.

I was delighted when Dave called me late in the evening on Monday, August 28.

"Mike, Dave Janssen. Did you see the show?"

"Of course! Tomorrow I'll, finally, find out the truth. Did Kimble kill his wife? Was the one-armed man innocent? Maybe he was a peeping tom and saw Kimble kill her, and Kimble tried to kill him!"

"No ... no ... no, Mike! It isn't gonna work; you can't make me talk. You'll just have to wait," he said with a laugh.

"Well, now that we both know you're no longer running in Dr. Richard Kimble's shoes, how do you like being George Beckworth? Is he a nice guy? Is he good at his job ... does he like his job?"

"Well, yeah! I've come to like him a little, respect him; he's an honest journalist determined to let the American people know what our government has gotten us into - a stupid war where our men are dying every day for absolutely nothing. We'll never win there," Dave said emphatically.

"Wow! Dave, you really mean that, don't you? I hope you do because that is exactly how I feel."

"Hell, yes! I do! Of course, my script downplays Beckworth's views. After all, this is *The Duke's* film, and I can tell you he is one hell of a big HAWK; he's gung-ho on this stupid war."

"I know what you mean. Obviously, he doesn't see the comparison with the Korean War. I hope Nixon is elected and brings our guys home ... no way we can win it with Johnson's plan. If they would send in a squadron of B-52s and bomb the hell out of North Viet Nam, they would surrender and our guys could all come home and have victory parades - like when Truman ordered the bombs dropped on Hiroshima and Nagasaki, the Japs gave up!"

"I have to agree with you, Mike," Dave said. "Nixon is already saying he'll end the war so he has my vote."

"Well, don't say anything like that to Wayne; he'll replace you in the film with some reporter whose as misguided in his opinions as he is," I said with a laugh. Dave laughed, too.

"Well, I just wanted to make sure you watched the show last week and you'll see the ending tomorrow. We'll be going back to LA this coming week so I'll give you a call next week."

"Okay, be sure you do. I may have some questions about my friend Dr. Kimble. Wait! How was your anniversary? Did you get to go home and see Ellie, have dinner with her at least?"

"She came here. We had a quiet dinner in a nice restaurant. I gave her a nice gift and she went back home the next morning. I guess you could say it was a pleasant anniversary."

"That's good to hear ... maybe things will get even better."

"Time will tell. Who knows? Okay, I've gotta go. Have a good week."

I felt good over this conversation. Dave sounded stone cold sober and in a very upbeat mood. He sounded like he was really into his character and was enjoying working on the film.

I made certain I was home in time to see the last episode ever of *The Fugitive* the next day. I made Baron his dinner and we rushed out to Riverside Park for his evening run. At ten o'clock we were on the sofa waiting for *The Judgment, Part Two*.

I was mesmerized as the minutes ticked by and the suspense built to the climactic end. The scene where Lieutenant Philip Gerard offers his hand to Dr. Richard Kimble and Kimble slowly reaches out and shakes his hand, was a very touching scene. The expression on Dave's face made Kimble so real.

To think Kimble had been on the run for four years all because the so-called war hero, Lloyd Chandler - who had obviously been having an affair with Helen Kimble - did not save her from the one-armed man's attack. I liked the ending as I saw Dr. Kimble and Jean Carlisle walk away; perhaps they have a future together. Special guest star, Diane Baker, gave an excellent performance as the beautiful Jean Carlisle.

I was extremely impressed by the writers, George Eckstein and Michael Zagor, for their very complex and suspenseful script and with

Director Don Medford for getting the right facial expressions, body movements of each cast member, even the battered bartender in the early opening scenes and the surprised look on Bill Raisch's face as the LA Police officer ordered him to drop the knife.

I knew immediately *The Fugitive* was not over, not by a long-shot. It would live on through re-runs and, even then, my opinion was *The Fugitive* would become an American Television Classic. It has.

Since I had come to know David Janssen and had first recognized him in his first starring role as *Richard Diamond – Private Detective*, I knew this role as Dr. Richard Kimble in *The Fugitive* had made him a world famous star and earned him the respect of everyone in the television and film industries. I felt so honored that he had chosen me to be among those he considered friends.

It was September 23 when Dave called again. He was back in Los Angeles and in the final stages of filming *The Green Berets*.

"How is it going, Mike?" he asked as I answered my phone.

"Great, Dave! How is everything with you? You're back in LA?"

"Yeah ... been here for a couple of weeks. Did you see the finale of the show?"

"Of course! Dave, I'm thinking you could bring back the show, make it another season or two. Dr. Richard Kimble and Jean Carlisle get married, he becomes a prominent pediatrician and they have kids and everything turns out rosy. Of course, Lieutenant Gerard and his wife become good friends with Kimble and Jean," I said.

Dave let out a big laugh. "I don't think so, Mike. I'm not ready to do another TV series ... not for quite a while. Did you like the grand finale?"

"I LOVED IT, Dave! I really did. It was perfect ... it will make *The Fugitive* a television classic, I am sure. I read in the *New York Post* that it shattered all the ratings in the Nielsen polls. Congratulations on that. As for bringing it back, I don't blame you. I was just pulling your chain," I laughed. "How are things on the home front?"

"Not that bad ... not perfect, but not all bad. We may be going to Europe again after I finish with this film."

"Really? That would be nice. I think you and Ellie deserve a nice, long vacation. Where are you going?"

"Don't really know yet, but I'll tell you when we decide something definite."

"Yeah ... at least I'd know you're not calling me because you're out of the country or something."

"No problem. So everything is good with you ... and Rose Marie?"

"Yeah, actually it really is, but I'm not rushing to get into anything. No commitment. I'm still legally married," I said.

"Well, take care and I'll keep in touch ... just wanted to know what you thought of the ending."

"Okay, you take care, too, and let me know where you'll be going in Europe."

We ended the call.

20

My next contact from Dave came on Saturday morning, November 25, 1967.

"Good morning, Mike! How was your Thanksgiving?"

"Good. I was a guest at Rose Marie's parents' home in Queens. They are really nice people and Mrs. Risatello is an excellent cook. I enjoyed a very good home-cooked meal. How was yours and Ellie's, and the girls?"

"It was good ... had dinner at home this year. Beatrice prepared a great turkey with all the trimmings. It was very relaxing. After dinner, Diane and Kathy had places to go so Ellie and I just lay around and watched television," he replied. "So Rose Marie took you to meet her parents ... starting to sound serious, Mike."

"Not really ... hell, I'm not even divorced yet and Rose Marie knows that nothing can get too serious. So is *The Green Berets* finished?" I asked.

"Oh, yeah! We finished it a few weeks ago. Now they're doing the editing, music ... all of the technical stuff."

"Good. I'm looking forward to seeing it. Do you have any idea when it will be released?"

"No, not yet, but you'll see the advertisements for it when it's about to be released."

"So things are getting better with Ellie?" I asked.

"Not really. She has her moments, but it is the holidays so I am trying to keep everything calm and, you know ... happy."

"Well, what is next ... now that you've finished the movie?"

"I'll be doing a few guest appearances on some of the talk shows and variety shows. Abby is getting me some scripts to read and consider. Right now, I'm just taking it easy," he said.

"So how are you doing on your drinking, if I may ask?"

"Hey, you can ask but will I tell you ... that is the question.

Actually, I've slowed down a bit, now that I'm not under the stress of the series ... and no real fighting with Ellie. Yeah, I've slowed down a bit ... not going out to as many parties as before," he responded.

"That's good to hear. What about your trip to Europe ... is that still on?"

"No ... at least not in the immediate future ... maybe spend some time in Palm Springs. We're just going to stay home. Ellie is decorating our apartment again and I just want to relax until Abby gets me into something I think I'll like."

"That's good ... you deserve a little break. Wish I could get a vacation ... take off and tour Europe ... must be a good life you have my friend," I said in a joking manner.

"You would not want to live my life, Mike. Believe me," he said, his tone serious.

"Yeah ... now if I could have your life without Ellie and her girls and without millions of women running after me, screaming and tearing my clothes off, I'd like your life," I said, again joking.

"Well, you have to give up something for this kind of life and privacy is it; it's a big price to pay."

"Yeah, I know, Dave. No, I would not want your life; I couldn't handle it. I notice when we're at a bar or restaurant how everyone stares at you ... that alone would drive me mad."

"Oh, you get used to that; I don't let it bother me. Hell, I don't even notice it anymore."

"I'm glad you don't let it bother you but, for me, if I were in your situation, I could not handle that. It just seems to me that you have sacrificed your privacy and, more important, your freedom to go anywhere you want without being mobbed."

"Mike, you are right, but I look at it this way. I owe my success not just to my abilities to give a good performance, the writers, directors, cameramen and all that makes the show; I owe everything I have and everything I am to my fans. They put me here and they deserve to be treated by me with respect and dignity, so I understand and my fans will always come first with me."

"I know. You are right and I understand. I am just glad I am not in your shoes; I could not handle it the way you do."

"It isn't as bad as you make it out to be. I love my fans and it's really nice to meet them; it only takes a few seconds or minutes, whatever. Ellie is like you, though; she hates it."

"Yeah, I got the impression from her the night she threw the wine glass at you. She isn't the kind of woman willing to share her man," I said jokingly.

"You don't know the half of it ... and, believe me, the old adage, *there's nothing worse than a woman scorned*, is very true."

"I can't understand her not understanding the business you are in. Hell, you were on your way to being a super star when she married you; she should be happy with, and proud of, you."

"Well, I have to take the blame ... for Suzanne," he said.

"Yeah, but the day you met, nothing happened ... and you told her at Mateo's the same night."

"Yeah ... but something did happen later and it was my fault."

"Okay, but from my perspective, Ellie drove you to it."

"That's not the way she sees it. Since I told her, she goes ballistic if I even look at another woman ... especially if it's one that's hired for the show."

"Well, Dave, all I can say is you have my sympathy. Damn, seeing you in this situation .. maybe I'm better off single," I said.

"I wouldn't say that. Every man needs a woman. By the way, how are things going with you and Rose Marie?"

"Good ... she knows I am separated and Joanne wants a divorce, which neither one of us has filed for, but since Joanne is in Connecticut, she feels it's okay for us to be dating," I said.

"You're lucky ... she has the right attitude, but do you feel anything for her? Do you think it could get serious between you?"

"I don't really know. I mean she's a lot of fun to be with, she's beautiful and she's smart. I just don't know. I don't want to really let myself fall for her, at least not until Joanne and I really decide we are ending our marriage. Joanne and I are Catholic and the church does not approve of divorce ... and, hell, I don't think Joanne has really given me a chance."

"We all have our mountains to climb, my friend, and it sounds like you are just putting on your boots," he said with a little chuckle.

"Yeah, thanks for the comparison. I'd expect a little more from a friend who has a helluva lot more experience than I, and millions of women chasing him all over the globe," I said with a laugh.

"Yeah, well, with all my experience, I have yet to figure any woman out. I just go with the flow and do my damnedest to keep everything copacetic," he said with a laugh.

"Well, Dave, I think I'll just take it slow with Rose Marie. I'm too young to make the same mistake twice."

"So it sounds as though you are accepting a divorce, if it is what your wife really wants," he said in a serious tone.

"Yeah, I am, Dave. It hurts but they say time heals all wounds and, at least, having someone like Rose Marie to go out with, have fun with ... that makes it easier."

"Have you made it to first base with her yet?" he asked.

I knew what he meant. "Not yet ... she's Italian and she's Catholic. I don't want to push anything ... not yet, anyway," I said.

"Well, I wish you luck. I have to go so let's stay in touch," he said before ending the call.

Dave sounded very good, more relaxed than usual. I attributed that to the fact he didn't have the daily grind of doing *The Fugitive*. Having finished work on *The Green Berets* and with the upcoming airing of the *ABC Sportsmen* African safari, Dave certainly would not be out of site for his dedicated fans.

I was certain that his unhappiness along with the stress and pressures of his marriage to Ellie was still eating away at him. I knew Dave to be a very kind and compassionate man; that was his character. I knew he was unhappy in his marriage. he felt Ellie's fits of jealousy, which had advanced to screaming at the top of her lungs and verging on violence, was boiling inside him.

As unhappy as Dave was - despite the emotional roller coaster he rode most days - he did not want to end the marriage because he hated divorce, having seen his mother go through it twice. Dave looked at a divorce from Ellie as telling the world he was a failure.

I had repeatedly told him that I felt, although a divorce would be costly to him financially, I was certain it would not have any adverse effect on his career. I felt it would have the opposite effect: millions of women already *in love* with him would feel they have a chance to be the next *Mrs. David Janssen*.

Dave was scheduled to have surgery on his knee again during the first part of December and was looking forward to getting it behind him and staying home during the Christmas holidays.

21

I was surprised to get a call from Dave on Saturday morning, December 23, 1967. I knew he was relaxing at home, aside from occasional business meetings with his agent and others involved with his career and business interests.

"Hey, Mike! Good morning!" he greeted in a cheerful voice.

"Good morning, Dave! This is a surprise! Did you have your knee surgery? How did it go? I thought you were going to relax the entire holiday season ... no work, no parties ... just golf and relaxation."

"Well, I had the surgery and all went well but it is too soon to know if it will make a significant improvement. I have been doing just that - relaxing at home - but I wanted to give you a call to wish you a Merry Christmas. What are your plans? Are you going to see your family or stay in New York?"

"Actually, I am going to drive out to Indianapolis, leaving today as a matter of fact. I bought my mother a Zenith console television-stereo combination so she can see you better in re-runs of *The Fugitive* or your other appearances," I said jokingly.

"How in the hell are you going to get it there?"

"It fits in the trunk of my T-Bird. Of course, I'll have to tie the trunk down but it will be okay. What are your plans?"

"We'll be staying home. We are committed to a couple of holiday parties with some of our close friends ... but mostly just relaxing. The girls will be here on Christmas day and we'll have Christmas dinner at home."

"That's nice. How are things with Ellie?" I asked.

"Fragile ... I feel like I'm walking on eggshells," he said in a firm voice.

"Well, I would think she would be happy having you home every minute - not out of her sight."

"Yeah, but it's driving me crazy; it's almost like being in a prison. The only way I can get out of the apartment is to schedule a meeting with Abby or Fred or someone; it's getting to be like before - pure hell."

"Damn it, Dave! I really feel bad for you especially during the holidays. You would think Ellie would feel secure enough and do all she can to make it a happy period. You don't deserve this kind of treatment; I hope you figure out a way to make her see that."

"I know, Mike, but it does not seem to me there is a way to get things back to the way they were before my little indiscretion with Suzanne. I am giving serious thought on saying to hell with everything and filing for a divorce ... no matter what it costs!"

"I don't blame you, and I know I don't have to even suggest that you have your business manager consolidate your financial assets. Get advice from Abby and get the best possible divorce attorney you can find," I advised.

"You're right; you don't have to tell me. After the holidays I will be making definite plans – actually, after I finish work on the next film Abby has set for me."

"Oh ... what is it?"

"It's a co-starring role with Anthony Quinn ... one of my favorite actors. It's called *The Shoes of the Fisherman* ... about the Catholic Church, the Pope dying ... quite an interesting script ... very well-written. It will be filmed in Rome so that makes it exciting for me; I loved Rome when we were there last."

"You playing a Catholic Priest ... now that will be interesting," I said.

"No, I won't be a priest. I'll be playing a journalist."

"A journalist? That's what you played in *The Green Berets*. See! I told you that your performance, especially in your disputes with Wayne, was absolutely perfect. You looked and sounded like a journalist ... that is probably why they want you in the same role in this movie."

Dave laughed. "Yeah, well, I have a little more work in this film and working with Quinn will be a great privilege for me. I am looking forward to it."

"When will you be going to Rome?" I asked.

"No date set yet ... after the first of the year. I'll let you know."

"Will you be able to take Ellie? How long will you be there?"

"I think Ellie will be going with me ... not that I really want that, but we'll be on location there for, at least, two to three months so I can't just leave her at home."

"Well, Dave, make sure and let me know when all this is going to happen. I like Anthony Quinn, too, so tell him I send my regards," I said, half joking.

"Yeah, Mike ... I'll do that. Okay, I've gotta go but I'll give you a call later. Have a Merry Christmas and, if I don't talk with you, have a great New Year."

"Thanks, Dave ... the same for you, Ellie and the girls."

We ended the call and I prepared for my trip. I had already loaded the car and it would only take a few minutes to make sure the apartment was closed up tight and take Baron down to the car. I was really looking forward to my trip and I was certain Baron would love it, too.

On the drive from New York City to Indianapolis, I had a lot of time to reflect upon the past few conversations with Dave.

I was beginning to feel seriously concerned for him. I was concerned the tension in his marriage was driving him to drink more than what I had assumed was his normal, manageable intake. I was not basing my concern on the articles I had recently read about him, or him and Ellie; I knew not to believe more than half of what was written.

I was glad to hear he had a starring role in the new movie with Anthony Quinn because I knew he was happiest when he was busy acting. I was hoping he could find a way for Ellie to remain in Los Angeles while he was in Rome for the filming. I felt that would give him a good break from the pressures she exerted on him and, perhaps, give her a chance to realize that she was, in fact, driving him away from her.

Actually, I think she had succeeded in driving him away. In reflecting upon our conversations, it seemed there was no way for Dave to recapture his love for her. I knew he did not hate her but his unhappiness had reached the depths where there could be no return. I was convinced that it would only be a matter of time before Dave felt he was in the position to end their marriage.

I spent Sunday, Monday and Tuesday in Indianapolis. It was a very happy Christmas and a pleasure to see my mother, brothers, sisters and their families. Baron loved meeting the family and made friends with my brother Jack's German Shepherd, Midnight. I left Indianapolis for my return drive to New York City on Tuesday, December 26.

The sun was shining, melting the snow in Indianapolis Tuesday morning. I had packed my car and Baron was as anxious to get on the highway as I was. The drive back to New York was uneventful; the highways were clear of ice and snow, unlike my drive to Indianapolis.

On the trip I again found myself thinking of Dave and wondering if everything was going smoothly for him during the holiday season. If it could be avoided, I knew Dave was not one to engage in confrontations. He would just walk away or respond in a quiet voice and ask for a civil discussion of a perceived problem.

From the last few conversations it was clear to me he had made the decision to end his marriage. Based on what I had witnessed of Ellie's temper, and what Dave had told me, I was certain a split from Ellie would not be easy nor smooth, nor remain a private matter.

I was trying to think of any sound advice I could proffer to help in what he would face. I also thought about his career. Would a divorce really hurt him or have little effect on how his fans viewed him?

Time would tell.

Credit: Tim Williams Art
E-mail: timwilliamsart@bellsouth.net

22
~1968~

I made the drive from Indianapolis to New York City in 18 hours, stopping only for gas, coffee and Baron's latrine breaks. I was actually glad to be home.

On Sunday morning, January 28, my phone rang. I flipped on my light; my digital clock read 3:20. I knew it had to be Dave. Who else would call me in the middle of the night?

"Good morning, Mike ... bet I woke you up, huh?"

"Yeah ... yeah, you did Dave, but it's okay. It's been a while since we spoke. How is everything with you?" I replied, shaking the sleep out of my head.

"Good ... everything is going good. We will be going to Rome the first week in February for that movie I told you about."

"You said *we*; does that mean you are taking Ellie with you?"

"Yeah ... I tried to talk her into staying here, but we'll be over there for about three months and I could not convince her to stay home."

"How have things been with her since we spoke last month?"

"The holidays were quiet ... in the last couple of weeks she is getting testy again. She is still going to the doctors so maybe that has something to do with it."

"I would think she would be treating you like a king since you agreed to take her to Rome. She'll enjoy the city. I'm sure she'll do some shopping and she'll be with you," I said.

"Yeah, but I think she doesn't want to risk me being alone around all those beautiful Italian women. She knows how tempting it would be for me," he said with a laugh.

"Yeah ... on that note, you'd better be careful. Ellie catch you doing anything there, she may just kill you," I said in a joking manner.

"Is this the movie with Anthony Quinn?"

"Yes, and I am really looking forward to it! The script is terrific. I have a lot of scene presence and, with the subject being the Catholic Church and the Pope, it should be well received at the box office."

"That is great; I'll be looking forward to seeing it. Now, if you are going to be there for three months, will you have a chance to call me? You could call me collect, you know," I said with a laugh.

"Yeah, I'll call you ... but it won't be collect. Have you ever been to Rome, to Italy?"

"No, I haven't; I've been to Paris and London, that's it ... while I was in the Air Force," I answered, then asked, "So have you been able to relax at all since you're not doing the series?"

"Oh, yes! Been playing some golf, some tennis, going to Delmar Race Track, but I'm getting anxious ... antsy ... I want to get back to work."

"I know what you mean. I'd go nuts if I didn't work. I hate rush hour traffic so I get to work before it begins in the morning and don't leave the office until the evening rush is over ... that way I get a lot of work done, keeps my mind off my marital problems ... keeps me out of trouble," I said.

"Have you made any decision on a divorce yet?" he asked.

"Yeah, that's what she wants, so that is what she'll get. I'm just not in any rush."

"Is it going to cost you? Is she demanding anything?"

"Not really. I mean we've only been married a few months. We don't have much in the way of assets ... as far as I'm concerned, she can have everything but my car and bank account."

"Well, I give you my sympathy but, hey! You're young. Don't be in a rush to tie the knot again. Enjoy your bachelor days; they go by fast," he said with a laugh. "How are things with you and Rose Marie?"

"Rose Marie is questioning me about when I'll file for divorce or if my wife is going to file ... that feels a little like she is pushing me ... and I think I'll follow your sage advice: I'll enjoy being a bachelor for a while."

"You will be better off ... believe me! Don't rush into anything. Really get to know her. Live with her for a few months. Marriage is a hell of a commitment and people change over time."

"I know. I know. Looking at what you have to deal with, I would be a fool not to listen to your advice."

"Good, Mike. You'll save yourself a lot of headaches, not to mention money."

"Speaking of which ... have you made your decision? Have you figured a way to protect yourself ... or maybe things will change for the better while you are in Rome."

"Mike, it wouldn't matter if she changed completely and started treating me like she did when we first met, or treated me like a king. It is over. We haven't even had sex in months, which is okay with me. She has this damn thyroid problem! Hell, it's one excuse after another!"

"Damn it, Dave! Then why even take her to Rome? You will just be putting yourself through hell."

"I can handle it; I'll be working long hours. She knows better than to bother me when I'm working ... especially on a film as important as this one."

"Well, I guess you know what you are doing."

"I do. When we get back, I'll be in a better position to put things in motion. Do you really think a divorce won't hurt my career?"

"I'm positive of that ... your fans love you ... your work ... not Ellie. Ellie is not an actress; she's not in the business. Now, if you were married to someone like Elizabeth Taylor or Suzanne Pleshette, then I would say it could hurt you because they have their own fans. Yes, I am positive it won't hurt your career.

"Dave, why in the hell are you asking me ... have you talked with Mr. Greshler, your publicist or business manager? How about your close friends in the business, people like Paul Burke, Jimmy Farentino or James Garner?"

"Yeah, I've told Abby and Fred. I haven't said anything to Liberman yet; I want to make certain I've got everything in order before he makes it public. I haven't said anything to Jimmy or Jim. I don't really talk about my private life with them; they read between the lines when they see Ellie and I out together. I've only told you."

"Why can't you just let her know now ... before you go to Rome?"

"No, can't do that; it would be a disaster," he answered firmly.

"Well, Dave, you know best. I just hope your trip to Rome and your work is not disrupted by her."

"Don't worry ... I can handle it. Now that I know it is over, it will be easy - well, somewhat easy - to play the game and keep her happy," he said.

"Okay, give me a call when you have a chance or just feel like talking. It doesn't matter about the time difference."

"Not to worry. I'll stay in touch," Dave said and ended the call.

In early February I read in the *New York Post* that Dave, Ellie and all the major stars of the upcoming film arrived in Rome to prepare for the filming. It was reported to be a *big budget* film with an *all-star cast*.

I did not hear from Dave the entire time he was in Italy. I dismissed it knowing how busy he must be. Besides, having Ellie with him, I was certain he was doing a lot of socializing and attending parties. I was aware he would most likely be working very long hours so he would not really have much free time to even think of calling me.

23

It was Sunday, May 19, when Dave found time to call me.

"Hey, Mike! It's me, Dave Janssen."

"Dave who?" I chided. "Oh, *the fugitive*! I thought I read somewhere that Gerard caught you and you're cooling your heels on Indiana's Death Row."

"Yeah, Mike ... okay, I deserve that. Sorry I didn't have a chance to call you while we were in Rome, but things were busy and chaotic there ... but we're back now."

"Well, tell me ... did you and Ellie enjoy Rome? How was your work on the film? What kind of guy is Anthony Quinn? I've always admired him as an actor."

"I loved Rome ... people are really nice to Americans. We had a lot of Italian movie people hired on our crew and they were great. Anthony Quinn is the best ... a really great guy; easy to work with ... very supportive, he's one of the best men I've ever worked with. He gave me a big compliment; he was a fan of *The Fugitive* and said I nailed it, every time in every episode ... that was very nice of him. I hope I have the chance to work with him again."

"How about the other stars ... they say it's an *all-star cast*.

"They were all great people to work with, really a great crew, from the big shots all the way down to the character actors."

"Well, how did things go with Ellie? Did she enjoy it? Did you have time to take her around, do the party thing?" I asked.

"Mike, to be honest ... she was a Bitch, with a capital 'B'. She had insisted on taking Kathy with us, which I did not mind. I thought it would be good for Ellie, having Kathy to go with her touring the city, do their shopping sprees while I worked - but she was very suspicious of where I was, even though she knew I was on the set."

"Damn it, Dave! I'm sorry to hear that, but I'm sure it did not affect your concentration on your work."

"No, that would never happen; you know that. We had a couple of very loud, acrimonious arguments ... which Kathy heard, even saw a little - that really pissed me off!"

"Dave, I really feel for you. How much longer are you going to take this? You don't deserve that kind of treatment ... not from anyone, especially someone you give so much to."

"Not much longer, Mike. Since we got back, I've started to get things in order; she will soon be in for a big surprise," he said in a firm voice.

"Well, Dave, as I said before, I don't believe for one second that your split with Ellie will hurt your career at all. Not one iota ... your fans love *you*, not Ellie."

"Mike, I don't know about that. She may try to make me out to be the really dirty bastard that cheats on her and all that crap - not to mention I drink too much, come home drunk, don't fuck her enough - but I have to do this. It is not worth driving myself crazy. I sure hope you are right, though."

"I'm positive that I am ... I know I'll be proven right. You'll see," I said, before asking, "So, tell me ... did you have any fun in Rome, I mean besides working on the film?"

"Oh, yeah! A couple of good friends of ours, Jimmy Farentino and Michelle Lee, came over and spent a few days with us at the villa. We sent the girls out shopping and Jimmy and I were able to relax at a nice little Taverna where we proceeded to get very drunk, had a hell of a good time, beautiful women all over the place - another little incident that pissed Ellie off. Michelle actually calmed her down," he said with a little laugh.

"So did you see the Vatican ... Saint Peter's Basilica ... have an audience with the Pope - the real Pope, I mean?"

"Went all over Rome, toured the exterior of the Vatican, Saint Peter's ... but the Pope was out of town," he said jokingly. "I don't really know where the Pope was. I'm sure he was there but he didn't invite us; his loss," he said jokingly.

"Well, are you glad to be back in the States?"

"Oh, hell, yes! Very happy!"

"When will the movie be coming out?"

"Sometime in the fall; I'll let you know."

"How did Kathy enjoy the trip?"

"She really enjoyed it, except when Ellie created her scenes; she did not like that at all. Kathy knows we have our little arguments but I have always stressed to Ellie we should not be doing it in front of the girls ... but, hell! They are old enough now to know what goes on in a relationship and they know their mother; she's a very domineering woman, always wants control of everything and everyone."

"I'm sure Kathy and Diane know what their mother is doing. I'm pretty sure they are on your side ... if push comes to shove. After all, they know it was YOU who insisted on bringing them into your home and out of the boarding schools they had been stuck in."

"I hope you're right; I have a feeling you are. The girls and I have always been close but I have never stepped in to discipline them ... not my place. If anything, when Ellie disciplined them, if I thought it was too harsh, I would defend them - not in front of them, but to Ellie in private. I'm sure they know."

"I just hope you can get out of this mess as easily as possible and that Ellie doesn't try and take you for every dime you've worked for."

"Oh, Mike! I'm not kidding myself; it is going to hurt - big time - and, knowing Ellie as I do, it's going to get downright dirty, really nasty ... but I have to do it. I want to be FREE ... and I damn sure won't make a mistake like this again ... at least, not for a while," he said with a serious tone, but let out a little laugh at the end.

"Well, I don't blame you there ... thinking the same thing myself."

"Speaking of that ... are you resolved to getting a divorce?"

"Well, I haven't filed yet ... haven't heard from her yet, so I'm just leaving it in a status quo."

"Well, that may be best for you. In your situation, my opinion is that if she truly loves you, she'll come around and accept your career. I wish you luck and hope it works out for you."

"Thanks, Dave, but then again, looking at your situation ... with Ellie, you must have loved her when you married her and you've been together for almost 10 years now. You even accepted her daughters, helped her raise them, provided for them. Now you are in one hell of a nasty marriage; I sure as hell don't want to end up in your situation."

"Yeah, you're right, Mike ... I was madly in love when we got married but, as I told you, people change. I don't think I have changed in the way I have treated Ellie. I believe in my heart I have gone out of my way to give her everything ... a good life, but it seems that isn't enough."

"I know what you're saying; it is just a damn shame the way things have turned out. I have a gut feeling that Ellie is developing, or has developed, some insecurity because she is so much older than you. Now you are loved by millions of women all over the world; I just think that could be the root cause of her treatment towards you."

"Well, you have a good point, and you could very well be right, but I've never made an issue of her age ... but that could be a reason for the changes in her personality. Mike, I have to run. It's been good talking with you. As soon as I know what my schedule is, I'll give you a call," he said.

"All right, Dave. Good talking with you, too ... don't be a stranger, okay?"

"Okay, talk soon." He ended the call.

I had not spoken with Dave since the end of January and was glad to hear from him. I really felt bad for him, knowing what he must be going through with Ellie. I felt from the tone of his voice and the little innuendo that he was making definite plans to end the marriage.

I was glad he was back in the States knowing that he would call more often and I would know what was happening with him.

24

I was really worried what would happen when Dave asked Ellie for a divorce. Having witnessed her anger first hand, I suspected it would be like the eruption of World War III. I knew he was making his plans and it would be just a matter of time; I was convinced it would be soon. I wished I were still in Los Angeles; at least, we could be sharing drinks together and he could vent to his heart's content with me. He sounded so depressed during that last call.

I could not believe he was in such a position with Ellie. If anyone knew how hard Dave had struggled and worked to achieve the level of success he had, it was Ellie. Couldn't she see that, perhaps, it was her insecurity - her suspicions of Dave's infidelity - that was pushing him to drink as much as he was, to find excuses to meet someone in a bar and have several drinks before he could go home to suffer her wrath?

I felt real sympathy for him and felt the old saying that *money cannot buy happiness* was so true. I had no doubt that I was a hell of a lot happier with my life, empty as it was at the time, than Dave was with his. I also wondered how he was able to do his work so well, to give outstanding performances. I just told myself there certainly wasn't anything I could do for him; the only thing I could do was be there when he called and to listen. I felt that did help him in some small way.

The more I thought about it, the evidence was overwhelming. Ellie had watched Dave's career explode with *The Fugitive* and had seen his popularity, especially with women, grow by leaps and bounds all around the world. He was 12 years her junior and, although she was a strikingly beautiful woman, I am certain the age difference was building inside her, making her feel very insecure.

Ellie was, at that time, feeling the pangs of insecurity which caused her suspicions and mistrust of Dave, which resulted in her becoming domineering and contriving attempts to exert control over his every move. When he was not working, she would not let him out of her sight. I think that precipitated his developing habit of stopping for drinks after many long hours on the set.

Dave was young, handsome and wealthy ... he could have had any woman he wanted. Women threw themselves at him and Ellie witnessed it. There was also Dave's guest star for two episodes of *The Fugitive*, the lovely and glamorous Suzanne Pleshette, who was much younger than Ellie.

In the first episode Suzanne was cast, she played the part of Ellie Burnett in *World's End*. Suzanne's character was the daughter of Kimble's defense attorney and, unbeknownst to Kimble, she was madly in love with him and believes in his innocence. It was an outstanding episode; it was aired September 22, 1964.

The second day of filming, after a long day of shooting, was when Dave invited Suzanne to dinner. Feeling somewhat guilty, he called Ellie and had her meet him at another restaurant where he blurted out that he had had dinner with Suzanne; that was the beginning of the end for their marriage, in my opinion.

A few months later, there were rumors put forth in the tabloids that an affair was blossoming between Dave and Suzanne. At the time, they were not true. It was perfectly innocent; there was no affair (at the time) with Suzanne. Dave and Suzanne had known each other for years when they were both struggling to make their mark in the industry. They were good friends and nothing more.

When Ellie learned Suzanne was cast to play Peggy Franklin in the episode, *All the Scared Rabbits*, she went ballistic. Dave told me that she instigated an argument which lasted from the time he arrived home from the studio until he left home at four o'clock the next morning; it was one of the more serious arguments during their marriage.

She even called Quinn Martin and pleaded with him not to use Suzanne, to find someone else. When Mr. Martin said he could not do that, Ellie screamed at him, asking him if he was trying to ruin their marriage - saying she would bring a gun to the set and *end it*!

Well, Ellie did go to the set, for three days in a row, and did everything to disrupt the filming. Finally, Dave took her into his dressing room and told her in no uncertain terms to go home; he was working and she was being a bitch.

Ellie's reaction to him confessing about a friendly dinner with an old friend was over the top. Now, a *Fugitive* guest star was fraught with a combination of jealous rage and suspicion; there was no way Dave could convince Ellie nothing was going on.

The episode was completed without further interruption and aired on October 26, 1965, right around the time Dave and I met; it was an excellent show. That is also when Dave made his move on a very happy Suzanne.

That night, after filming for almost 16 hours, Dave had dinner with Suzanne again during which an affair evolved between them. He would tell me later that he had really fallen in love with her and had wished so badly to be a free man. He would have married her in a *New York Minute,* he told me.

However, Suzanne was a genuine lady, one with moral principles. She couldn't continue to engage in a steamy affair with a married man, not even with a married David Janssen.

The affair was very brief, contrary to the rumors of the Hollywood tabloids which have a long shelf-life. It was Suzanne who told Dave she couldn't continue a relationship with him as long as he was married. "IF you get a divorce, call me," she had said. It was a blow to him, even frustrated him, especially considering the state of his marriage to Ellie.

It was during the early days of his affair with Suzanne when I had met Dave and, for me, it was an honor and, somewhat exciting, to be invited by him to have a few drinks. In the early days of our friendship, we did not really discuss his marriage or his relationship with Ellie and we certainly did not discuss his having an affair with Suzanne or any other women.

It was quite obvious to me that Dave could have any woman he wanted; the line of beautiful women would stretch for miles. It was fodder for the media, the tabloids and fan magazines that *The Fugitive* had its pick of beautiful and talented actresses for guest starring roles. I had no doubt many would have jumped at a chance to share Dave's bed; no doubt, Ellie knew that, too.

In spite of the on-going rumors and Ellie's suspicions and mistrust of Dave, I believe his close friends knew he was no longer cheating on Ellie, that the affair with Suzanne had been brief and was, indeed, over.

I don't think anyone, even the Pope, would have succeeded in convincing Ellie that Dave was being faithful to her. I do believe that when the affair was developing with Suzanne in October of 1965, Dave was coming to the realization that the happiness of married life with Ellie was eroding and he was feeling trapped in what would soon be a loveless marriage.

I would learn from Dave that many times he used me as an alibi. He would call me for drinks, immediately after leaving Suzanne's bed, knowing he would have an iron-clad witness for Ellie, that we were just a couple of guys talking war and politics over a few drinks.

Ellie and I, of course, knew David Janssen was not *just another guy*. Could Ellie have any reason for jealousy or suspicions over Dave and a young kid from the Midwest having drinks and talking war and politics? In retrospect, I learned from Ellie that she did! She actually thought he was using me to cover up his infidelities.

The thing is, I was completely in the dark and, had I known, I would have done it anyway. The vision and the sound of Ellie's fury the morning I drove Dave home and she threw a wine glass at him, hitting my car window instead (thankfully) was seared into my mind. I witnessed her wrath and realized what Dave had endured for years.

In the process of writing HER book about their life together, their marriage, the bitter divorce and his tragic death at such a young age, I firmly believe Ellie loved Dave to the end. From what I know, through the years after the divorce, Ellie had dates but every man she knew, for her, it was nothing more than a platonic relationship.

I also learned she enjoyed men spending their money on her. By that, I mean dinners in the finest restaurants, small gifts of adoration, but that was the extent of it. I don't believe Ellie allowed herself to even consider falling in love with another man.

On a side note, by the time Dave and Ellie's long, drawn out divorce was finalized, Suzanne Pleshette was a happily married woman.

In the midst of his and Ellie's nasty divorce, Dave had become completely involved with Rosemary Forsyth - his co-star in the film, *Where It's At* - which was filmed at Caesar's Palace in Las Vegas. Caesar's Palace became a favorite of both Dave's and mine – but I digress.

My next call from Dave came in the wee hours of Thursday, June 27.

"Hey, Mike! Wake up! You're sleeping your life away!"

I quickly came fully awake. "What time is it, Dave? Never mind; I know it's three hours earlier where you are ... so what's up? I haven't read anything about Ellie throwing things at you so I guess you're still a happily married man," I joked.

"Well, still married ... you got that right; everything else you got wrong," he laughed aloud. "What's going on with you? Are you still a happily married man?"

"Now I know you must be drunk ... I'm still a married man, living a bachelor's life ... and loving it!" I replied.

"No, I'm not drunk ... fooled you, didn't I? I don't have to be drunk to call a friend, or do I?" he asked jokingly.

"No, you know I was kidding ... so what the hell is going on with you? I feel like an abandoned kid, only hearing from you a couple of times a year. I'm only kidding."

"Sorry, I've been very busy ... doing as much as I can to stay out of the house. I'm going to Vegas; we're doing a film at Caesar's Palace ... I'm the owner."

"WHAT? YOU bought Caesar's Palace!" I almost yelled into the phone.

"HELL, NO! I couldn't afford that. We're just doing a film there called *Where It's At*. I play the owner and I have an estranged college boy son and a beautiful girlfriend."

"Okay ... that sounds interesting. I'd sure love to come out there. I love Vegas and it would be great to see you work again."

"Why don't you? Don't you get a vacation? Just do it! Come out for a few days ... it will be fun."

"Hey, I think I will. I'll see if I can get a few days off."

"Great! Just let me know. I'll set up a prepaid plane ticket for you."

"No, that's not necessary ... I can afford that."

"Well, let me know. We'll be there for several weeks."

"Is Ellie going with you?"

"HELL, NO! She is wrapped up with doctor appointments and that suits me fine. If you can make it, I'll get you a comp for a room at Caesar's."

"Okay! Can I call you? I don't like calling you; never know where you are or if I would be interrupting you ... or if Ellie would answer your phone."

"When you make your plans, just call my office and leave a message. I'll be sure to get back to you. Okay ... I have to run, but we'll talk soon."

Dave ended the call and I was excited at the possibility of making the trip. It would be great to see him again, to just sit and talk over a few drinks.

25

When I got to the office I made plans to fly out to Las Vegas on Friday night and return to New York the following Sunday night. I had not taken a real vacation in over two years and Vegas would be a fun place to relax and have some real fun even if only for a long weekend.

I landed at McCarran Field just after seven o'clock in the evening Las Vegas time, which is three hours behind New York.

I called Caesar's Palace reservations desk and gave my name. Yes, they were holding a room for me, compliments of Mr. David Janssen. I wondered if that meant Dave would be paying for my room, which I would not allow. I hailed a cab and headed for Caesar's Palace.

Arriving at the Front Desk, I was treated like a VIP. I asked if Mr. Janssen was in the hotel. I was informed they could not give me his suite number but I could leave a message for him. I left a message to let him know I was in the hotel and would look forward to seeing him.

Once in my room, I unpacked and took a quick shower. As I was dressing, the phone rang and it was Dave.

"Welcome to Sin City, Mike."

"Thanks! I am really glad to be here. How are things with you; have you started filming yet?" I asked.

"We start tomorrow ... been doing the preliminaries the last couple of days. How about joining me downstairs for a drink ... dinner?" he asked.

"I'll meet you for drinks; I had dinner on the plane. What time shall I meet you?"

"Now ... I'll be in the casino bar, right inside the casino."

"I'll be down in a minute."

It was just after nine o'clock when I entered the small open bar inside the main casino. Dave was seated at a small table with bar stools.

"Hey! It's great seeing you, Dave!"

"Good to see you too, Mike! I'm glad you could make it out here. You look like you can use a little rest from the hectic pace of the city."

"Yes, I can and seeing you was a great excuse to make it here."

"One thing: I didn't know this when we last spoke but the filming we will be doing here is a closed set. That means I won't be able to get you in to watch any of the scenes being shot. Everything we do here will be on the main casino and show room floors and it'll be done in the off hours, so we don't cause too much disruption to Caesar's," he informed.

"Damn it, Dave! You mean I came all this way and I can't watch you work! I'm disappointed ... I may as well pack up and head home," I said jokingly. "You're the *star* ... tell them I have to be there!"

"It isn't that easy ... tell you what, when the movie comes out I'll send you a ticket and you can see it at your neighborhood theatre," he said with a broad smile.

"Yeah ... just let me know when the premier is and, Dave, I can afford a ticket." I laughed. "At least I can enjoy Vegas, maybe win a million or two on the slots."

"Well, we'll have dinner tomorrow night, if that's good with you," Dave suggested, apologetically.

"I'd enjoy that; it will give us a chance to catch up. How are things with Ellie?" I asked.

"Getting so damn intolerable I can't stand it! She is sick. Now the doctors think it has something to do with her thyroid glands, but she keeps hammering me with her suspicions and I really haven't done anything; it's a hell of a way to live."

"Have you really made up your mind to ask for a divorce?"

"I'm not going to ask for a divorce; I'm going to file myself! I'm already working on it with my lawyers ... haven't discussed it with my agent or anyone else, but I have to get out of this marriage."

"I sure hope it won't become a nasty brawl that drags you through the tabloids. No doubt it is going to cost you a heavy price, but you can't live like this; it isn't good for your mind."

"I know, Mike, but I have to have everything lined up ... or I will be really screwed."

"You must know what you're doing ... and I'm sure your lawyers will do their best to protect you and not be too hard on Ellie."

"I don't want to drag her through the gutter, but I can't take her jealousy anymore; we just don't have the love between us we did before."

"Do you think she'll put up a big fight? Would she try and bring you down ... damage your public persona?" I asked.

"I don't really know IF she'll try that. Do I believe she is capable? HELL, YES! I've seen her anger ... hell, so have you ... and what you witnessed was mild," he said with a serious look on his face.

"Well, let's talk about something nice ... tell me about this movie," I said with a smile.

"It's called *Where It's At* and that means Las Vegas - Caesar's Palace, specifically. I OWN it. Actually, I'm the resident owner; I have some other investors and they're in Baltimore so out of my way.

I have a son from my first marriage; he's graduated from Princeton and we're a little estranged. I wasn't a good father as he was growing up. Anyway, he comes to visit, has his own ideas for his future. I want to teach him the business ... and, boy, do I! I have a girl and we're going to get married; she is played by Rosemary Forsyth ... a real beauty."

"Who plays your son?" I interrupted.

"Robert Drivas. He's a young actor who seems to have a bright future. In the film, he doesn't want anything to do with me, much less running a casino. Anyway, Rosemary is my soon-to-be bride and things go from there."

"So, since I can't watch you filming ... tell me the rest of the story."

"No ... I don't want to spoil it for you. I've already told you too much. I think it's going to be a good film, especially for people who have been to Vegas."

"Okay ... I'll wait 'til it comes out ... I'm a very patient guy."

"So what room are you in?" he asked.

"Eight-forty, facing the fountains ... really nice. I am paying for my room; they said it was compliments of Mr. David Janssen. I don't want that; I can pay my own way."

"Nonsense, Mike! They've comped you because I'm doing the film here; it isn't going to cost either one of us a dime," he said.

"Are you sure? I really don't want you to be paying for my room."

"I'm telling you like it is, no bull. I'm not being charged for your room or your meals. The hotel figures you'll drop some cash in the casino and that's just fine with them," Dave said.

"Yeah ... well, what IF I win a bundle and decide to take it with me?" I asked with a sly smile.

"So be it ... they have a thousand others that will be dropping a lot more than you'll be taking away," Dave added with a grin.

It was now just before eleven o'clock and we had each had at least five drinks in two hours, give or take a few minutes. I was feeling the time change from New York and was ready to call it a night. I was kind of proud of myself; I had not even played a single slot machine since I arrived.

"Well, Dave, I think I'm ready to call it a night ... it's been a long day."

"Okay ... let's plan on dinner tomorrow night - say around nine o'clock, in the lobby?"

"Yeah, that will be great! Looking forward to it," I said.

We shook hands. Dave signed the bar tab and left a cash tip. I headed for the elevators and noticed Dave walking into the casino.

I went up to my room, took a quick shower, opened the drapes and enjoyed the fantastic view from my room. I was feeling the jet lag and my busy day and went straight to bed.

I awoke just after eight o'clock and realized it was eleven o'clock in New York. I took a shower, dressed casually and headed downstairs for breakfast. I assumed Dave was working hard on the closed set.

After breakfast I decided to try my luck in the casino. I am not a gambler in any sense of the word. I do like to play the slot machines, the one-armed bandits. I had once heard the slots had a higher pay-out than all other games in the casinos. In less than two hours, I dropped two hundred dollars. I told myself that was my limit for the morning and mentally told the machine I would return and get my revenge.

I left Caesar's and decided to walk around the famous strip and maybe even try my luck at other casino's slots. The plan was for Dave and I to meet for dinner around nine o'clock in the lobby. I assumed we would be having dinner in one of the hotel restaurants.

26

I spent all day Saturday roaming the Las Vegas Strip, in and out of all the famous casinos, and losing a few dollars at each. It was okay; I kept reminding myself I was on vacation.

I was back in my room at Caesar's Palace by three o'clock, wanting to take a short nap before getting ready for dinner.

I went down to the lobby at 8:30 and walked around for a few minutes, then headed for the casino but, fortunately, Dave walked up to me and saved me from my stupid temptations.

"Hey, Mike! How was your day ... did you win a bundle?" he asked with a broad smile.

"Are you kidding? These one-armed bandits see me coming and start spinning their wheels laughing at this sucker," I said with a half-hearted laugh. "How was your day ... tough on the set?"

"Yeah, it was, but that's to be expected when you first start filming with all the actors, director and crew just getting to know each other and what to expect from each other. It'll ease up in a few days," he said. "So what did you do all day?"

"Just walked around the strip, in and out of casinos, counted my losses and forced myself back to my room," I said jokingly.

"Then you must be ready for a good dinner." He smiled.

"You bet I am ... are we eating in one of Caesar's restaurants?" I asked.

"No, I thought we'd go over to the Sands; they have an excellent restaurant. Most of the cast and crew will be crowding the restaurants here and I need some break-time."

I had been in the Sands Casino earlier in the day and knew it was a very short walk from Caesar's. As we exited Caesar's, a Cadillac limo pulled up and the doorman opened the rear door and Dave slid in. I followed suit.

"Dave, it's a short walk ... you really think we need a limo?" I asked with a slight laugh.

"Yeah, I want to get there with all my clothes on," he said, letting out a big laugh.

I realized that his instant recognition on the street would mean fans approaching him for autographs and just to have the chance to touch him. This fortified my mindset that being in his position, with the fame and instant recognition, is something I would never want to experience.

Oh yeah! It was a cool experience to have a limo at your service, but for a couple of blocks! I felt sorry for Dave and then admonished myself. Why should I feel sorry for him? He had it all.

We entered the Sands and Dave led the way straight to the main dining room. He was greeted like royalty by the Maître D" and we were ushered to a table in the back of the vast room. The Maître D" took our drink orders and left menus for us.

Our drinks arrived within moments and Dave raised his glass: "To good friends, good food and good booze," he said, smiling.

"I'll drink to that. It's really good to see you, Dave."

A waiter arrived and asked if we needed more time to peruse the menu. Dave nodded and ordered another round of drinks. We had barely taken a sip of the first one.

We looked over the menu and I decided on a filet mignon steak, baked potato and broccoli. Dave ordered a salmon, with rice pilaf and asparagus.

"So tell me more about the movie. Do you think you are going to like it? Have you ever worked with any of the other cast members?"

"I've worked with Brenda Vaccaro and Don Rickles; all the others are new to me. Yeah, I like the script; it has a good plot and it has a consistent flow. I think the finished product will be a hit."

"I could fall in love with Brenda Vaccaro in a New York minute ... you're very lucky ... you'll have to tell me all about her. Is Don Rickles as much fun to work with as he seems on TV?"

"I'll tell Brenda you're a big fan. Yeah, Don is one hell of a good guy; he's perfect for his role here."

"When will it be released? When can I go see it in New York?"

"I really don't have an answer for you. It will be several months. Don't worry! I'll let you know the minute I know."

"So, how are things with you and Ellie?"

"I'm nearing 'D' Day ... 'D' as in DIVORCE," he responded.

"Damn! That sounds pretty ominous for Ellie; does she have any clue you're going to file?"

"Not yet ... I've got everything in place. Now it is just to pick the right time to tell her. It will be after this film is finished," he said.

"You are going to tell her? I thought you were just going to leave and let her be served the papers."

"No, I'm going to tell her face-to-face, as gently as I can, but I won't tolerate another fight," he said in a serious tone.

"Are you going to be all right ... financially, I mean? I know California is a community property state and I don't think you'll have any need for her dress dummies or any of her property," I said in a joking way.

"Yeah, I'll be okay. My agent and lawyers have been careful so I won't take a catastrophic hit ... and I do want to be fair to her. I won't leave her destitute and I'll take care of Kathy and Diane."

"Wow! You sure have a lot on your plate."

"Well, you know, when we were married, I really felt it would be my first and last time doing it but, as I've told you, people change. Hell, I know I have changed; I know it and I admit it, but she has really changed. I don't know where her domineering and jealous traits came from but it's like she woke up one morning and decided not to trust me as a husband anymore."

"Not that it is any of my business, but do you think the fact that you are always working with beautiful actresses, always having love scenes, has caused Ellie's mistrust?"

"Oh, yeah! I don't doubt it one bit ... but it is just part of my job; it's just acting. Mike, as I've said before, it has reached a point that I don't feel any love for her anymore ... and I don't think she feels the same about me as she did before. The way she treats me, it's like I'm just a piece of her property, that she owns me ... and I can't and won't tolerate any more of it."

"What about her daughters; do they realize you guys are having problems?"

"Hell, yes! They've known it for years and I know it hurts them when Ellie starts screaming and yelling ... but I can't help that."

"Well, if you need a place to run and hide, I've got room at my apartment."

"Thanks, Mike, but I don't think I'm going to have to run and hide ... at least, not that far," he said with a laugh.

"What about all the things you guys have collected over the years, furniture ... you know household things, art ... are you going to split it or are you just going to get your own place and start all over?" I asked.

"I'm going to start from scratch, Mike. I'll get a bachelor pad and furnish it to my taste ... won't be fancy, just a place I can call home, and come home to relax ... even get drunk if I want to and not worry about someone nagging me."

"Well, I sure know how to do that, so if you need any advice, just give me a call."

"Speaking of that ... what's going on with your wife? Are you still holding out hope of reconciliation or are you headed down my path?"

"I'm probably headed down your path; we haven't even spoken on the phone in months and I've opened my eyes. There are plenty of women in the Naked City. I think when the time is right, I'll find the right one, and I'm in no rush."

"Just take it slow and easy, Mike; you're young enough you don't have to rush into anything."

"I agree with you, Dave ... I am taking it slow and easy. Getting back to your situation, how do you think the news of you getting a divorce will affect your career?"

"It'll be all over the tabloids. It may hurt a little but people forget, so it won't hurt for very long."

"Well, I'm sure you know best but keep me informed. Remember, I'm a fan ... so I want to know," I said with a smile.

"Yeah, Mike, I'll let you know ... you'll probably know before it hits the papers," he said with a broad smile.

We finished dinner and Dave ordered us coffee and another round of drinks. I glanced at my watch and noted it was already 10:55.

"Have you done much gambling?" Dave asked.

"Not really, and all I've done is give the casinos my money ... maybe tomorrow."

"Well, I'm going to go in and play a little Blackjack. I'm usually pretty lucky there," Dave said.

"I'll come and watch you ... maybe your luck will rub off on me," I joked.

David motioned for the check and our waiter brought it over within a couple of minutes. Dave signed the check and left a one hundred dollar bill as a tip.

"Are we going back to Caesar's or play a little here?" I asked.

"Sands is good ... let's see if we can take some of their money back to Caesar's," Dave invited.

We entered the casino and I followed Dave to a Blackjack table with only two players. I noticed the man and woman staring at Dave with obvious recognition. Dave smiled and nodded, sat down and ordered $500 worth of chips. He then placed a $100 bet. He won and doubled his bet. He won again.

I went to the row of slot machines behind the Blackjack tables and started playing with 50 cent coins. I lost another $50. I decided to try another $50; by my fourth pull of the bandit's arm, I won ... $48. I continued and my winnings were growing.

Dave came over and asked if I was ready to go back to Caesar's. I was.

27

On the short ride back to Caesar's, Dave asked, "When do you have to go back to New York?"

"I have a reservation for tomorrow afternoon. I have to be at the airport at two o'clock, flight leaves at three, non-stop," I answered.

"I'm sorry I couldn't get you on the set, but I know you'll like the film when you see it. We break around noon for lunch so maybe we can meet for a farewell drink," Dave said with a smile.

"That would be great! I'll have already packed so I'll check out of the hotel. Where should I meet you?" I asked.

"In the lobby, by the Bell Captain's desk."

"I'll be there," I said.

We arrived at Caesar's and said goodnight at the elevators. I was in my room and in bed by 1:20. I was hoping for a good night's sleep and was really looking forward to going home Sunday.

I was awake just after six o'clock Sunday morning. I took my shower and packed my bags before eight o'clock. I was sure Dave was hard at work so I headed downstairs to have breakfast. I decided after breakfast I would spend some time in the casino, to seek revenge on one specific one-armed bandit.

I entered the casino a little past nine in the morning. I was surprised to see so many people gambling at such an early hour. I could only assume they were like me, tourists who were enjoying all that Las Vegas had to offer.

I told myself I would be happy to just break even, especially since the machine I was going to had toyed with me Saturday, letting me win modest amounts, then taking it all back - tempting me to put more of *my* money in his slots.

I sat down in front of my one-armed friend and told him I was there to collect. I could swear he winked at me.

The time flew by and it was 11:30 before I knew it. I took my buckets full of coins to the cashier. She smiled and took my four buckets and started emptying them into a counter. In less than five minutes she was counting out hundred dollar bills. When she had counted to 18, she placed a 50 and 20 on top. She then re-counted it in front of me. I pocketed the cash, leaving the 20 for the cashier, returned her smile and headed back to my machine. I patted the machine and told it I'd see it again.

I entered the lobby and headed for the Bell Captain's desk. There I would just stand around and wait for Dave.

Dave arrived a few minutes past noon, appearing to have just showered and changed clothes. He seemed very relaxed as we shook hands and he pointed to the lobby bar. As we slid onto the bar stools a bartender appeared, smiling at Dave.

Dave ordered our drinks. "So, Mike, are you anxious to get back to New York or have you decided to spend a little more time here?" Dave asked.

"Yeah, I have to admit I'm tempted to stay here ... but I want to still have something in the bank when I get home. As it is, I just won $1,870 on my favorite slot machine and that puts me $1,100 ahead so, basically, I've made money on this trip," I said, smiling.

"That's great. I didn't do so good last night, dropped a couple of thousand ... but, hell, there's still time to get it back," he smiled. "Are you hungry? Want some lunch?"

"No, I had a big breakfast. I'm fine."

He ordered another round of drinks and a Reuben sandwich. Our drinks appeared instantly and soon afterwards Dave's lunch arrived.

"It's really been great seeing you again, even if I did not get to watch you work. Thanks again for getting the room comped, and for dinner last night," I said.

"You're more than welcome; it was good seeing you again. We will get together again and probably be sooner than a few months."

"So how has your day been, so far?" I asked.

"Not bad. We've finished a few of the opening scenes, getting to know each other. Actually, everything is going smooth. My co-star, Rosemary, is quite a beautiful gal and I can tell she likes me already," he said, smiling.

"Is she married ... involved with someone?" I asked, returning Dave's smile.

"Yeah, she's married, but I don't think it's a very happy situation."

"Man, Dave! Be careful! You sure as hell don't need to get involved in a love triangle. Ellie would drag you through the mud."

"Yeah, I know you're right. Hell, nothing has happened - not yet anyway," he said with what I observed to be a mischievous smile.

"I just don't want to see the headlines: *David Janssen Involved with Married Starlet,*" I said with a serious look.

I knew Dave usually refrained from drinking alcohol when he was working and wondered to myself if he was changing. I wondered if the stress of his imminent divorce from Ellie was weighing on him more than I, or others close to him, could see.

It was just after one o'clock when Dave signed the tab and we walked back out to the lobby. I had already checked out of the hotel and my bags were at the Bell Captain's desk. Dave walked me over to the desk and we shook hands.

"Okay, Mike. Have a good flight home. I'll be in touch," he said. With that, he turned and waved as he walked toward the elevators.

The Bell Captain signaled a Bellman who came to take my bag out to the driveway where I intended to catch a cab to the airport. As we arrived outside, the Bellman signaled and a white Cadillac limo pulled up, popped his trunk and the Bellman placed my bag inside. I noted the Caesar's logo on the rear door.

"Compliments of Mr. Janssen," the Bellman said. I slipped $20 into his hand and smiled.

"Good afternoon, Sir! What airline are you taking?" the driver asked.

"TWA and I have plenty of time," I said.

"No problem, Sir. Just sit back and enjoy the trip. There is a bar if you would care to take advantage."

"No, I'm fine, but thank you," I said.

The ride to McCarran Airport was less than 20 minutes. I gave the driver a $50 tip and thanked him. I carried my bag to the TWA counter and checked in. I was advised the flight would be taking off on time.

I headed for the bar. I was thinking how nice and considerate it was of Dave to arrange for me to have a comp on the room and food, but the best was arranging the limo to take me to the airport.

I did feel slighted; I had not had the pleasure of meeting Ms. Rosemary Forsyth. Although, at the time, Dave spoke of her as just his co-star; he said she was a beautiful blonde but gave no hint that they were falling in love.

My plane took off on time and landed at JFK 10 minutes early. I retrieved my bags and headed out to catch a cab to my apartment in Manhattan, a good 45 minute ride.

It had been really good seeing Dave again. It had been too long since we last saw each other. I had to admit he looked good and was in shape and, although he appeared cool, calm and collected, I knew the stress had to be reaching a crescendo.

Although I did not know precisely when Dave was going to tell Ellie he was filing for divorce, I had a feeling it would be soon. I was concerned about his drinking even though I knew he always controlled his actions and seemed to know when to stop.

I entered my apartment just after 10:30, unpacked and took a shower. I wanted to be up early so I could prepare for work and then stop at the kennel to pick up Baron; it was the first time we had been apart since I got him and I knew he would be excited to see me.

I would take him to the office to hang out with me. I had taken him to my office before and everyone loved him. I put on a Dionne Warwick album and decided to go to bed early; I had no problem falling into a deep sleep.

I woke before five o'clock and prepared a fresh pot of coffee then flipped on the news on WNBC Channel Four. I took my shower and dressed for work. I called the kennel at seven to let them know I would be there to retrieve Baron. As expected, he was extremely excited seeing me, knowing I had not abandoned him. He was even more excited when I told him he would be going to work with me.

We arrived at my office at 8:30; no one else had arrived. I got a bowl of water for Baron and made a pot of coffee for the office. I started perusing the new executive resumes that had been placed on my desk.

Just before nine o'clock, my boss, Norman, peeked his head into my office. "Hey, Bear! Good morning, boy. How was it in Sin City?" Baron looked at him and gave a little bark.

"Well, the only sin I committed was armed robbery. A one-armed bandit attempted to rob me; I turned the tables on him and took him for over $1,800 ... yeah, and I enjoyed it."

"How was your friend, Mr. Janssen? Did you get to see them filming, meet any of the stars?" he asked.

"No, it was a closed set. He only had time for dinner on Saturday night and we had drinks before I left yesterday. What was really a surprise and great for me: he arranged for my room and meals to be comped and a limo to take me to the airport yesterday. I didn't spend a dime ... actually made money."

"That's great! Good to have you back ... now you can make us money," he said with a smile as he went out, closing my door behind him.

I sat back and my mind drifted back to Dave. He looked good, relaxed and full of energy. Still, I had the feeling in my gut that the stress from all that was going on with Ellie was a heavy burden.

Dave had a hard rule when I saw him in Los Angeles for the several months we would meet for drinks: he would never drink while he was working - yet he had at least three doubles over lunch the day before.

I was glad to know Ellie was tied up with doctors' appointments in LA; otherwise, she would have insisted on being in Las Vegas with him, which would not have been good for him.

I knew Dave was close to making a move on his divorce but I did not know when. I decided to keep an eye on the newspapers and TV news in case it might be announced that Dave and Ellie were heading for divorce court. I would wait until I heard from him again and hope it would be good news.

28

I did not hear from Dave again for well over a month and had seen nothing in the newspapers or on television news about Dave. I knew their tenth wedding anniversary was Friday, August 23.

It was just after two o'clock on Sunday morning, August 25, when my phone rang. I had just gotten home a few minutes before so I was wide awake and answered on the first ring.

"Mike, Dave ... you don't sound like I woke you ... you awake?"

"Of course, I'm awake! It's Saturday night ... been out partying," I said with a laugh.

"Well, I told you I would let you know ... it's happened. I left Ellie, moved out; she'll be served the papers early this week," he said with a serious tone.

"WOW ... you did it! How did she take it?"

"She was speechless, but I know that won't last," he said.

"When did you tell her? I mean, you just had an anniversary ... did you do it gently?"

"Yeah, I was gentle. Actually, we were at the Greco's apartment; they hosted a party for us ... small party, just a few close friends. I took Ellie onto the balcony, gave her a couple of nice gifts and told her it was over ... that I was leaving her."

"DAMN, DAVE! You did this on your anniversary! MAN, that's just unbelievable ... so what happened? What did she say?"

"I didn't give her a chance; I walked back inside, excused myself, went down to our apartment, grabbed some clothes and left before she got down there."

"Have you spoken to her since?" I asked.

"No, she's been calling the office, the studio ... leaving all kinds of messages for me. I'm gonna let the lawyers handle it from here," he said.

"Where'd you go? Did you get an apartment somewhere?" I asked.

"Not yet. I'll be staying with a friend for a few days; I'll have Victor find me a rental for a while."

"How about Kathy and Diane ... do they know?" I asked.

"Oh, they probably know by now, if they've spoken to Ellie. I haven't seen them so I don't know."

"How do you think they will take the news?"

"They'll probably wonder what took me so long. Hell, they moved out the minute they could. I really think they know and they will understand."

"Yeah, I guess you're right. Has it hit the tabloids yet? I haven't seen anything in the news here."

"Well, I haven't heard anything or seen anything here yet either. I'm sure Ellie is trying to keep a lid on it. She probably thinks I put my tail between my legs and will come running back."

"Well, do you think those at the party know?"

"Hell, yes! I haven't spoken with any of them but they are friends so maybe they are being protective ... of both of us."

"Did you tell your agent, studio ... all of those on your *need to know* list?" I asked.

"Yeah, they all know and, so far, everyone is keeping their mouths shut which, in this town, is just plain fucking amazing!"

"So this just happened ... what, Friday?"

"Yeah, so I'm spending my first weekend as a bachelor," he said with a hearty laugh.

"So I guess everything went well with the filming in Las Vegas and you felt it was the right timing to make your move," I said.

"Yeah, perfect timing. You remember I told you about Rosemary Forsyth, my co-star in the film?"

"Yeah, I remember ... but you didn't introduce us ... or even introduce me to Brenda Vaccaro," I said with a slight, intended sarcastic tone.

Dave let out a laugh. "Well, the opening was there, so I made a move on Rosemary and things look pretty good there. I think I kind of like her ... a little."

"DAMN, DAVE! You move fast but, hey, slow down! You're not out of the frying pan yet; don't rush into the fire!"

"Ahh ... don't worry my friend. I am not that damned stupid. I want a chance to enjoy my freedom - for a while, at least," he said with a slight laugh.

"Man, I can't believe you did it on your anniversary! I mean, *why* on your anniversary ... supposed to be a happy day," I said.

"Hey, you really want to know? I figured *10 fucking years* was enough and I couldn't think of a better day to tell her!"

"When do you think it will hit the papers, the tabloids?"

"Hell, I don't know ... soon no doubt. Mike, I told you I'd let you know and I kept my word ... and I'll tell you, I feel like I'm breathing clean, fresh air for the first time in years!"

"Man, Dave! All I can say is that I hope all goes smoothly. Maybe Ellie won't try to drag you down."

"Mike, I know her. When she sees I'm serious, that I'm not coming back, she'll be out for absolute revenge. She'll be after blood ... she'll go after my flesh, she'll try and strip me for as much of MY assets as her grubby little lawyers can grab ... you can bank on it!"

"Dave, at least you have the ball rolling so I guess you know what to expect, and I'm sure your people will handle it in the best way for you. IF, at any time I can do anything for you, just call!"

"Thanks, Mike! That's good to know. I'll be in touch."

"Hey! Now that I know you've done this, keep me informed. Don't wait and call me a month from now." I wondered if he heard the unspoken plea in my voice.

"Yeah, okay ... I'll call you in a few days. You take care." With that, Dave ended the call.

I went to my bar and fixed another scotch and water, a double. I sat down in my living room in a state of shock. I reflected upon his call. Dave sounded perfectly sober and I detected what I was certain was a big sigh of relief in his voice.

I finally went to bed. Baron jumped up on the bed and gave me a kiss goodnight, then plopped down at the foot of my bed. It took a while for me to fall asleep, thinking of all that was going on with Dave. If he told her this last Friday night, then I figured she would not be able to even contact a lawyer until Monday.

I thought about Dave's words, the tone of his voice. He was very relieved. He sounded confident and, for the first time – really since I had gotten to know him - he sounded truly happy.

How in the hell could he be happy knowing this foray was going to be very, very costly - financially and, possibly, for his career - an unknown factor at this stage?

I last glanced at my digital clock at 4:10 before falling into a deep, alcohol-induced sleep.

Baron was licking my face, waking me just after eight o'clock. It was his way of telling me to get out of bed and take him to Riverside Park for his morning run. I staggered into the kitchen and hit the button to turn on the coffee pot then went to the bathroom to brush my teeth and wash my face.

My conversation with Dave early in the morning came rushing into my mind. *WOW!* I thought to myself ... *he really did it!*

I thought of his choice to tell Ellie on their *tenth* anniversary and, again, wondered why. The more I thought about it, the more I realized it was Dave's way of saying: "It's over! I'm starting over...alone!"

Yes, that was just like Dave. He was a very methodical man and he chose his actions as carefully as he chose his words. I poured a cup of coffee and got Baron ready for his run. I was anxious to stop by the corner newsstand and grab all the papers, see if there was any news about Dave and Ellie.

I took Baron for his morning run and picked up the *Sunday New York Times* and *Daily News*. I looked at the most recent Hollywood fan movie/TV star magazines; nothing on their covers. There were no sordid headlines on *The National Enquirer* or the other rag sheets, either.

I would scan the newspapers over coffee in my apartment. I would watch the television news because I was certain there would be some report, if it had leaked out to any media, which I was certain it would have by now ... certainly by Monday.

I didn't ask Dave who he would be staying with but, knowing Dave had so many friends there, he could bounce around from place to place for an endless amount of time. Still, Dave was the kind of guy who would not want to impose on his friends for anything.

I tried to envision how Ellie was reacting. I believed she did love him but, from the few glimpses I had and from what Dave had related, I wondered if her jealousy and tendency to want control over him had blinded her love, making his life far more miserable than any man could withstand.

I felt the age difference between them may have been weighing on her mind, creating feelings of insecurity which resulted in uncontrollable jealousy.

It was obvious all the money Dave had spent for Ellie (and his) therapy was wasted money. In a way, I felt sorry for Ellie to be in this situation. I wondered, for a fleeting moment, if Dave would reconsider and return to Ellie. I dismissed the thought instantly; there was no way he would.

29

Since Dave's call Sunday morning, I had been grabbing every fan magazine, all the tabloids and *The Los Angeles Times* as well as the New York papers. On Wednesday, there was a short article in *The New York Daily News:* 'DAVID JANSSEN'S SPLIT.'

The article basically said: *David Janssen has moved from his Sierra Towers apartment and left his lovely wife, Ellie. Is a divorce looming? Close friends of the couple have stated, on condition of anonymity, this may be the case.*

David Janssen, best known for his starring role in The Fugitive is staying at an undisclosed location. Ellie seems to be in seclusion in their luxury apartment and could not be reached for comment.

Once considered one of the happiest, and most successful, marriages in Hollywood, the couple celebrated their tenth wedding anniversary on August 23. Frank Lieberman, David's publicist, has refused to comment, saying only, "This is a private matter and David and Ellie will appreciate you respecting their privacy."

I read the short article several times and realized Dave was finally free, in a manner of speaking. He would not be going back and he would be facing some very tough months ahead as the divorce moved through the long court process. There would be a considerable amount of publicity and I felt certain it would not all be good for Dave.

I found myself thinking of him almost on a daily basis, wanting to call him. I refrained from calling him because I knew he was constantly busy and I continued to fear I'd be interrupting him, especially at this time in his life. I kept telling myself that he'd call when he wanted to talk.

I kept picking up the newspapers, adding *The Los Angeles Times* to my New York papers and scanning the covers of the fan magazines and tabloids to see if there was any breaking news. Not speaking with Dave was driving me nuts. I was not concerned about him because he was a TV-Movie star; I was concerned because he was a good friend.

I picked up all the newspapers en route to my office Monday morning. Once in the office, a fresh cup of coffee on my desk, I perused each paper, starting with *The Los Angeles Times*. I was both surprised and disappointed not to find anything about Dave. It had been five days since the small article appeared in the *Daily News*. Oh well! I told myself it would soon be big news and I would just have to wait. I then concentrated on my work.

I left the office at 6:15 and went down to the Oyster Bar in Grand Central Terminal for a well-deserved drink. I took a sip of my scotch and water, lit a Winston and David immediately appeared in my mind.

I could not help but feel anxious, wanting to hear from him ... wanting to know what the hell was happening with him. I also wondered why nothing had hit the newspapers or even television news about his leaving Ellie since the small blurb I had seen in *The New York Daily News*. I could only surmise his studio and publicist were doing an excellent job for him.

I left the Oyster Bar just after seven and headed uptown to Sparks Steakhouse for dinner. I had a quiet dinner with a couple of Brandy Alexanders, ordered a prime rib for Baron and was home by 8:30.

Baron was very happy with his dinner and there was enough left over for the next night. Although I was tempted to call Dave, I knew it would be a waste of time. I would just wait until he found time to call me; he had both my home and office numbers.

Finally, on Friday night, August 30, Dave called just after ten o'clock, New York time.

"Mike, Dave ... how's it going for you?"

"Great ... but the big question is HOW in the hell is it going for you?" I asked.

"So far all is calm ... won't be for much longer, I'm sure."

"Your people, Mr. Liberman, and the others must be doing a super job for you. I've been scouring all the newspapers; there was just a very small article in the *Daily News* a week or so ago, then nothing. I even buy the *LA Times* ... nothing. Have you changed your mind and made up with her?" I asked, partly joking.

"Not a chance of that! She has not been served the papers yet, but it will be soon, then I expect World War III will begin."

"Are you still staying with your friend?" I asked.

"No, I checked into a hotel ... the Beverly Hills ... until Victor finds me a place. I have him looking for a nice, secluded house."

"May I ask if you've spoken to Ellie? I'm sure there is a lot of gossip flowing among your friends," I said.

"Hell, yes ... a lot of gossip ... but the feedback I'm getting, at least from those who really know Ellie and I, is that most are wondering how our marriage lasted as long as it did," he said with a laugh.

"Have you spoken with Kathy and Diane? What's your mom think about you leaving Ellie?"

"I spoke with Diane; she gave me her heart-felt congratulations. My mother is happy, which I expected she would be; they never got along."

"That doesn't surprise me. How about everyone else ... your agent, all the people you pay to protect you ... have they given you their opinions?"

"Yeah, they have ... and I take it with a grain of salt. The only one I truly respect is Abby; he knows what I'm facing and he knows how I have to handle it. He says it will be rough but I'm a big boy. I can take it ... as well as give it, if it comes to that."

"So how are you enjoying bachelor life, or do you have to learn it all over again?" I joked.

"Well ... it's not like that. Rosemary and I have hit it off and things are hot and heavy ... so I'm having a hell of a lot of fun," he said with a laugh.

"Damn, Dave! Do you think that's smart? Ellie could go after you for adultery or something," I said.

"I don't give a damn ... she can try. I am happy right now and, after 10 years ... well, after about five years of pure fucking hell, I am happy and that's all I care about now."

"I have to agree with you on that ... your happiness is what counts ... you've worked hard, you deserve it. So how is it with Rosemary? Do you love her? Do you think she loves you?"

"Well, a little problematic there. I love her ... but I'm not in love with her. I think she has the same feelings but she is still married ... and she has a two-year-old daughter ... so a lot of complications ... have to take it one day at a time."

"Man! Are you sure you know what you're doing? What does her husband say about this; does he even know? Dave, are you sure you want another step-daughter?" I asked, amazed that I was even saying the words. I instantly felt I was over-stepping my bounds as a friend.

"Yeah, her husband knows ... I'm not a home-wrecker; their marriage was already headed for divorce-court. I don't think he gives a damn who she sleeps with. Her daughter is a bundle of joy; I love her. Mike, don't think for a minute I'm jumping out of the pan and into the fire ... I'm not ... plenty of time to let things play out."

"What kind of work does her husband do? Is Rosemary still taking roles? Who takes care of her daughter?"

"Her husband is Mike Tolan; he's an actor. I know him; he's a decent guy. Rosemary has a nanny for her daughter. She still takes roles ... no problems there."

"Man ... I sure hope you are right about all of this. It does look like you're jumping out of the frying pan and into a very hot fire ... at least, it looks that way to me. I still think it's going to give Ellie a hell of a lot of ammunition when you guys get into court."

"I know and you have a point, but I sure as hell am not going to hole up in a hotel room, become a monk ... I'm FREE, even if it's not set in stone yet. I'm going to enjoy life."

"I know ... you have to live your life and you deserve to enjoy it. I just don't want to see you get hurt. What does Mr. Greshler and Mr. Liberman think ... about how the divorce will affect your career?"

"Oh, hell! We all know it will have an adverse effect, to some degree. I mean there will be a lot of people, especially women, who may be pissed off at me, blame me. I'm sure I'll lose some fans but, over time, I hope they'll understand and maybe forgive me for getting a divorce."

"Speaking of fans ... do you have anything in the works, any movies or television roles coming up that I don't know about?"

"Yeah, Abby's got a few irons in the fire ... nothing certain, but I'll let you know. One thing is for sure: I gotta work. I'm gonna need all the money I can lay my hands on," he said, letting out a big laugh.

"Well, if you really need a few dollars after you walk out of court ... let me know. I can send you a few hundred," I said with a laugh.

"Yeah, right, Mike! Hey, you may be in my position ... better save your money. You'll need it," he said with another big laugh. "All right, Mike. I have to go but I'll touch base with you in a few days ... try and keep you abreast of things as they happen so you don't have to spend your money on all those newspapers and magazines."

"I'd really appreciate it, Dave; it's not so much the cost of the newspapers but they're heavy when you have to lug them from the newsstand. Besides that, I worry about you, not knowing if Ellie has slit your throat or not," I joked.

"Hey, if that were to happen, you'd hear the news ... that would be news! Okay, take care and we'll talk soon."

"Thanks, Dave! I appreciate your call and I will be waiting for your next one," I said.

30

I would not hear from Dave again until Sunday morning, September 15. It was just after five o'clock in the morning when I was awakened by the loud ringing in my ear, followed by Baron licking my face.

"Hello. I know it's you, Dave. No one else would have the balls to call me at this ungodly hour," I asnwered with a hoarse laugh.

"Time to get up anyway, Mike ... your dog needs to go out," he said, returning a laugh.

"Yeah, you're right ... and I am glad you called. I've been going crazy wondering what the hell is going on with you and Ellie. I'm sure you read the papers, too - all the nasty bullshit they're saying about you and Rosemary."

"Oh, yeah! I read them and you're right ... 98 percent is plain BS ... all fabricated, not an ounce of truth to most of it."

"Are you - Mr. Greshler, Mr. Liberman or your attorneys - worried about the 2 percent that may have a grain of truth in what they're writing?"

"Yeah, they seem to be a little concerned, but I'm not. I told you I'm not going to hole up in a hotel room and play like a monk. I'm going to LIVE!"

"Are you still staying in the hotel?" I asked.

"No ... I leased a small house on La Collina Drive ... didn't do this on purpose, but I can see my old apartment from the driveway," he said with a chuckle.

"Unbelievable ... does Ellie know?"

"Hell, no! At least, I don't think she does - not yet anyway."

"I hope she doesn't find out; she'll be screaming in your driveway," I said. "What about all of your things in your apartment; were you able to get them out ... your clothes and personal things?"

"Yeah, I made sure Victor got them when he knew Ellie was out for a while. Luckily she had not changed the locks yet. She called Victor a couple of hours after she got home and read the riot act to him; she obviously knew he had been there to gather my clothes."

"Poor Victor," I said.

"No, not poor Victor; he's known about my plans for quite a while. I think he's as happy about it as I am. Ellie always treated him like a servant," Dave said in a serious tone.

That was one attribute I truly respected of Dave: he treated everyone, those who did things for him, shopped for him, even the crews on his shows, as equal to him. He always treated everyone with whom he came into contact with utmost respect.

"So are you still seeing Rosemary?" I asked.

"Hell, yes, and we're having a hell of a lot of fun; I'm going to ask her to move in with me."

"Dave, are you sure that would be okay? Don't you think it would create problems you don't need right now? I haven't seen anything in the papers about you and Ellie being in court yet."

"You will. She's hired a bunch of lawyers so things will be happening ... most likely this coming week. My lawyers are ready for it so I don't really give a damn."

"Okay ... I know you'll be able to handle anything Ellie throws at you," I said with a slight chuckle.

"No, that's what I'm paying the lawyers big bucks to do. At this point, I don't give a damn what it costs as long as I'm free and can live and breathe again. Hell, Mike! I can always make more money," he said with a big laugh.

"What are you working on now? All the crap that's been in the papers hasn't said anything about what you're working on."

"Well, *The Shoes of the Fisherman* is about to be released and I've gotten a script for a space film with Gregory Peck, Gene Hackman, my friend - Jim Franciscus - and some others; it may start around the end of the year."

"Good. At least, you're keeping busy; that'll help you. I can't wait to see *The Shoes of the Fisherman*. I think Anthony Quinn is a great actor. What was it like to work with him ... or did I already ask you that?"

"You did and I'll tell you again: he's a great man, very fine actor, great gentleman. I've always liked him. Yes, you're right; I'm keeping busy - sure I'm going to need all the money I can make. Ellie never was cheap and she's gonna want to continue living like a queen now," he said, again with a laugh.

"So how are things going with Rosemary; do you think things will turn serious? You know what I mean."

"Mike, I'm taking one step at a time, one day at time. Hell, this divorce will probably take a year or so to get through the court so I'm not too worried about being forced into a marriage again and, seriously, I don't think I want that anyway."

"Well, I'm clipping all of the articles from the papers here. Maybe you'll want to read them; I could send them to you," I said.

"Hell, no! It's probably like all the crap here. I don't need to read them. Besides, that is what I pay Liberman for; you can trash them."

"I'll just put them in a scrapbook ... might be worth looking back on them down the road," I said with a slight laugh.

"Yeah, sure ... maybe for a laugh. By the way, you haven't told me about your situation; are you headed for divorce court, too?"

"I haven't heard from her or any lawyers ... actually, I try not to think about it."

"Well, if you're out there playing the field, you'll think about it when you meet someone you want to get serious with ... just like me."

"Yeah, you're probably right, but I didn't think you'd get so serious right out of the gate. I would have thought you would want to play the field a little yourself."

"Actually, so did I ... but, working with Rosemary in Vegas, things happened. I'll just enjoy it while it lasts," he said.

"I hope you do ... and you're smart. Leave it all in the hands of your lawyers and the others ... enjoy life. You've earned it."

"All right, Mike! Are you wide awake now? I bet your dog wants to run so take it easy and we'll talk soon."

It was almost 5:30 and would not be light for at least another hour. I decided I would have some coffee and watch the news before taking Baron to the park. With a fresh cup of coffee, I went out on the balcony and gazed out over the city.

I reflected on our conversation. Dave was sober. I had no doubt about that and he sounded strong and confident and, of course, he sounded very happy.

I would not hear from Dave for another two weeks. During that time I continued to scour the newspapers and the Hollywood fan magazines - not to mention the tabloids - looking for articles on the machinations occurring in the Los Angeles divorce court in 'Janssen -v- Janssen.'

It was apparently in the public eye as well as the court system. David's lawyers had filed citing *irreconcilable differences;* I had yet to see anything filed by Ellie.

Could it be she was still closed up in their apartment trying to convince herself that Dave would return to their marital bed with his droopy, sad eyes asking for her forgiveness? I told myself, if that were the case, Ellie would have a very long wait.

Dave called me early on Saturday evening, October 5.

"Hey, Mike! How are things going for you in the big city?"

"Good, Dave ... and how are things going for you in Tinseltown?" I joked.

"Great! Couldn't be better!" he almost shouted.

"Ahh ... does that mean you are officially divorced?"

"Hell, no ... but, just like in the movies, I have a mistress," he said with a deep laugh.

"Dave, that sounds awful familiar to me ... actually sounds like the script for the movie you did in Vegas. Is it out yet?"

"No, it's still being put together; it won't be out until sometime in the spring, but you have a good memory. Rosemary was my mistress in the film and we're just turning art into reality," he said with a sly laugh.

"Oh, boy! I guess something really happened on the set ... the set I was not allowed to be on. Okay, Dave, tell me. Don't keep me in suspense."

"Well, yeah, something happened. I don't want to spoil it for you but there were a couple of scenes ... a couple of nude scenes ... and, I'll tell you, it wasn't all an act. It was, if I say so myself, pretty damn good," he said with a deep laugh.

"What? You must be kidding! At least, now, I know why you couldn't get me in to see you work; I don't think I'd really have wanted to watch that anyway. Are you serious? I mean, how in the hell can you make love in front of a hundred people watching you? How in the hell could you even get it up?"

"Mike ... when you meet Rosemary, you'll know. Getting it up was no problem; getting it to go down when Garson called for a 'cut' ... a kid brought us both robes. I had a little problem with the front of mine, but the take was perfect. You'll see."

"Dave, you have to be kidding me ... that didn't really happen ... did it?" I asked, as I was beginning to believe him.

"I'm just kidding, Mike, but the truth is it wasn't all an act; that's where it began with Rosemary and me."

"Man, I can't wait to see the movie now! They don't really show everything, do they? I mean, no frontal nudity, right?"

"No, not really ... you'll see more of Rosemary than you do me." He laughed.

"So you mean the entire world will see what you cuddle into bed with each night?" I asked with a genuine laugh.

"Hell, yes! Everyone that sees the film will."

"Doesn't that make you mad?" I asked sincerely.

"Hell, no, but it will make every lecherous old man jealous of me!" he said, letting out a big laugh.

"Okay ... I can't wait to see it. I'm still clipping out articles; you and Ellie are getting a lot of press here on the east coast."

"Yeah, but it's all bullshit, so don't believe it. I have to go. We're going out to dinner and I'll call you later."

"Okay, Dave ... thanks for calling and be careful," I cautioned.

31

Over the next two weeks there were numerous articles in *The New York Post, The New York Daily News, The National Enquirer, Photoplay* and *Radio/TV Mirror* magazines. I had scoured *The New York Times* and found nothing, even on the television pages. I guess *The Grey Lady* did not find Janssen -v- Janssen part of their *all the news that's fit to print.*

The consensus was not at all flattering to Dave. I could only surmise Ellie was doing a little public relations of her own. The media was making it sound like Ellie had been the perfect Hollywood wife supporting Dave's career, making an eloquent, tastefully decorated home and doing everything for her husband.

The articles I was reading made it sound as though Dave had been playing around on Ellie for years and had really fallen head-over-heels with his *Where It's At* co-star, Rosemary Forsyth.

Rosemary was married to actor Michael Tolan and they had an infant daughter when she and David met for the filming of *Where It's At* in Las Vegas.

Dave had told me that she was very unhappy with her marriage to Tolan. I had the feeling she was also unhappy about being a mother, but I could have been wrong and quickly dismissed the idea. I never told Dave my feelings about that.

I could not help but notice that Rosemary was 12 years younger than Dave, and Ellie was 12 years older than Dave. Of course, that provided the tabloids with more than enough fodder to make it appear that the break-up of his marriage was entirely Dave's fault. There was also detailed attention to Dave's drinking habits, insinuating he was a full-blown alcoholic.

In reflection, I had been sitting with Dave and watched him drink, at least, 20 scotch and sodas within three to four hours, yet I could not say that he even appeared to be drunk to the extent he was unable to control his faculties.

Knowing David Janssen as I did, I felt anger at some of the stories and allegations I knew to be false and totally without merit. I could only imagine how Dave felt. There was no doubt in my mind Frank Liberman would be earning his money.

The tabloids were making a big deal of Dave and Rosemary being seen out on the town, acting like newlyweds. There was an article alleging Dave was showering Rosemary with expensive gifts of jewelry and clothing and spending a large sum on gifts for her baby.

Ellie had filed for an increase in her monthly maintenance; Dave had told me she was receiving over $8,000 per month. "Hell, we never spent $8,000 a month when we were living together and had her daughters with us," he had lamented.

"Hell, $8,000 a month - that's only about $4,000 less than what I earn in an entire year," I had responded. I could not conceive how one person could spend $8,000 in a single month - but I didn't have that worry. I laughed to myself.

It appeared Dave and Ellie would not be parting as friends.

Dave called me again early Sunday morning, October 12. I was glad he called because the breaking news articles had waned over the past month.

"Mike, it's Dave. How are things with you?"

"Not bad ... progressing slowly but surely. How are things with you ... are you and Rosemary still making love?"

"Oh, yes, and I am truly enjoying it."

"Well, I haven't seen anything about you and Ellie in the papers lately. How is that going?"

"Slow ... too damned slow and it gets more costly as the days pass. Damn lawyers are not cheap, I can tell you that."

"I can imagine ... have you had any contact with Ellie?"

"Hell, no! She's called and left messages all over the place. I'm doing exactly what my lawyers say, leaving it in their hands. Listen! I'll be coming to New York next month and wanted to make sure we could get together and have a few drinks, maybe a lunch or dinner."

"Hell, yes! That would be great. It's been a hell of a long time. I'd love it! What's bringing you to New York?"

"They are having the east coast premier for *The Shoes of the Fisherman*. It will be a short trip, maybe two days tops, but it will be good to see you and we can have a few drinks."

"What date will you be here? I'll put it on my calendar now."

"Not certain yet ... I'll know in a few days and I'll give you a call."

"I'll mark off the entire day. Just let me know. It would be great - breakfast, lunch or dinner. Is Rosemary coming with you?" I asked.

"Okay, I'll let you know. I'll be at The Carlyle. We can meet somewhere around there. No, Rosemary's not coming this time; she's busy here," he said.

"That's too bad. I really hoped I would get to meet her, especially since I didn't get to see her in Vegas ... on the set," I joked.

"Ahh ... come on, Mike! You'll meet her, eventually ... and I know you'll like her, too," he said with a laugh.

"I'm sure I will ... maybe I'll be invited to the wedding," I said jokingly.

"Of course you will ... IF there ever is one. I'm not in any rush to get tied down again," he said in a serious tone.

"Well, I'll tell you now: if there ever IS a wedding, I'll be there for sure," I said.

"Okay, Mike ... so how about your marital situation - still status quo or are you waiting to see how mine ends up?"

"Right now, still status quo... I haven't heard from her so I'm just taking one day at a time. I'll get something done, hopefully at the right time. I can't decide based on your divorce; there sure as hell isn't that much money involved in mine," I answered laughing. "So are there any new developments?"

"Not really. So far, things are at least civil. I'll keep you informed," he said.

"What about Rosemary and her husband?"

"She's already filed for a divorce - looks like he's not going to contest it so it should be quick and easy for her."

"What about their baby ... custody?"

"They'll have shared custody. When their schedules work together, Rosemary will have her, then when he's in between work, he'll have her. He seems to be a pretty reasonable guy."

"So he's not angry with you ... he doesn't blame you?"

"Oh, no! Not at all ... neither one of them were happy with each other, going back to when they found out she was pregnant."

"That's a shame! I mean, in a way, it's a shame. She's not going to be like Ellie is she, putting her daughter in schools ... not being the mother to her baby?" I asked, knowing it was none of my business.

"No ... she's really a good mother; she loves Alexandra very much. I'm sure things will be fine with her."

"I hope you know what you're doing, Dave. You married Ellie and she had two young daughters. You've helped her raise them ... and now you are with Rosemary and she has a baby daughter. Are you sure you're ready for this?"

"No ... no, I'm not sure and, no, I'm not ready for this," he said, letting out a big laugh. "But I'm having a hell of a lot of fun right now; that's what I'm looking at."

"I'm really glad to hear that, Dave. I think you deserve it and, more important, you need it! Do you know when it's really going to get started in court, the hearings I mean, where you will have to be there?"

"Not yet ... Crowley says it may be a couple more months. He'll try and work things around my schedule, and that's good."

"Well, I hope you will let me know. Maybe I could fly out and watch the fireworks," I said joking. I knew that was highly improbable.

"I'll let you know ... I can't guarantee you any fireworks. I've told Crowley to play nice; I just want to get this over with ... move on."

"I sure don't blame you. I hope Ellie plays nice, too; it would sure be a lot easier on her ... on both of you."

"Mike, I have a gut feeling she won't be nice. She is a very poor loser ... and it's not about money, it's me. She can't stand the thought of losing me."

"That's a real shame ... she should have thought about that when she was pushing you so hard, being suspicious ... trying to control you.

"Honestly, Dave, do you think your heavy drinking has something to do with the way Ellie treated you in the past? I'm not trying to get personal here but, when we first met and I started joining you for drinks, I couldn't help but take count ... you can really put 'em away, and you handle your booze quite well. Hell, I've learned from you!"

"Mike, to be very honest, I was always a heavy drinker. I learned to control ... to know my limits. There is a lot of pressure on a guy in my position ... not knowing when your next job would come, always needing money, wondering if your work will be appreciated, worrying about having fans ... and keeping the fans you have.

"No, I can't blame Ellie for my drinking. I can't blame anyone but myself. However, the last four years or so, Ellie sure hasn't kept me from drinking; she's been an excuse I made to myself, but it's not really her fault," he said in a very serious tone, as if taking a reflective look at himself.

32

I continued searching through the New York papers and the Los Angeles papers and TV-Movie fan magazines almost on a daily basis looking for articles concerning Dave and Ellie.

There were sporadic articles, most of which appeared to me to be complete fabrications of what was really going on.

Everything I read was purportedly "according to a close friend of David's" or "a very close friend of Ellie's" and Dave's friends were only saying he "wanted to move on." Ellie's "close friend" was saying, "Ellie loves David with all her heart and is sure he will come to his senses and come home to her."

Although Dave had introduced me to a few of his fellow actor friends during our drinking sessions at The Formosa and Polo Lounge, I had never spoken with any outside of Dave's introduction.

I knew that he considered Paul Burke, James Farentino, Rock Hudson, Milton Berle and Jackie Cooper to be real friends. I also knew Dave was a very private man and had serious doubts as to whether anything said by "a close friend of David's" was authentic. I was positive that Dave would not make comments to anyone unless he had total trust in the individual.

It was exactly a week later when Dave called me at 10:30 in the morning, New York time.

"Mike, how are you? I just wanted to let you know I'll be in the city on the 12th and 13th of next month. That's a Tuesday and Wednesday. Is that okay with you?"

"Hell, yes! I can't wait to see you! When is the premier?"

"Wednesday evening ... I'll have a ticket for you."

"That's great; I appreciate that ... so you'll be at The Carlyle?"

"Yes. I don't have my flight information yet, but I'll be at The Carlyle and we could meet and have some drinks there. I'll be making it an early night; I have to be fresh for the premier."

"That would be great. So who is coming for the premier?" I asked.

"Just about everyone: Anthony Quinn, Laurence Olivier, Barbara Jefford - she plays my wife in the film - Isa Miranda ... several others."

"Will I get to meet Mr. Quinn?" I asked.

"I think that can be arranged; I'll let you know when I'll be coming in and we'll meet Tuesday evening."

"I'd be happy to pick you up at the airport."

"No, that won't be necessary; the studio has a limo service. I'll give you a call before I get to the hotel."

"Okay, I'll be waiting. So, how are things going with your divorce?"

"Getting nasty ... Ellie knows about Rosemary. Of course, she has known for several months but her lawyers are getting mean ... and I'm sure it's because she's telling them to screw me."

"Yeah, but California is a *no fault* state. I mean, you could have a hundred mistresses and she couldn't do a damn thing about that ... right?" I questioned, wanting him to confirm I was right about the divorce laws.

"Well, she's trying every damn thing she can and it's just costing more money and time. I just want to get this over with."

"How is Rosemary handling it? Is she holding on or is she getting upset?"

"She's handling it very well, better than I expected. I wish I could handle it as well as she is ... but then I am the one losing big bucks."

"How is her situation with her husband?"

"He is being very amicable ... no problems. He wants liberal visitation rights with Alexandra, and that's not a problem with Rosemary. She's not asking for any alimony or community property; they realized they both made a mistake and they're handling it like civil adults."

"Well, I saw how Ellie reacted to you missing a party ... if she acted like that over a simple little thing, I can only imagine how she is going to be when she realizes you're not going back to her."

"Yeah, I knew it would get nasty ... maybe that's why I stayed as long as I did. I don't have a stomach for this kind of bullshit."

"I know, Dave, but you were only hurting yourself. I could see your moods change and you were not happy at all ... except when you were at work."

"That's the only thing that kept me sane ... working and, of course, hiding out and having a few drinks with you, my friend. I wish you had not moved to New York."

"I seriously doubt I had any role in you maintaining your sanity but. to be honest, I enjoyed your company and the free drinks," I said with a laugh.

"Well, I meant it. You have proven to be a good friend ... you've never betrayed me ... never taken from me ... you've always treated me as a friend, not just a celebrity."

"Thank you, Dave! That's really nice of you; I appreciate that and I'm glad you know I am your real friend," I responded humbly.

"Well, it will be good to see you again and we'll have some fun. I'll call you and let you know the time table. Talk to you soon."

"Okay. Thanks for calling, Dave," I said and ended the call.

I was really excited to know of his unexpected trip to New York, to have the chance to sit down and talk with him again. It had been a long time since he was in New York.

I was also excited that he had invited me to the premier of *The Shoes of the Fisherman*. I was looking forward to meeting Anthony Quinn, as a fan.

I fixed myself a cup of coffee and thought back to my conversation with Dave. He sounded very happy, very sober and relaxed. Of all the time I spent with Dave when I lived in Los Angeles, I had never heard him sound so relaxed and happy. I felt his relationship with Rosemary had a lot to do with his happiness.

On Monday, I advised my boss, Norman, that I would have to take the 12th and 13th of the following month off. He did not ask why but told me to enjoy. I was determined to get as much work done as possible to be able to enjoy the days off without feeling guilty. I was counting the days and anxious to see Dave and to see the movie, too.

The days dragged by but the weather was nice, an Indian summer. I hoped the weather would remain good for Dave and the movie stars' visit. I had never been to a premier of a film but, from what I had seen of them on television, it was a big deal with the stars all dressed to the nines and stepping out of their limos onto a red carpet. I was sure it would be that way for this premier; after all, this is New York.

Dave called me at my office on Monday, November 11, just after nine o'clock.

"Mike, it's Dave. I'll be landing at JFK tomorrow afternoon at three o'clock. I should be in the hotel by 4:30; will you still be in your office?"

"I was going to take tomorrow off but, since you're not going to be in until that time, I'll go to the office and get some work done."

"That's good ... so I'll call you once I'm checked into the hotel and we can set a time and place to meet ... maybe have dinner."

"Perfect! I'll be here. I'm looking forward to seeing you."

"Great ... then I will see you tomorrow," he said and hung up.

Tuesday, November 12, Dave called me at 4:45 in the afternoon.

"Mike, I'm in my room at The Carlyle ... going to shower and freshen up. Can we meet in Bemelmans bar, say around eight?"

"Yeah, Dave, that would be great. I'll be there."

I left my office and went home to walk and feed Baron. I would then take a shower and change into a fresh suit.

I was at Bemelmans in The Carlyle lobby at 7:50. The Maître D' seated me and I told him I was expecting Mr. David Janssen. He nodded and took my order for a J & B Scotch, water with lemon wedge.

The Maître D' escorted Dave to the table at 8:20 and immediately left to get his drink. Dave was wearing a custom-tailored navy blue suit with white shirt, French cuffs and a red-white striped tie. He looked very refreshed, especially after a five hour flight.

"It's great to see you, Mike," Dave said, reaching over the table to shake my hand.

"It's my pleasure, really. Thank you! Damn, Dave! I don't know what Rosemary is doing but you really look great! I don't think I have ever seen you looking so well."

A waiter appeared with Dave's drink and menus.

"Are you ready for another?" Dave asked, pointing to my nearly empty glass. I nodded and the waiter left the table.

"I'm feeling great ... never felt so good. Yeah, Rosemary has worked wonders for me and I'm drinking it all in," he said with a big smile.

"I can't wait to meet her ... of course, I'm sure I'll see *Where It's At* before I have that opportunity," I said with a laugh.

"Yes, probably so ... and I know you'll love the movie. I'm pretty proud of it," he said.

"I'm glad you didn't really buy Caesar's Palace, though."

"Yeah, right. Let's order dinner. Is that okay with you?"

"That would be nice; I'm hungry ... but you're still on California time. Is it too early for you?"

"No, just an early dinner for me. I'm hungry, too; I didn't eat on the plane."

We perused the menus.

Dave motioned for the waiter and ordered another round of drinks. The waiter smiled at Dave and left the table. I glanced around the room and saw that many of the women were just plain staring at Dave. I thought it was cute. I wondered how Dave could act like he was just an ordinary guy having dinner; I know he noticed the ladies stares.

33

We ordered dinner and another round of drinks.

"So, Dave, tell me ... what should I expect tomorrow? I am really looking forward to this. Can I bring a date?"

"Of course you can bring a date! You can dress casual if you want to. All of us will be seated in the front rows; it will all be roped off and, of course, there will be security. We'll have some time after the showing so I'll introduce you to Anthony and the others. There will be an *after party* at The Plaza and you're welcome there. Are you going to bring Rose Marie?"

"Well, of course! I know she would be thrilled to meet you and the others."

"Good! I'm glad I had the foresight; here are your tickets," Dave said, reaching into his jacket pocket and pulling out two tickets for the premier. I noted the seat selection was right behind the three front rows.

"Thank you, Dave ... this is really nice of you; I sincerely appreciate it."

"Your seats are right behind mine, I think. They have the first three rows roped off for the cast and VIP guests. I think you will like the film. You're Catholic, right?"

"Yeah, but not a very good one," I said with a smile.

"Well, this film is very realistic ... shows a lot of the Catholic Church, the process of selecting a Pope ... it's a very moving film - one that is sure to provoke a lot of controversy and bring attention to the political ramifications the Church has on the world."

"What role do you play? You haven't told me much about it."

"I'm a journalist ... my wife is with me and I am to report on the selection of a new Pope. Of course, I am having problems with my marriage and I also enjoy a drink or two ... pretty close to my role in real life. It's a very good role and the plot is excellent; I'm glad to be a part of it," he said.

"You told me you enjoyed working with Mr. Quinn ... how is he as a person? Is he really a nice guy?"

"He's a real prince, a damn nice guy, dedicated to his craft, humble and kind."

"Wasn't Ellie with you during the filming? Didn't you film it in Italy?"

"Oh, yes! I told you that when we went over there. She and Kathy ... yeah, Ellie was with me and it was pure hell! The only peace I had was while on the set ... or when Jimmy and Michelle visited us for a few days. Ellie did nothing but complain ... about the heat, the long hours of filming and the people on the crew ... just anything."

"How did you manage? How did you keep from sending her home on the next flight?" I asked.

"It wasn't easy. I just stayed away from the house we rented until I was too drunk and too tired to argue with her," he said and let out a little laugh.

"At least it's over ... and you won't be taking her on any future locations where you're working," I said with a sincere smile.

"You're right about that. You know, Ellie is not - has never been - an actress; she does not understand what it takes. Yeah, she knows it takes long hours and a lot of preparations but all she really cares about is the night life, the party life ... the nice things the money can buy her. She doesn't understand the hard work, that when I come home, I am usually exhausted and I still have to read the scripts for the next day's shoot," he said.

I saw his mood change from being relaxed to being disgusted just thinking about her.

"You're right, Mike; that part of my life is over ... well, almost over. I want to put that all behind me and live again," he said in a serious tone.

"Do you think you and Rosemary will get married?" I asked.

"Whoa, Mike! Don't rush me! I want a chance to breathe a little before I do anything. Rosemary and I have a good thing going ... I love her and I'm crazy about Alexandra. We have a good life together but I'm not going to be in any rush to tie the knot again."

"I was just wondering - not rushing you at all. I haven't even met her yet. I just think if I were in your shoes, which I'm not and never will be, I would just want some real freedom, without any obligations, without being tied down with just one woman. I'd want to play the field a little," I said with a smile.

"Ordinarily, I would agree with you - and that thought had been in my mind for the last couple of years, but then came Rosemary ... and, when you meet her, you will understand my willingness to give up the carefree life of a bachelor."

"She must be one hell of a woman. She's a little younger than you ... isn't she?" I asked.

"Yeah, as a matter of fact, she's your age ... but, like you, she's mature."

"I can't help but think that is why Ellie is so enraged ... and maybe convinced that you will come back to her. She's a few years older than you, then you get rich and famous and leave her for the younger woman ... man!"

"Yeah, you could have a point there but, at least, Rosemary was honest upfront about her age," he said.

"How does Rosemary feel about the age difference?" I asked.

"She thinks exactly as I do ... age is only a number. It's how you live that matters."

The busboy cleared our table and the waiter brought us desert menus, on which we both passed. We both ordered coffee and Dave ordered us a last round of drinks.

I glanced at my watch and noted it was just 10:40. I mentally counted our drinks; seven each, not that bad. I was still feeling completely sober and Dave looked and spoke as if he was, too.

"Well, Dave, I am really, really looking forward to tomorrow night. I'll bring Rose Marie and I am sure she will enjoy it, too. I can't thank you enough ... and for this wonderful dinner - and the drinks, of course."

"Yeah, it was nice ... good to see you again ... just like old times," he said. He motioned for the check and the waiter was there in seconds. Dave signed the check and we walked out of Bemelmans. Dave walked me to the entrance; we shook hands and he headed for his suite. I retrieved my car from the valet and headed home.

I was awake at my normal hour of four o'clock. I made a pot of coffee and watched the early morning news on NBC. I would take Baron for his run at daybreak. I laid out my tuxedo for the evening. I showered and shaved and dressed in Levis and a Pendleton shirt.

Dawn came just after seven o'clock and Baron was anxious to go to Riverside Park for his run. The park was only two blocks east of our apartment and he enjoyed the brisk air. We stayed in the park until 8:30 and then returned to the apartment.

I was taking the day off so I decided to go have a leisurely breakfast at the corner coffee shop and read the morning newspapers. There was a big article in *The New York Daily News* announcing the premier of *The Shoes of the Fisherman* at the Demille Theatre on Seventh Avenue in Manhattan. Among the stars who would be attending were Anthony Quinn, David Janssen and Sir John Gielgud. I must admit I was excited to be attending a movie premier, that my date and I would be guests of David Janssen.

Just after three o'clock I called Rose Marie and told her I would have a limo pick her up first. Rose Marie lived in Queens and I did not want to fight the traffic so I rented a limo. After all, this was a special occasion. The limo would pick Rose Marie up and then me for the short ride to the theatre.

At 3:30, Dave called and asked if I could meet him at The Carlyle for a quick drink. Of course I could!

"Hello, Mike! I'm glad you could make it."

"My pleasure, Dave. I'm really excited about tonight ... and so is Rose Marie. She is really looking forward to meeting you and, if it's okay with you, we'll go to the after party but just for a few minutes."

"You're welcome to stay as long as you like; there will be food and an open bar," Dave said.

"That sounds really good. I rented a limo for us tonight and I don't want to rack up a big bill so we'll just stay there for a few minutes. I know Rose Marie will be thrilled."

We enjoyed two drinks and Dave returned to his room to get ready and I went back home.

34

The limousine arrived at my apartment at six o'clock sharp. As I entered, I complimented Rose Marie on her hair and the stunning evening gown she was wearing. She looked like a movie star. Rose Marie was more excited than I was; I had gone to several Broadway plays and it was normal to dress formal.

Our limo pulled up several car lengths north of the Demille Theatre. There was a large NYPD presence for traffic and crowd control. There was a red carpet leading from the curb to the theatre entrance, with velvet red ropes on either side of the entry way. The space directly in front of the entrance was kept clear for arriving stars and VIPs.

I believed us to be among the first to arrive. I guided Rose Marie as we walked to the entrance. A large crowd was gathered on either side of the velvet ropes. We threaded our way through to the ticket box and I presented our tickets. The young lady gave me our stubs and we walked over to the entrance and stood inside of the theatre. Rose Marie was anxious to observe the stars and VIPs as they arrived.

John Gielgud, accompanied by a beautiful young lady, was the first we saw arrive. The crowd erupted in applause as they exited their limousine. They nodded and smiled to all on either side as they walked slowly into the theatre.

David's limo arrived within moments. As he exited the car, the crowd went wild ... many young women shouting his name, many reaching over the ropes to grab at him, just to touch him. I was amazed; this was the first time I had seen anything like this!

It was a privilege and an honor to witness how gracious Dave was as he flashed a sincere smile and spoke a few words in acknowledgment of his fans. I was very impressed with how he handled this adulation of his fans; David had built up a very large fan base as a result of his role on *The Fugitive*.

As David entered the theatre, I stepped over and we shook hands. Rose Marie blushed as he took her hand and placed a gentle kiss on it. We shook hands and he asked if I knew where our seats were. I did ... the center of the fourth row. He was seated right in front of us.

We walked over to the cash bar and I ordered, and paid for, our drinks. Rose Marie opted for a glass of champagne. We watched as many of the stars arrived, then entered the theatre - including Mr. Anthony Quinn.

Rose Marie and I were surprised to see such a gathering of film and television stars who were attending the premier. I must admit it was exciting to be a spectator, but to feel as though we were *insiders*, it was genuinely fun. The lights dimmed and the screen came to life with the title page and opening credits; the din in the theatre hushed.

The Shoes of the Fisherman is an excellent film, exciting and gives the feeling as if it was a real story. It's based on the novel by Morris West. I had not read the novel but, seeing the film, I made it a priority on my reading list. It was over two hours long, with no intermission.

The film was nominated for Oscars in two categories: Best Art Direction (Set Decoration) by George Davis and Edward Cafagno and Best Music (Original Score for a Motion Picture) by Mr. Alex North.

As the credits ended on the screen, the theatre lights came to life and I noted the paying customers began an orderly exit. Rose Marie and I exited to the theatre lobby and waited for Dave. He arrived shortly afterwards and we agreed to meet up at the after party.

As we exited, the crowd - many of whom had paid to see the film's premier - were applauding and yelling at all the celebrities as they exited the theatre, the celebrities smiling and waving at the crowd as they rushed into their waiting limousines.

Our limo had parked across the street from the theatre and our driver waved at us when he caught my eye. We crossed the street and people in the crowd were waving at us, too.

"That's funny ... maybe they think you are one of the stars," I said to Rose Marie.

"Should I wave back?" she asked, giggling.

"Of course ... after all, YOU are a star to me," I said.

Rose Marie laughed as our driver opened the rear door for us.

I told him we were going to The Plaza Hotel but I intended we would be there for only about a half an hour. I was determined to keep the cost of the limo and tip for the driver less than $175. I actually liked the new Lincoln limousine. I still had my 1966 Thunderbird, but I told myself my next car would be a Lincoln Continental.

We arrived at The Plaza within minutes. I escorted Rose Marie into the hotel and to the second floor ballroom. A full orchestra was playing music from *The Shoes of the Fisherman* as we entered. I scanned the crowd, looking for Dave.

There were four open bars and two large buffet tables stacked with a wide assortment of finger foods. I spotted Dave as he was talking with Mr. Quinn and two ladies I did not recognize. I took Rose Marie by her hand and walked directly to him. He spotted us as we approached and extended his arm.

"Tony, this is my good friend, Mike Phelps, and his lady, Rose Marie Aiello," he said.

"It is a great pleasure to meet you, Mr. Quinn," I said as we shook hands. He smiled and gently shook Rose Marie's hand.

"It is my pleasure and you look stunning, Ms. Aiello. Did you enjoy the film?" he asked.

"Yes, sir! It was magnificent. I must say YOU actually looked like a real Pope," I said.

"Yes, it was very exciting; I will see it again," Rose Marie added.

Dave took my bicep and led us over to a bar to make certain we had a drink, as well as getting another for himself.

"There's a ton of food here so don't let it go to waste," he said with a smile.

"Thanks, Dave! We will take advantage," I said, to which Rose Marie smiled.

"Mike, we'll meet at The Carlyle in an hour or so; is that okay with you?" Dave asked.

"Sure! I'm going to take Rose Marie home; she has to be up early in the morning."

"Okay, I have to excuse myself; it has been very nice meeting you, Rose Marie." He smiled as he shook her hand.

"I have enjoyed it, Mr. Janssen ... Mike has spoken so highly of you, and now I know why," she said, smiling.

"He lies ... don't believe what he says, unless it is good – and, please, call me Dave; all of my friends call me Dave."

Dave left us and I watched as he walked over and began talking to a small group of people.

Rose Marie and I had another round of drinks and meandered over to one of the buffet tables and filled our plates with jumbo shrimp and cocktail sauce.

We stood together eating our shrimp and enjoying our drinks as we watched the large gathering of celebrities and Hollywood executives drinking, talking and laughing. To me, it was a sign that each of them was quite pleased with the premier of the film. I was certain the film critics who were in the crowd would be sure to give excellent reviews in the morning papers.

It was just after midnight and Rose Marie wanted to go home. I did not spot Dave so we left the party without a formal goodbye, but I knew I would be meeting him a little later at The Carlyle.

I directed the driver to take us to Rose Marie's home and then return me to The Carlyle.

I kissed Rose Marie good night and thanked her for honoring me with her presence for the evening. The driver pulled up in front of The Carlyle around 12:45. I knew the bar would be closing at two o'clock so I felt the night would be over after having a couple of more drinks with Dave. I paid the driver and gave him a nice tip. I would take a cab from The Carlyle to my apartment.

To my surprise, Dave was already seated in Bemelmans when I entered. As I approached his table, he motioned for the waiter and ordered me a drink before I even sat down.

"So, Mike, what do you think of the film? Did you and Rose Marie really enjoy it?"

"Of course we did! I think it was great ... very enlightening for those not of the Catholic faith, and for Catholics who do not really know the inner workings of the hierarchy or how the church conducts business," I answered.

"Good! I'm glad you liked it. I've got an early flight back to Los Angeles so let's relax and enjoy our drinks."

We had enjoyed two drinks by the time the bar prepared to close. Dave went to his suite and I went home.

35

I received a Christmas card from Dave on Saturday, December 21. It was not one that his secretary sent to business associates or fans; it was from Dave, personally, and he signed it from he, Rosemary and Alexandra. I thought that was a nice touch and it made me think he and Rosemary were truly in love.

Just after five o'clock on the morning of December 29, I received a call from Dave.

"Good morning, Mike! It's Dave. How is everything?"

"Good, Dave ... how is everything with you?"

"Couldn't be better. We've started filming the movie *Marooned* and I'm having a blast. I just wanted to give you a call and wish you a Happy New Year. What are your plans for New Year's Eve?"

"Joining some friends for dinner, then for the countdown in Times Square; this should be a lot of fun."

"That's good ... good to know you'll be celebrating with friends. Rosemary and I are going out to a couple of parties so I'm sure we will have a fun evening as well."

"How far along are you in the filming? How is Gregory Peck to work with ... and Gene Hackman?" I asked.

"We just started ... will have a little break over New Year's Eve, then start up again. We'll be going down to Florida - Cape Canaveral, or Kennedy they call it now. We'll be doing some actual scenes there. NASA has given us the green light and they are cooperating; it should be fun."

"That's great ... wish I could be there. I'd love to see that ... the Space Center. They don't have you playing an alcoholic, do they?"

"No ... no, I'm an Astronaut; they even make me a hero," he said with a laugh.

"Well, that's good to hear. I'll look forward to seeing it. Speaking of movies, when is *Where It's At* going to be released?"

"I think sometime in April or May. I'll let you know for sure when I know."

"So how are things going with you and Ellie?" I asked.

"I'm just playing it cool ... letting Crowley handle it all and, of course, Fred is handling the money end of it - and Frank is handling the publicity part.

"Ellie's lawyer filed a motion asking the court to give her an unconscionable amount of money for monthly maintenance; they said I've been extremely cruel to her ... and that is plain bullshit!"

"Damn! I guess the holidays don't stop the lawyers in LA; here in New York the whole city seems to stop working; it's like nothing but party time here," I responded.

"Yeah, I know ... but this divorce thing has to happen here and I can't do a damn thing about it."

"So is everything going well with you and Rosemary? I got your Christmas card, thank you ... and noted you added Rosemary's name and her daughter's ... sort of like you've eased into a family life."

"You're welcome for the card; I signed all of them that way ... the ones I sent out to my friends, which were not many. My secretary sent out boxes full to people I do business with and, of course, my fans," he said.

"I appreciated it, Dave! Sorry I didn't send you one but I'm not big on sending cards for anything."

"I know what you mean; it's really a pain in the butt."

"So do you know when you're going to Florida for the filming? Will Rosemary go with you?"

"Yeah, sometime in the next few weeks and, yes, Rosemary and Alex are going with me. It will be a fun, working trip."

"That's nice. Has Mr. Greshler lined anything else up for you after this movie?"

"Not yet, but he will. You know I'm suing DeLaurentis over the film I was supposed to do in Italy, but he cancelled it and I lost out on a couple of other opportunities. Anyway, that lawsuit will be coming to a head soon. I'm sure I'll have something lined up for soon after this one is finished."

"Don't you think you might take a few weeks off, take a vacation? You've been working a lot lately."

"No time for a vacation ... I'm going to need the money. Ellie's lawyers are out to clean me out," he said with a laugh.

"Dave, I'm sure Fred can protect you - at least, to where Ellie won't get all you have. I mean California is a community property state; she can't get more than half of what you made since you got married," I said.

"Yeah, you are right ... problem is everything I have has been earned after we got married," he said, this time in a serious tone.

"Man, I feel sorry for you. I guess I better think about a divorce. I'm making a hell of a lot more money here than on the police department; I'd hate to have to give it to my wife. After all, she left me; I didn't leave her."

"Mike, I don't know how New York divorce laws are but you may want to look into it," he said.

"Yeah, I better. I damn sure don't want to be in a position like you are."

"Yeah ... believe me! You don't want to be in my shoes. Okay ... I have to go but I'll be in touch soon," he said.

"Well, thanks for calling, Dave, and my sincere, best wishes to you, Rosemary and the baby for a great 1969!" I said.

"Thanks, Mike! You take it easy and we'll talk soon."

The call ended and, since it was almost 5:30 in the morning, I decided to make some coffee and watch the news waiting for daybreak to take Baron for his run in the park.

I had still been getting all the newspapers and looking for articles about Dave and especially about his imminent divorce but had found nothing over the past few weeks. I figured after the holidays things would heat up.

I was off work until Thursday, January 2, so I was going to take full advantage of it to enjoy time with Baron, do a thorough cleaning of my apartment and go out and enjoy all Manhattan had to offer in the dead of winter.

I did not hear from Dave again until the end of January of 1969. He called me from the Space Center in Florida where he was wrapping up the *Marooned* film.

"Hey, Mike! Dave ... we're on the same time so don't tell me I woke you up." He laughed.

"No, actually Dave, I've been awake for a couple of hours, already been to the park with Baron. How's it going?"

"Great! We are finishing the film and I decided to take your advice. Actually, I mentioned it to Rosemary and she is all for it; we're going to take a little vacation."

"That's great, Dave! You deserve it! Where are you going?"

"I'm chartering a boat and we're going to Paradise Island, just the two of us."

"That is really great! I'm happy to hear it! I'm sure you will both enjoy it, especially the weather," I said.

"Yes, we will ... only be a couple of weeks, though - but I wanted to let you know. After all, you're the one who planted the bug in me and now I agree with you: I need a vacation."

"You do, Dave, and things will probably be heating up soon with your divorce, so it's good that you will relax, sort of recharge your batteries, and be ready to fight."

"I know ... and with Rosemary I will be able to totally relax and put everything else out of my mind."

"That's good, Dave. I am happy for you ... and Rosemary."

"Well, sorry to be so short, but I have to go on the set now. I'll give you a call when I'm back in Los Angeles."

"All right, Dave! Thanks for calling. I'll be thinking of you in the sun while I'm freezing my butt off here in New York."

Dave laughed. The call ended and I smiled. It was good to know Dave and Rosemary were taking a vacation.

36
~1969~

The only articles in the newspapers were about Ellie's attorneys filing for *separate maintenance* and allegations that Dave was having an adulterous affair with Ms. Forsyth. Ellie's attorneys made a point of informing the Court that Ms. Forsyth was still legally married to her husband, Michael Tolan.

I could only assume that Dave and Rosemary would not see the garbage being printed since they would be in the Bahamas. The thought then occurred to me that either his agent or publicist may be keeping him advised by telephone.

My next call from Dave came on Friday evening, March 7; I was surprised it was early, just after nine o'clock. I had just arrived home from dinner.

"Hey, Mike! It's Dave. How are you?"

"Fine, Dave ... how was your vacation?"

"Just great ... very relaxing and a hell of a lot of fun; we both enjoyed it. Listen! We are coming to New York in a few days so you and Rosemary will have a chance to meet."

"That's great! Are you coming here to relax, see a Broadway show, do some shopping?" I asked.

"No. Actually, I'll be doing a film; it's called *Generation*. I'll be playing an old man ... well, not really an old man, but a sort of young grandfather," he said.

"A grandfather? Dave, you're not old enough to be anybody's grandfather; you've gotta be kidding me."

"No, I'm not. Kim Darby plays my daughter and she's pregnant ... in New York. I'm in Chicago but I go to New York to get to the bottom of the situation and I find she's married this joker, played by Pete Duel ... and it all gets crazy from there."

"Whoa! Dave, I know Kim Darby and Pete Duel; she played in

Run For Your Life and he played with Sally Field in *Gidget*. NO ONE will believe you are her father; that's about the same as you being old enough to be my father," I said with a laugh.

"Oh, no, Mike! You are forgetting about make-up; they can make me look like I'm 50 or they can make Kim and Pete look like they are in their late teens, but I'll be a young grandfather," he said.

"Yeah, I guess you're right about that but you - a young grandfather! What were you, about 13 when your daughter was born? So is this going to be a drama or what?"

"No, it's a comedy ... and I love comedy so it'll give me a chance to show my funny side. I've worked with both Kim and Pete on *The Fugitive* and they're great, talented actors. I'm really looking forward to it."

"That's great ... so is the whole movie being made in New York? How long will you be here?" I asked.

"Yeah, almost all of the filming will be done there in Manhattan. We will probably be there at least eight to ten weeks, so we'll get to see each other more often," he said.

"I'm glad to hear that ... looking forward to it. Is Rosemary bringing her daughter? I can't wait to meet Rosemary. So things are still going well with you two?"

"Oh, yeah! Everything is going great; I couldn't be happier. Yeah, we'll be bringing Alex and her nanny," he said.

"That's good to hear; you sure deserve it. So what is going on with Ellie?"

"I don't really know. She fired her lawyers and is bringing on some new ones, so they have to get brought up to speed. Who the hell knows what they have up their sleeve? I'm just being patient and hoping Crowley can move the process along faster than it has been going."

"Well, Dave, I don't know about your lawyer, but I know most lawyers will drag a case out as long as they can, especially if they are charging hourly. Is your lawyer charging you an hourly rate or a flat rate?" I asked.

"Hourly ... and he isn't cheap ... but I figure, no matter what it ends up costing me, my freedom is worth it."

"Yeah, but you've been with Rosemary several months ... right after you left Ellie; it doesn't look to me like you're going to be free after your divorce ... at least not for long."

"Hey, I can assure you I am not going to jump into tying the knot with anyone ... at least not for a while. IF, and when I do, I will make certain it is the right one for me."

"That's good to hear! I sure don't want to see you get hurt again ... or be with someone who treats you like you're their property ... like Ellie," I said, then asked, "So when will you be in the city?"

"Within the next week or so. I'll be sure to call you. We'll be staying at The Carlyle. We'll get together for dinner. You and Rosemary can meet, and you'll meet Alex, too," he said.

"I'll really be looking forward to it," I replied. "You know, Dave ... I'm surprised to hear from you. I mean, at a normal time of day, even with the time difference between here and LA. You sound pretty good. Have you cut back on drinking?"

"Yeah, actually, I have ... I'm having so much fun with Rosemary and the baby, I don't have the desire to screw it up with alcohol."

"I am really, really glad to hear that. I remember when we first started having drinks together; I could never keep up with you and, yet, I never saw you what I would consider drunk."

"Surely you are jesting. I have mastered the art of drinking and controlling my consumption to where it doesn't show that I am really fucked up," he said with a big laugh.

"Well, when you get here, I don't want to be the one that leads you back into your wicked ways. I don't want Rosemary to get pissed off at me before she even gets to know me."

"Don't even give that a thought. You are my friend; she's going to love you," he said.

"Thanks, Dave! I'm sure I'm going to love her, too."

"Okay. I'll give you a call when we get into the city. Take care."

"Thanks, Dave! I'm looking forward to it and thanks for calling."

The call ended and I was excited to know that he would be in New York for such an extended period of time. I was also really enthused at the chance to meet Rosemary, having heard so much about her.

With Dave and Rosemary coming to New York City, it reminded me that I had not seen anything about the release of the movie they did together in Las Vegas, *Where It's At*, so I made a mental note to ask Dave when he called again.

I recalled him telling me Rosemary and he had several nude scenes and I surmised that is what made him fall for her so fast, right after leaving Ellie on their tenth wedding anniversary.

Dave did not know their exact itinerary so I would just have to wait for his call when they arrived in New York. I would make certain that my schedule would be flexible so I could enjoy as much time with them as they would allow.

I planned a relaxing weekend and wanted to stay around my apartment so I would not miss his call. Even so, I knew if he called and I wasn't home he would leave a message on the answering machine. Besides, I did not want to feel as though I would be a prisoner in my apartment for the entire weekend. I remembered then that he had said they would be here in a few days, so I doubted it would be over the weekend.

Dave called me on Sunday afternoon, March 16, just after four o'clock.

"Mike, Dave ... we're at The Carlyle. Can you join us in the lounge ... say, around six?"

"Welcome to New York! Yes, I'd be happy to. Did you have a good flight?"

"Oh, yes! TWA is a great airline; we all enjoyed it. So we'll see you at six?"

"I'll be there ... looking forward to it."

37

I arrived at The Carlyle at 5:45 and left my car with the valet. I had never seen a photo of Rosemary so I was not certain what to expect but I knew, if Dave had fallen in love with her, she must be very special.

As I entered Bemelmans, I told the Maître D" I was to meet Mr. Janssen. He immediately led me to the back of the room and there was Dave and Rosemary seated at a table for four. I did not see the baby or nanny.

Dave stood as I approached and we shook hands. "Mike, this is Rosemary Forsyth and, Rosemary, this is my friend, Mike Phelps," Dave said with a broad smile.

Ms. Forsyth extended her hand and I shook it gently. "It is a real pleasure to meet you, Ms. Forsyth," I greeted.

"Please, call me Rosemary. Dave has spoken of you often; it is my pleasure to meet you," she said.

I was in awe of her beauty. She was a tall young lady, at least five feet, eight inches. She had a beautiful figure and a warm, friendly and sincere smile. Her hair appeared to be natural blonde.

I could easily see why Dave was so attracted to her. I could tell her personality was genuine; she was not one to put on airs. She had a warm and inviting personality and I was very impressed with her.

Dave ordered a drink for me and another round for him and Rosemary.

"It is good seeing you again, Mike. How has the city been treating you?"

"It has been good to me. I enjoy living here - unlike you when you were a struggling young actor here."

"That was ages ago ... I enjoy it much more when I visit now. Now I can afford it," he said with a smile.

"Do you enjoy the city, Rosemary?" I asked.

"Oh, yes! Very much ... the diversity, the excitement ... it truly is the city that never sleeps. I have been here many, many times. I love it!" Her response reminded me of my own feelings about the city.

"We are going to have an early dinner. Can you join us?" Dave asked.

I appreciated Dave's invitation but it was their first night in the city and I felt they should enjoy it alone. "No, not tonight, Dave, but thank you. Where is Alexandra? I thought I would be meeting her," I said.

"Alexandra is upstairs with her nanny. You will meet her; she is my doll," Dave said with a broad smile. Rosemary smiled as she gave a loving look at Dave.

"So when do you start filming here?" I asked Dave.

"In a couple of days. We wanted to get here a little early, do some shopping and relax," Dave said.

"It takes a while to get adjusted here; it is so different from California," Rosemary said.

"I certainly agree with you there. The only thing I enjoyed in California was the weather. The smog was too much for me ... and it's so spread out; you meet someone, become friends and you have to fight traffic and drive for hours just to meet for dinner," I said.

"Yes, that's true, but Los Angeles has so much to offer and, after all, it is the film and television capital of the world," Rosemary said.

"I don't think you gave Los Angeles enough time, Mike. You have to get into the feel of it; it grows on you," Dave said.

"The traffic, the smog ... I could never get used to that, Dave - and you know I have no interest in your industry."

"I know ... but, hey! Look at the traffic here in New York. Look around at the filthy streets. How do you acclimate yourself to that?" Dave asked.

The waiter brought another round of drinks.

"Yeah, I know, Dave, but there is so much excitement here, so much culture ... and, like Rosemary said, such diversity here. I found that anything you could want, 24 hours a day, is within a few steps of your apartment," I said.

"Yeah, you're right there, but you will have to agree that each city has pros and cons. Los Angeles has the weather and so much more. New York has the change of seasons but I would say LA has more pros than New York," Dave replied with authority.

"Well, I have to tell you, Dave - I like New York much better. I grew up with snow and cold in Indiana so I am used to it."

"Okay ... to each his own." Dave smiled, which brought a smile to Rosemary's face as well.

"So tell me ... how was your vacation in the Bahamas?" I asked.

"It was heaven ... so beautiful, so relaxing. It was as if we had not a care in the world. I loved it!" Rosemary answered.

"Yes, Mike, it was truly paradise. We needed it and we will be doing it again ... soon," Dave added.

"So, this new movie ... do you think he can pull it off, Rosemary? Does he look old enough to be a grandfather?" I asked with a smile.

"Well, they may give him a little bit of grey around his temples," she said, then added, "No, he doesn't look old enough to be a grandfather, but you know Dave; he'll pull it off ... and it is a comedy, and he so enjoys comedy, this will be a good vehicle for him," Rosemary replied.

I noted Dave had a mischievous smile and I could tell he liked her response.

"Dave, I still haven't seen anything about the release of your film, *Where It's At.* When is it coming out; do you know?"

"Oh, yeah! It should be coming out the end of next month or the first of May. Make sure you see it and let us know what you think," he said.

"Oh, you can count on it. I have been watching for it but haven't seen anything in the papers," I replied.

I glanced at my watch; it was approaching seven o'clock. I had two drinks and decided it would be a good time to leave them alone for what was sure to be a romantic night in the city.

"Well, Dave, I had better get going. I hope you both enjoy your dinner and evening," I said.

"All right, Mike. We'll get together again soon and next time you have to join us for dinner," Dave said.

"Thank you! I will be looking forward to it. Rosemary, it has been a genuine pleasure; now I know why Dave is so happy," I said as I shook her hand.

She smiled. "It was nice meeting you too, Michael."

I retrieved my car from the valet and drove down to Greenwich Village to have dinner. I would get a prime rib for Baron, mixing it with his dry food; there would be enough for at least three nights.

Dining alone at One Potato, I reflected upon Dave and Rosemary, how happy they both looked. Dave looked better than I had ever seen him, on or off screen. He was so relaxed and seemed content. I was happy for him. I knew it would only be a matter of months before he would be caught up in what was sure to be nasty, and very public, divorce proceedings in California.

I felt certain his divorce and his relationship with Rosemary would not turn any of his fans away from continuing to adore and appreciate him as an actor.

The thought occurred to me that he was working as much as he could to build up his financial resources in preparation of the permanent split from Ellie. With Dave's lifestyle, and I was certain his spending on Rosemary, he would need a substantial amount of money to continue his lifestyle after his divorce.

I was comfortable in my mind that Dave would come through the divorce fine - a little bruised perhaps, especially his bank account – but, to me, with Rosemary by his side, he would be stronger and happier than he had been since I met him.

The last three years of his marriage to Ellie had put a lot of stress on him and, although I did not believe it showed in his roles on screen, I was certain it was the driving force behind his excessive drinking. I was looking forward to seeing Dave again and for the chance to get to know Rosemary a little more and to meet her daughter, Alexandra.

38

The following week passed without my hearing from Dave. In my mind, I was hoping I had not made a bad impression on Rosemary. Then, out of the blue, he called me at my office just before 4:30 Friday afternoon, March 28.

"Mike, Dave ... do you have time for drinks?"

"Of course! It would be a pleasure; where shall I meet you?"

"How about some place near your office?"

"That would be fine. Why don't you come here and we can just go downstairs to the Oyster Bar?"

"Good. I'll see you in about 20 minutes; is that okay?"

"Perfect. In case you forgot, I'm in suite 303 East, in the Pan Am Building."

"I know ... I'll be there," he said, then ended the call.

He arrived at 4:55. Since it was Friday, Norman and everyone else had left the office. I ushered him into my office.

"So this is where you slave away all day, huh?" He was smiling.

"Yeah, this is where I spend 90 percent of my life," I said, returning his smile.

"I could never do this, Mike ... being tied down to a desk all day ... every day; I'd go crazy."

"It's not all that bad; you would get used to it. Still, I'd rather be a cop on the street ... much more interesting. I certainly could not do your job ... I mean, acting; I'll never know how you do it."

"Now, let's go have a drink ... or two. I'm ready for that!" Dave said with emphasis.

I locked the offices and we took the elevator down to the mezzanine and entered The Oyster Bar. I could not help notice all eyes turned to Dave as we headed for a vacant table. Dave smiled at several ladies, but said nothing. We found a small table near the bar and a waiter appeared and took our order.

"So, how are Rosemary and Alexandra?" I asked.

"Great ... they are enjoying the city."

"How is the filming going? Are you happy with it so far?"

"It's moving along very nicely. I love the script and everyone is attuned to their lines and expressions. We do a quick run-through and then do the scene for a take so it makes the director happy and saves a lot of time getting the takes he wants."

"Yeah, but are you happy with it? Do you ever want to do it over, after the director says it's okay?"

"If the director says it's a take ... then I don't question it. I'm ready to move on to the next scene."

"So how much longer will you be filming in New York?"

"Maybe two, maybe two and a half weeks, then we'll move back to the studio in LA."

"Well, hopefully, I'll get to meet Rosemary's little girl before you leave."

"Yes. Can you join us for dinner next Saturday?"

"Yes, I can ... that would be great."

"You can bring Rose Marie; I'm sure Rosemary will enjoy meeting her."

"Thank you! I'm sure she will enjoy it, too; she has become a great fan of yours," I said. "I plan on taking her to see *Where It's At* when it opens."

"Okay. I'll give you a call and let you know the place and time," he said.

The waiter brought us another round of drinks and a fresh bowl of bar mix nuts.

"Well, I wasn't going to ask, but I've seen nothing in the papers recently so I *must* ask ... how are things going with your divorce?"

"To tell you the truth, Mike, Ellie's being a downright bitch and I'm starting to think it is not just her lawyers. I've been hearing from our mutual friends that she's making a lot of lurid comments ... allegations about me that just aren't true; I've instructed my lawyers to put a stop to it. It has me so damned disgusted ... and to think I once loved the bitch!"

The expression on Dave's face had changed in an instant and I deeply regretted even mentioning the matter. "Whatever she's saying to those who know you, they will know not to believe it. Chalk it up to a woman scorned," I said.

"Yeah, I know that; it just infuriates me that she would even think she could say the crap she's saying and get away with it. I think she is just looking for sympathy."

"The best way for you to handle it is to ignore it. Let your lawyers fight it out with hers. Let your publicist make certain the media highlights your work. YOU should concentrate on your life ... your relationship with Rosemary and Alex ... and put Ellie and the divorce out of your mind."

"That's a hell of a lot easier said than done, Mike! When I'm home in LA, not a day goes by that I don't have talks with my lawyers ... relaying Ellie's demands through her lawyers; it's a living hell. I have to sell my property in Palm Springs; I won't find another like it at anywhere near the price I paid."

"I cannot imagine what you are going through; just keep a cool head and let your lawyers handle it. If it does go to trial, let your lawyers do the fighting for you; that's what you're paying them for."

"Yeah, don't I know it! I thought it would be so simple: 'Ellie, I want a divorce; let's be civilized.' Well, that didn't work ... she is out to cut my balls off!"

"I'm sorry I even mentioned it, Dave ... I didn't mean to upset you."

"No, Mike, you didn't upset me. I live with this every day and you are one of only three friends I dare talk to about it. Of course, Crowley knows all the dirt and he deals with that for me."

"Yeah, and here I am offering you advice on how to handle it. Who am I to even think I can offer advice to you? I won't mention it again but, if you want to blow off some steam about it, I'm here for you ... I hope you know that."

"I know, Mike ... and, believe me, I appreciate knowing I can let out my frustrations with you, and feel secure in your confidence."

Dave motioned the waiter for another round of drinks. I noticed he glanced at his watch. "After this round, Mike, I'll have to go. We're having dinner at the 21 Club with some people from the studio," he said.

"That's nice, and I have to stop for a quick bite at the Friar Tuck and take Baron his dinner, too."

We finished our fourth round of drinks and I could tell Dave had recovered his composure from our brief discussion about Ellie and their divorce. I offered to drive him to his hotel but he insisted on taking a cab; I knew Dave had been provided a car service but he seldom used it.

I retrieved my car from the garage and headed for the Friar Tuck Inn where I grabbed a quick meal. I was late getting home for Baron's run in the park and his dinner.

Dave called me the next day early to advise he would be working half the day and he and Rosemary had a dinner to attend that evening but he had set eight o'clock the following Saturday evening, April 5, for Rose Marie and I to join Rosemary and him for dinner at Joe Allen's Restaurant on West Forty-Sixth Street.

I told him I would make certain we would be there and even offered to pick him and Rosemary up at The Carlyle, but he told me it wouldn't be necessary.

I decided I would tell Rose Marie about the invitation when we were together for dinner. She was quite excited and looked forward not only to dinner with Dave, but meeting Rosemary as well.

The week passed and I picked Rose Marie up at her parents' home in Queens and made the 25 minute drive to the restaurant. She looked lovely in a royal blue gown - just as stunning as any movie star, in my opinion.

We arrived at Joe Allen's at 7:45; Dave and Rosemary had not. I told the Maître D' we were there to meet Mr. Janssen. He ushered us to a nice table in the back of the room.

Dave and Rosemary entered the restaurant at eight o'clock sharp and were escorted to his table. We both stood and Dave smiled as we shook hands and took our seats.

Dave ordered a round of drinks and Rose Marie chose iced tea; I think that surprised both Rosemary and Dave, as it did me. Rosemary's baby was not with them.

39

"Good evening, Rose Marie. Mike ... uh, Rosemary, this is Rose Marie Aiello, Mike's lady friend," Dave said, introducing Rose Marie. The ladies shook hands and exchanged smiles.

I had told Rose Marie that Rosemary was also an actress and she had co-starred with Dave in the film *Where It's At*. I think Rose Marie was impressed at meeting a super star like Dave and, now, a strikingly beautiful starlet.

We placed our drink order and made small talk about the vast differences between the city and Los Angeles and how Rosemary and her daughter were enjoying their visit. Rose Marie, a native New Yorker, was very animated about her city and she and Rosemary seemed to really hit it off.

After placing our dinner order, the discussion turned to *Where It's At* and how Dave and Rosemary met on the set and found instant attraction.

"I'm sure the storyline had a lot to do with you falling in love with each other," I said.

"Not really ... I've loved David for a long time, albeit from afar. When I was cast for the role, I was as excited as a little girl meeting Santa Claus for the first time," Rosemary responded.

"Yeah, and I took one look at her ... in the flesh ... and I knew we were meant to be," Dave said with a wide grin.

"You are a lovely couple. I'm sure you will have many years of happiness together," Rose Marie predicted.

Rosemary and Dave looked into each others eyes and smiled then, almost in unison, said, "Thank you," to Rose Marie.

I knew the age difference between Dave and Rosemary was the reverse of his and Ellie's, and I felt that was a much needed ego boost for him, one he needed. Still, at age 38, Dave still looked to be in his late twenties. Rosemary looked to be in her very early twenties.

We enjoyed a delicious meal and conversing over a range of subjects. After coffee, we all enjoyed a nightcap and the evening ended just before midnight. I offered to drive Rosemary and Dave to The Carlyle as it was on my way to the Fifty-Ninth Street Bridge to Queens, but Dave had the car service. We all bid goodnight on the sidewalk in front of Joe Allen's Restaurant.

Rose Marie and I walked the half-block to the Eighth Avenue parking lot. She was so happy over meeting such glamorous people as Dave and Rosemary; she talked non-stop all the way to her parents' home.

I called Dave at The Carlyle just after nine on Sunday morning to thank him for the wonderful dinner the night before - but he and Rosemary were not in his suite so I left a message.

I took Baron for his run in Riverside Park and returned to my apartment, brewed another pot of coffee and read *The New York Times*. I always looked forward to Sundays as a do nothing day - just clean my apartment, relax and spend quality time with Baron.

I was about to go out for dinner when Dave called.

"Hi, Mike ... got your message. You are quite welcome for last evening. We enjoyed it and Rosemary likes Rose Marie. We'll have to do it again sometime."

"Thanks, again, Dave! I wish you would have let me pay, at least for Rose Marie and me."

"Nonsense! I invited you and that's that! Besides, I make more money than you ... at least, that's what you tell me," he said with a laugh.

"Yeah ... well, thanks again but, next time, you and Rosemary will be my guests. I'm sure I can save up a few dollars for a nice dinner," I said in a joking manner.

"We will be wrapping up here in the next two weeks or so - that is if we stay on schedule, so we'll see."

"Oh! Does that mean you'll be going back to LA?" I asked.

"Yeah ... and I am anxious to get back. Crowley tells me things are heating up with Ellie and my presence may be required there in court."

"Damn! I hope we can get together again before you leave - at least, for a couple of drinks. MY treat!"

"I'll do my best to squeeze it in somewhere ... I'll let you know."

"Well, promise me you'll at least call before you leave the city, even if we can't get together for drinks or something," I said.

"Yeah, of course I will ... so take care and I'll be in touch." With that, the call ended.

I would next hear from Dave on Saturday, April 12. He called just after three o'clock in the afternoon and invited me for drinks.

"Sounds good, Dave. How about the Playboy Club? It's on Fifty-Ninth just off of Fifth Avenue and it's close to your hotel," I suggested.

"Yeah, I know where it's at ... fine, I can be there in about 15 minutes," he said.

"Great ... then I'll see you there in the lobby."

I took a cab rather than fight with traffic and try to find a parking space and was there in 10 minutes. Dave's car pulled to the curb as I was paying my cab driver. We entered the club and I showed my card; we went to the second floor main bar.

I had to smile inside my head as all of the *bunnies* swooned quite openly over Dave. A couple asked for his autograph; as always, he smiled and readily signed his name, asking each her name to make his greeting personal.

I had noticed when Dave and I first began having our drinking sessions how he reacted when approached by fans - mostly women, of all ages; he was so humble and genuine.

On countless occasions after signing autographs, we sat down for our drinks; he never complained or made any disparaging remarks about his fans who approached him. He always asked them something personal: their name, where they were from, things like that. He made each one feel special.

He was keenly aware his fans were the key to his success. There were a couple of times when I reminded him it was HIS work – his determination to give his best in each performance, in each scene, that made him such a star. He agreed and had told me that fans will remain only as long as the actor delivers what they want ... what they expect.

"I didn't know you belonged to the Playboy Club; is this where you look for your girls?" Dave asked with a grin, bringing my thoughts back to the present. We ordered our drinks.

I laughed. "Not really ... Hefner has a rule: you can't play with HIS *bunnies* ... but, they have great food, excellent service. I mean, just look at all this eye candy - and they have a great room upstairs for big-name entertainment, comedy. I saw Rodney Dangerfield here a few weeks ago; he was hilarious. Haven't you been here before?"

"No, actually, I haven't. I've been to the main club in Chicago and, of course, the mansion in Los Angeles," he answered.

"I guess you know Mr. Heffner then. I've never been to the LA mansion, but I have been to the one in Chicago; it is great ... better than this one," I said.

"I've met Mr. Hefner but I don't know him. I've just attended a couple of parties there ... no big deal."

"I don't come here that often, but it is a good place to bring male clients to, for lunches and sometimes just drinks at cocktail hour," I added.

"Yeah, I can see that ... I bet a lot of business is done here. It has great ambiance," Dave said.

"So do you know when you're going back to Los Angeles?" I asked.

"Yeah, we will be wrapping up here by the middle of the week and we'll be heading back home - at least, Rosemary, Alexandra, her nanny and I. Some of the people will be here for a couple more weeks and, when they get back to LA, we'll finish filming there."

"Well ... I hate to see you go. It's been fun, just seeing you and having drinks together like old times and, of course, meeting Rosemary. She is beautiful and anyone can see she is madly in love with you. Damn, Dave! I didn't get to meet Alexandra!"

"Oh ... sorry about that! Here, I have a photo of her," he said, pulling out his wallet and showing me a cute photo of Rosemary's adorable little girl.

We had three rounds of drinks and Dave checked his watch and let me know he had to leave.

I motioned for the check, signed it and, as I learned from Dave, I left a cash tip for our bunny.

"Well, Dave, it's been great seeing you and thanks again for the dinners and all the drinks. Tell Rosemary I am deeply honored to have met her and I wish you both all the happiness in the world," I said as we shook hands on the street.

"It's been good seeing you again, Mike ... and we'll get together again, either here or in Los Angeles - if you find your way out there again. You take care and I'll be in touch," he said.

Dave's car pulled up and he left. I took a cab and headed home.

40

I did not hear from Dave again until Wednesday, April 30, just a few minutes after four o'clock in the morning.

"Hi, Mike! It's Dave ... are you awake yet?" he asked with a chuckle. I could tell he had been drinking.

"Yeah, I'm awake ... just having my first cup of coffee; how about you? You should be just about going to bed about now," I replied.

"Yeah ... just about. I've been pretty busy and just thought, hell, I haven't called my friend Mike in a while, so I put a dime in the phone and called. How is everything going with you? How's Rose Marie?"

"All is well; I've been keeping busy. Rose Marie is fine; at least, she's not pushing me to get my divorce and marry her," I said. "How are things with Rosemary?"

"Going well ... she is a fabulous cook and she likes for us to have dinner at home, which is really nice. I like it."

"Have you finished the filming on your movie?"

"Not completely; a couple of more weeks and we should wrap it up. It's going to be a good film; I like it ... good people to work with all around."

"I see *Where It's At* is, finally, coming out next week. I can't wait to take Rose Marie to see it."

"Oh, yeah ... it's opening here, too. Rosemary and I have to attend the premier and that will be a hell of a lot of fun; we're looking forward to it. Let me know what you and Rose Marie think of it, will you?"

"Of course I will ... you already know we're going to love it!" I exclaimed. "How could we not?"

"Yeah ... I know you really want to see Rosemary in the flesh."

"Hell, yes, I do! I'll probably reach over and cover Rose Marie's eyes, especially when they show your naked butt." I laughed. "How are things going in divorce court?"

"Getting hotter than Hades! I can't believe she is being such a fucking bitch! Although I should have known she would put up a fight, I sure as hell didn't think she would be so damn nasty ... accusing me of things she knows damn well I never did. She's fabricating a bunch of pure crap. I am getting fed up with it!"

"What's your lawyers say? Can't they stop her? Maybe they could get the judge to issue a gag order."

"What do you mean?"

"Ask your lawyers to file a motion for a gag order; what that means is Ellie, her lawyers, your lawyers, even YOU cannot discuss the case outside of the court room. That would protect you and, if Ellie violates it, even saying something about you to her (or your) friends, she would be in contempt of court," I proffered.

"Why in the hell didn't my lawyers think of that? God knows I'm paying them enough; I'll call them in the morning."

"Well, just ask them. I don't know how California laws work or even if a gag order is applicable in a divorce action," I added.

"I sure as hell hope it is! Liberman is having a hell of a battle trying to keep all of the crap out of the media. It is starting to really piss me off!"

"Have your lawyers said anything about a trial date ... pre-trial depositions or motions?" I asked.

"Yeah, she wants more money ... to maintain her lifestyle. Damn it! I'm the one who busted my ass to give her the fucking lifestyle; she never had the kind of lifestyle I gave her even with her first husband in New York."

"Yeah ... not even her brief dating time with Sinatra. You have to admit, Dave, that you spoiled her ... and I got that from the fan magazines. I think Ellie even said it," I joked.

"Yeah, but she isn't going to have it anymore - at least, not with me ... and whatever she takes from me in the divorce won't last her long, unless she latches onto someone else with money," Dave said.

"Well, I hope your lawyers can do something to stop her from spreading all the bullshit about you. I hope they can get a gag order."

"So do I ... that would be great; if they do, I hope Ellie violates it! I'd love to see what the judge would do to her," Dave said with a slight laugh.

"Well, if your lawyers get a gag order and Ellie violates it, the judge could put her in jail - which I doubt he would - or levy a fine against her, or both ... but no matter what he would do, the publicity of her violating such an order would be great publicity for you."

"Yeah, I think Liberman could have a field day with that kind of material," Dave said.

"Yes, Dave, but I still think I am right. I don't think the divorce is going to have any adverse effects on you ... at least with your fans," I added.

"I'm happy to agree with you, Mike, at least so far. People who like me - my work, at least - they don't seem to care about my little marital problems."

"Dave, you are the one they care about, admire and appreciate. Ellie is not an actress, a star. The only thing your fans know about Ellie is what they've read in all the articles Liberman has arranged," I said.

"Yeah, I know. You're right ... and I'm glad you are."

"If anything, your fans are going to have sympathy for you. They're going to see Ellie as the bitch she is acting like. Your fans aren't going to like seeing you in pain ... and, no matter who you are, a divorce is painful."

"You don't have to tell me that, Mike ... I'm feeling it," Dave said.

"Well, at least, you have Rosemary to ease the pain and, at least, take your mind off it, even if it is only for a moment."

"Yeah, and I am very fortunate there. Okay, Mike, I'd better turn in so thanks for your advice and for listening. I'll give you a call later," he said.

"Okay, but keep in touch ... otherwise I'll start to worry about you."

"Don't worry about me ... I'll make it. We'll talk later," Dave said and the phone clicked.

That was a very interesting call. It was the most in-depth conversation to that time we had regarding Ellie and their divorce. I could tell in his voice he was really starting to feel pressure ... the stark reality of what was to come.

It had been eight months since he left Ellie on their tenth wedding anniversary.

He was not hiding his relationship with Rosemary and it had been reported he was spending a lot of money buying her gifts ... expensive gifts. I could not help but think he was wrong in doing this; he was giving Ellie's lawyers plenty of ammunition to really take him to the cleaners, financially.

However, I knew Dave was not the type of man to have a secret affair; he had filed for divorce and he was not the kind of man who would stop living his life just to wait for the legal proceedings to be over. He knew what he was doing.

I was sure Ellie and her lawyers knew about his little vacation with Rosemary in the Bahamas and I'm sure chartering the yacht was not cheap, plus all the people he had working for him on the trip.

I was really looking forward to taking Rose Marie to the opening of *Where It's At*. I planned on taking her to a nice dinner and, then, the movie.

Yes, I admit I was really looking forward to seeing Rosemary *in the flesh*, as Dave had put it. Film and TV stars were not cast doing nude scenes as a general rule, so this was a brave step - I know, for Dave, and I had to believe for Rosemary, as well.

My observations of Dave since we met were that he was actually a shy man; he had to force himself to project the TV-Film Star persona. I think that is the main reason he enjoyed places like The Formosa and other public places that the general public did not know about, or as a rule, would not normally gravitate towards.

I could not figure out how he chose to be an actor and, when he became such a mega star, how he dealt with his fame. It only bolstered my admiration for him as being the down-to-earth ordinary guy he was.

41

Dave called me early Saturday morning, May 17, 1969. He was stone cold sober and excited.

"Hey, Mike! How the hell are you, my friend?"

"Fine, Dave ... and I'm awake! You sound good; is your divorce final?" I asked, not having noticed anything in the media.

"Hell, no ... not yet ... I'm not that lucky. I'm getting a new plane and I can't wait for it. Hell, I can fly to New York as fast as a commercial airliner ... "

"What the hell are you getting?" I interrupted.

"It's a Lear Jet, a 24A, top of the line. Wait 'til you see it!" he exclaimed.

"You mean you'll take me for a ride in it?" I laughed.

"Hell, yes ... first class all the way. It is a real beauty; you'll like it," he said.

"Have you obtained your pilot's license?" I asked.

"Not yet, but that's in the works. I'll get it soon. I have already taken this baby up for a test flight; it is a dream to fly."

"What does Rosemary think about it?" I asked.

"She's excited, too ... she loves flying. We can use it to go almost anywhere in the world," he said.

"How will that figure in your settlement with Ellie? Have you talked it over with your lawyers? I mean, Ellie could demand half of it ... or, at least, the value of it. I hope it doesn't present a problem for you."

"Well, I had not given a thought to that, but you make a good point. I'll run it past Crowley. By the way, Crowley can't get a gag order, can't do it ... so Ellie can keep on running her mouth and being the bitch she is, so I just have to grin and bear it ... but that's okay. I'm letting Frank handle it."

"Well, I'm sorry to hear that. I wasn't sure you could get a gag order in a divorce case, but it was worth asking. Dave, your fans don't give a damn about Ellie; if anything, she will be turning them against her and bolstering their love for you - and I don't think it will stop the studios from hiring you for movies."

"Mike, you are right. I'm still getting tons of fan mail, I've got several projects in the works and I feel free for the first time in years ... and I have a gal who loves me and doesn't try to dominate me, or show the insecurity and jealousy Ellie has for years. I'm HAPPY!" he exclaimed.

"That is the best news I've heard from you since you left Ellie! How are Rosemary and Alexandra?"

"They are great. Alexandra is talking so much now ... she is precious! As for Ellie ... even though I hate the bullshit she is putting me through, I know it will end and I will have a good life. Sure, I will have to work a hell of a lot to get back what I'm losing ... but I love working."

"So when do you get your plane?" I asked.

"Sometime in the next few days. I'm trading in my Piper and they will be checking it out in a day or two. I'll be sure to let you know. We may even fly to New York to sort-of break it in. I'll let you know."

"That's great, Dave! It will be good seeing you again and, of course, seeing your new toy. Promise me you'll give me a flight over the city," I said with a laugh.

"Yeah, that would be fun. Of course, that depends on the FAA; that's a pretty busy air traffic corridor so we'll see. So how are things going for you? How is Rose Marie?"

"All is well. We are going to see *Where It's At* this coming weekend. It's already been out a week but, between Rose Marie's family commitments and my schedule, we couldn't get to see it sooner," I said.

"Well, you be sure to let me know how Rose Marie likes it. I think you both will get some laughs from it," he said.

"I will, the next time you call. Hell, Rose Marie and I may just send you and Rosemary fan letters," I joked.

"Okay, you can do that, but it may take a month before you get a response; I'm way behind answering my fan mail." He laughed.

"I thought you had a secretary for that," I said, laughing.

"Oh, I do, but I take a handful home with me and answer them myself."

"I know that ... I was just kidding," I said, then added, "Although Rose Marie may send you and Rosemary one."

"All right, Mike. I have to go so take it easy and I'll be in touch."

"Okay ... let me know when you get your plane and your schedule for coming to the city," I replied.

"I'll let you know. It may be a couple of months before I can fit it into my schedule but I'm looking for a three day weekend," Dave said and we ended the call.

I was very glad to hear him sounding so happy, genuinely happy and excited about his new plane. I was thinking how good Rosemary was for him. I was certain they would marry shortly after they obtained their divorces.

I also gave thought to their age difference and I was positive it would not be a factor for Dave, but when he would be 60, she would be 48. Would she still be attracted to, and in love with, him? I would hate to see him hurt again and to go through another nasty divorce. I was being too judgmental, I told myself.

May passed into June with no calls from Dave. I was still checking the newspapers and fan magazines to see if there were any stories about Dave, Ellie and Rosemary.

Dave called just after nine o'clock on Tuesday morning, June 17.

"Hi, Mike ... Dave. How the hell are you?" he asked in a happy voice.

"Great, Dave! How about you and Rosemary?" I responded.

"All is well on the home front, my friend. I'm playing golf today. She's out shopping. It's been a while since we talked. I've been pretty busy, just wanted to touch base with you."

"Hell, I've been expecting you and Rosemary to fly into LaGuardia on your new jet and give me a fly-over of my city," I said, joking.

"Well ... I thought about what you said - the plane and the effect it would have on the divorce - and the expense so I decided not to buy it. Actually, I'm selling the Piper."

"I hope to hell I am not the reason you didn't get it; you sounded like you really wanted it. Hell, I'd love to have a Lear Jet; I could fly out to LA and have drinks with you every weekend," I said with a laugh.

"Yeah, but you'd get tired of it ... and the fuel costs are on the rise. No, I thought about your point regarding the divorce and mentioned it to Rosemary, and she agreed with you ... and then Fred agreed with you, so I was overruled," Dave said with a hearty laugh.

"Well, Dave, look at it this way: it does not mean you can't get the plane; it just means you have to wait a little longer. Put it on your Christmas list. Maybe Santa will surprise you."

"Yeah, I'll do that ... but I also want a new car. Just kidding! My Rolls still has a few miles left on her."

"I'll stick with my T-Bird. Maybe I'll ask Santa for a Lear," I said, joking. "How are Alexandra and Rosemary doing? Are you keeping them happy?"

"I hope I am; they seem to be. Alexandra is growing so fast. I'm going to have to fight all the boys to keep them away from her in day care," he laughed.

"So who are you playing golf with?" I asked.

"My friend, Milton Berle, and a couple of guys from the club."

"How is your game ... getting better?"

"Hell, yes ... if I can keep my knee in place. I'll never be an Arnold Palmer but I just do it for the relaxation."

"That's the best reason to play. I just don't think I could have the patience to play. I'm more into football and basketball ... but only as a spectator," I laughed.

"Yeah, me too. I don't think I could play basketball like I did as a kid, but I love the game."

"Well, how are things getting on with Ellie?" I asked with hesitation.

"Her asshole lawyers came to Crowley's office the other day. She is crying ... demanding more money for her monthly allowance.

"Crowley told them to go to hell so they are filing something with the court demanding Ellie get almost $10,000 a month! She is doing her damnedest to ruin me and it is really getting under my skin!"

"Ten grand a month ... wow! In two months, she would be getting about what I make in an entire year ... and she doesn't even work!" I exclaimed.

"Yeah ... I'm the one who works his ass off. She has never worked a day in her miserable life. I told my business manager to cut her off completely ... see what she does then."

"Did you run that by Crowley? Does Ellie have any court order that you have to give her anything on a monthly basis?"

"I only cut her off from the restaurants and clubs that I have a monthly tab with - and the department and jewelry stores. She's still getting a couple of grand a month and that's from my blood, sweat and tears!"

"Does Crowley give you any idea when this whole nightmare is going to end?"

"He has no idea. She's changed lawyers and they have asked for continuance after continuance and the judge gives it to them. I'm praying it will be over soon; I'm getting so fed up with her lies and crazy demands!"

"Well, I wish you luck. Remember: take one day at a time and, when you get really pissed off, take a deep breath and keep your cool."

"Yeah, I know Mike, that's good advice ... and I'm following it. You know I usually take deep breaths between sips of scotch." He laughed.

At least he could still laugh.

"Okay, well stay in touch. I'm still looking forward to your next visit to the city."

"All right, Mike ... talk soon!" Dave ended the call.

I could tell by Dave's voice that the demands Ellie was making, either herself or through her lawyers, was beginning to cause him a tremendous amount of stress. I concluded he was handling it well, so far. Although I felt sad he was not getting the plane he wanted, I was happy to hear both Rosemary and his lawyer agreed with my opinion.

42

Dave called again on Sunday, June 29, just after one o'clock in the morning.

"Mike, did I wake you?"

"No, I was just about to go to bed. How are you?" I replied.

"I'm good ... just wanted to give you a call. My grandmother passed away a few days ago. Ellie has filed another complaint with the court wanting more money. I'm not working right now ... just a bunch of bullshit I'm contending with ... other than that, I'm good."

"I'm really sorry to hear about your grandmother; was she your mom's mother? Did you go to the funeral?" I asked.

"No, it was my father's mother. I did not go to the funeral. I sent a floral arrangement and I didn't really know her," he said.

"Sorry ... but, at least, you sent flowers. What does your lawyer say about Ellie's latest demands?"

"He thinks he'll win ... the judge won't give it to her, so I'll just have to wait and see."

"You're not working? What is your next project? When will it start?" I asked. I knew Dave was restless and worried when he was not working on some film or TV project.

"I don't have anything lined up for the immediate future, but Rosemary is doing a film in Miami, so I'm going down there to spend time with her and Alexandra ... sort of a mini-vacation for me."

"Well, that sounds good. I'm sure you will enjoy it. Miami is a great place to relax," I said. "Put Ellie and the divorce out of your mind; just let your lawyers fight it out for you."

"Yeah, that's what I'm going to do. So how are things with you? Have you decided on a divorce yet? How are things with Rose Marie?"

"No, I haven't filed for a divorce yet - don't know if I should do it here, or in Connecticut where we were married and she's at now. Still thinking about it. though. Everything between Rose Marie and me is going great."

"That's good ... I'm happy for you. In my opinion, you better think about getting your divorce or you may end up losing her."

"Hey, Dave, don't rush me! If I get a divorce, I don't think I'm going to jump out of the frying pan into the fire," I said with a laugh.

"Well ... I think you and Rose Marie make a good couple. I just don't want to see you lose her ... if you know what I mean."

"Coming from you - I really appreciate that, Dave."

"Okay, Mike, I have to go. I'll give you a call later in the week."

"All right, Dave ... be sure you let me know if you go to Miami," I said. The call ended.

I thought to myself it was rude of me that I did not ask what the film was about, who the stars were that Rosemary would be working with in Miami. Oh well! I'd be sure to ask the next time he called.

I didn't have any knowledge of Dave's finances, other than what was reported in the newspapers and fan magazines as the divorce proceedings moved slowly through the court, but I knew he was, at least, a millionaire and Ellie was fighting to get as much of his hard earned money as she could. I felt sorry for him.

Dave called again on Sunday, July 20, just after eight o'clock in the morning.

"Hey, Mike! It's Dave. How are you doing?"

"Fine, Dave. How are you, Rosemary and the baby?"

"All good. We are in Miami; Rosemary is doing a film here."

"Yeah, you mentioned that when we spoke last, but I didn't ask you what it was about or who is in it," I said.

"It's a comedy with Rosemary, Jackie Gleason, Shelley Winters and Maureen O'Hara; it's called *How Do I Love Thee*. You and Rose Marie will love it ... make sure you go see it," he suggested.

"Don't worry! We will. Does Rosemary have any nude scenes in it? I can just see her and Jackie Gleason in bed together," I said with a big laugh.

"No ... no nude scenes ... and certainly not with Jackie Gleason," he said, laughing.

"So how do you like Miami?"

"Oh, it is great! When she isn't working, we are having a fabulous time. We're staying at the Fontainebleau, right on the ocean ... magnificent views."

"That is really nice ... glad to hear you are finally able to take some time out for yourself, Dave."

"Yeah, it is nice ... and I'm really enjoying it."

"So when will you be going back to Los Angeles?" I asked.

"In a few weeks - whenever they finish the location shooting here."

"So how about you ... do you have anything lined up, movies or TV?"

"Yeah, Abby has me lined up for some television guest appearances and there's a possibility I'll be doing a film sometime in the fall. I'll be busy and that is good."

"Glad to hear it, Dave."

"So everything is good with you?" he asked.

"Yeah, it's going great. So tell me, have you met Jackie Gleason?"

"Yeah, I met him."

"Do you like him? Is he a nice guy?"

"Oh, yeah! He's a really nice man ... funny as hell and a really good actor, for a comedian."

"That's good to hear. My mother and I used to watch his show, *The Honeymooners,* and we loved it. Good to know he's a good man."

"Yeah, Mike, everyone in this film are really good people ... nice to be around and very good at their craft. Remember it; you're going to want to take Rose Marie to see it when it comes out."

"Any news from your lawyers?"

"Yeah, Ellie didn't get the 10 grand a month she was seeking – actually, she got cut off at the knees. I only have to pay her three grand a month now so I'm happy about that! I have to run ... just wanted to give you a quick call and see how everything was on your end."

"Okay, thanks for the call. Glad to hear you are having such a good time in Miami ... keep in touch."

"I will. You take care," he said, then hung up the phone.

It was good to hear him so happy and to know he was winning, at least, part of his divorce battle with Ellie.

It was August 10, 1969, when Dave called again. He and Rosemary were back in Los Angeles at their home.

"Mike, it's Dave ... how is everything?"

"Good, Dave ... I see you are back in LA. How are Rosemary and the baby?" I asked.

"Good, everything is good. We will be moving to a larger home soon; I'll let you know the address when it is confirmed. I've taped a couple of guest appearances with Lena Horne and Dean Martin ... so watch for them and let me have your opinion."

Dave knew I was not a regular television viewer but, like a good fan and friend, I watched everything I knew he was appearing in.

"Great ... so you are back in the business ... working."

"Oh yeah ... and more projects in the works. I'm reading a script now, a civil war era film. I'll let you know about it later."

"Okay ... and are you any closer to being a free man?"

"Hell, no! The bitch has fired her lawyers again ... more damned delays and, the more delays, the more it is costing me, and she fucking knows it!"

"Damn it, Dave! This has been going on for a whole year! Most divorces are done and over with ... final ... in six months," I said.

"Yeah ... but not mine. Listen! I have to run. I'll call you back later," he said and the call ended.

I heard a female voice in the background calling out to Dave, but I wasn't sure it was Rosemary.

43

On August 20, I was awakened by the loud, incessant ringing of my phone. I rolled over and noted it was 3:15 in the morning.

"Hello, Dave," I said in a very sleepy voice.

"How did you know it was me, Mike?" Dave asked.

"Because you are the only person in the whole wide world I allow to call me after midnight. No one else would; they know I would reach through the phone and strangle him or her," I joked.

Dave sounded like he had been drinking - not quite drunk, but getting there. "I'm at The Formosa and, since you're on the east coast you can't be here, so I decided to call you," he said.

"Sounds like you're having a good time ... is Rosemary with you?" I asked.

"No, we had a little 'tiff earlier this evening so I decided to leave the house for a while ... give her time to cool down."

"Uh ... uh that doesn't sound good. Was it a serious disagreement or something minor, something you'll both laugh about tomorrow?" I asked.

"No, it wasn't a knock-down-drag-out fight ... just a little clash of opinions. I've discovered Rosemary has a temper and I know when to just leave," he said.

"Well, I'm glad to hear that ... so things are okay with you and Rosemary?"

"Oh, hell, yes ... but everyone has a little argument or two ... keeps things interesting. Making up is always great, if you know what I mean," he said with a laugh.

"Yeah, I know what you mean. So are you any closer to getting your divorce? I haven't seen anything in the papers lately."

"Hell, no ... and in just a few weeks it will be a year since I filed ... and she just won't let me go. It's costing me a fortune; everything I'm earning goes to fucking lawyers and her," he said with hostility in his voice.

"Doesn't your lawyers have any idea when it will be over ... can't they push it along?" I asked.

"Not really ... her lawyers keep filing motions demanding my financial records, who I'm fucking all the way to how many drinks I had in the past week. It is just plain stupid ... waste of time ... way for the god damned lawyers to keep gouging me for money." He was really angry and with good reason, in my opinion.

"Dave ... don't let it get to you. Remember ... take a deep breath."

"Yeah, yeah, I know, Mike, but it isn't easy. She keeps saying bullshit. She's dragging this out for as long as she can because she wants to hurt me and anyone close to me," Dave said.

"I'm sorry I even mentioned it," I said.

"No ... I was going to cry on your shoulder about it, anyway. I'm going to be moving on the first of the month; it's a much larger house, great for entertaining."

"You said *you* ... isn't Rosemary and her daughter moving with you?" I asked.

"Hell, yes! That's why we're getting a larger home ... room for Alexandra and her nanny. It is a beautiful home in Coldwater Canyon," he said.

"I don't think I know where that is; I wasn't in LA long enough to learn my way around."

"It is in Beverly Hills ... a nice area," Dave said with a chuckle.

"Dave, I know Beverly Hills is a nice area. I didn't have any reason to go there ... knowing damn well I could not afford it," I said with a laugh. "So is it a very large home ... a mansion?"

"Yeah, it is a mansion ... not really, but it is nice and will give us plenty of space and it will be great for entertaining friends and business associates."

"That is nice. Send me some photos ... and your address so I'll know where to come if I decide to drive back out there," I said. No doubt, Dave knew I was joking.

"I'll do that ... and don't worry! There are several guest rooms so you won't need a hotel."

"Thanks, Dave, but I doubt I'll be going out to LA anytime soon."

"Well, how are you doing with Rose Marie? How's your work going?"

"All is well with Rose Marie, but I'm not in a rush to get a divorce, and she knows that – and, believe me, I am not about to rush into marriage again. Work is good ... keeping me very busy and I love it."

"How's your Baron?"

"Getting big. He's over 75 pounds now ... but don't worry! He'll remember you the next time he sees you. So ... any plans on coming to New York?"

"I don't know when I'll be in the city again, but I'll be sure to let you know. I'm reading a script now for a movie that will be made in Mexico so, if I take it, I'll be spending some time south of the border."

"Hey, if you do go down to Mexico ... can't you get one of those quickie divorces? I've heard a lot of movie stars do that."

"Mike, if I could've done that, I damned sure would have a year ago, but there is too much involved ... we were married 10 years ... a lot involved financially."

"Yeah, I know, Dave. I was just kidding. What's the movie about?"

"It's sort of a western, actually deals with the period just after the Civil War. Good script ... I think I might like the role," Dave said.

"Yeah, it sounds good. Be sure to let me know if you decide to do it."

"I will, Mike. Well, I guess I better go home, see if the little lady has calmed down and go to bed. Hey, you have to get up and go to work! I didn't think about that when I called you. I'm sorry!"

"Hey, Dave, don't give it a thought. I get up early anyway. Besides, it's worth it to hear from you," I said.

This was the first time Dave gave any indication of a problem in his relationship with Rosemary. I shuddered at the thought he was finding himself trapped in a relationship already; I really could not see Rosemary having a temper, at least not where Dave was concerned. I knew for a fact he would do anything for her, give her anything she wanted. After all, it was now public knowledge he showered her with expensive gifts.

I decided to take Dave's word that it was just a little argument. Every couple has arguments. What's to worry about? I told myself it was nothing.

My next conversation with Dave came at one minute past midnight on September 18.

"Happy Birthday, Mike!" he yelled into the phone.

To say I was very surprised would be an understatement. "Gee ... uh ... thanks, Dave! I sure wasn't expecting your call. How in the hell could you even remember my birthday?"

"I have a good memory, but I forgot to send you a card. Anyway, are you celebrating? You must be about 26, right?"

"Yeah, 26 ... but I don't feel a day over 19," I joked.

"Well, you're catching up to me. Before you know it, soon you'll be 38 pushing 40," Dave joked.

"Yeah ... well, when I'm 38, you'll be 50 ... so let's just let time pass, one day at a time, and make the best of it," I joked.

"That's the right attitude ... the way I look at life," he said.

"So, how are things with you? How's the court case going with Ellie? Have you locked in any new films?"

"Things are good. We have on-going depositions, Ellie and her lawyers are still being nasty, pains in my ass ... but, Rosemary is being a real trooper; she is helping me maintain my cool. We've moved into the house in Coldwater Canyon, getting settled in. I got the role in the movie *Macho Callahan*; I think I told you about that."

"Great! I'm glad to hear everything is going so well with you and Rosemary. Didn't you say that film was going to be shot on location in Mexico?"

"Yeah, we start filming the first part of December. I have to grow a full beard. I'm *Macho*," he said with a laugh.

"Hell, Dave! It damn sure won't take you three months to grow a beard, maybe three days," I laughed, then asked, "What takes so long? If the script is all done, all the actors are under contract ... why don't you just fly down to Mexico and get it done?"

"A lot of technical stuff ... finding locations, building sets, making costumes, a bunch of work. At least, I know I'm back to work and that makes me happy."

"Yeah, and I'm sure you can use the money." I laughed.

"You better believe it! I'm supporting two women and a battalion of lawyers - hardly have enough for a bottle of scotch for myself," he said before releasing a deep laugh.

"Well, Dave, if you need some scotch, just let me know. I'll send you a case by UPS."

"Okay, I'll do that. I have to go so you have a great day and don't get into any trouble," Dave said.

"Okay, Dave! Thanks for the call. Keep in touch."

"I will, Mike ... you take care," Dave said and ended the call.

Dave sounded really upbeat, really happy. I was glad to hear from him when he was so positive.

44

The New York newspapers and the fan magazines were starting to publish bits and pieces of Janssen -v- Janssen - what a nasty divorce it had become, and how long it was taking to get through divorce court.

I was no longer clipping the articles. I would read them and mail them to my older sister, Judy - a big fan of Dave's.

I followed the news as much as I could about Dave, the divorce proceedings, his relationship with Rosemary and, of course, any television appearances he was scheduled to make.

On Sunday, October 26, Dave called just before noon. I was surprised, not having heard from him since my birthday in September.

"Hey, Mike! It's Dave. How the hell are you?"

"I'm doing well, stranger ... how about you? How Are Rosemary and Alexandra?" I asked.

"They are doing fabulous; we love the house and things here could not be better. We took some friends on a short vacation to Mexico ... had a really good time," he said.

"How long was the flight from LA to Mexico City, or wherever you went?" I asked.

"No, we didn't fly. I chartered the boat we used to go to the Bahamas - great accommodations, great crew ... it was a lot of fun."

"I'm glad to hear that Dave. I'm sure with all the BS you're going through with Ellie, you needed it, and you damn sure deserved it."

"So how are things with you? How are Rose Marie ... and Baron?"

"All is well. Rose Marie and Baron are both fine, madly in love with each other. It's beautiful Indian summer weather here, but it won't be long before we'll have freezing cold and piles of snow."

"Yeah ... well, that's what you wanted. You could still be here in the warm sunshine and palm trees, and having drinks with me at The

Formosa," Dave joked.

"Dave, the only thing I miss about LA is having drinks with you!" I exclaimed. "So, how about all this crap I've been reading about Janssen -v- Janssen? It sounds like there is no end in sight."

"About 99 percent of what you're reading is plain BS ... not a scintilla of truth in it. Crowley says we are making progress and he is convinced the judge is a big fan of mine."

"Well, that's good to hear, that your lawyer is making progress - but I'm not surprised the judge is a fan of yours and, seeing Rosemary, he may even be a little jealous of you."

"He hasn't seen Rosemary in person yet; maybe he's seen her pictures. I don't care what it takes to get this mess over with."

"One day at a time, Dave. This too shall pass ... and all that stuff, but it is true. Remember to take a deep breath ... in between sips of scotch," I said half joking.

"Yeah, I know, Mike ... and I'm doing it. Rosemary has been a rock for me, so I guess I'm lucky."

"You are, Dave ... I just don't think you realize it."

"Yeah, I know, Mike. I do count my blessings and I do take a deep breath when the moment demands," he said and let out a little laugh.

"So tell me ... what is up next with you? You are in the middle of a testy divorce, you've just had a short vacation and you're going to start a new movie in Mexico in a couple of months. So what are you doing tomorrow?" I asked.

"Hell, I don't know! I don't plan that far ahead. No, just kidding. I'll be playing some golf, going to the track, spending time with Rosemary and Alexandra, making some guest appearances, but I'll be busy and that's good, what I like."

"What about Ellie's daughters; are you still in touch with them? What the hell do they think about their mother, what she is doing to you?"

"I stay in touch, mostly by phone, especially with Diane. They know what is going on; they think their mother is acting in a disgusting way and they don't like it. They know me and they know I love them, and they know their mother."

"Maybe your lawyer could call them as witnesses on your behalf ... that would show the judge that you are not the philanderer, the adulterer Ellie claims," I suggested.

"That's a good point, but I would not want to put them in that position. They've been through enough with her; they are young ladies now – teenagers. They need some peace and a chance to mold their own lives," Dave said in a serious tone.

I had already learned what a compassionate man Dave was, how he always considered the feelings of others and was always willing to help, no questions asked. I thought about one incident I knew.

Dave had read about a single mother with six kids whose home was burned to the ground. She had no home insurance, nothing, and was struggling and working two jobs. Dave sent a check for $10,000 to her, and he did it anonymously. I learned later he did that type of charity many, many times.

"I see your point, Dave; you are right. However, do you think they would do it if you or your lawyer asked? I mean, couldn't they testify to some of the arguments Ellie started - testify how you always did what Ellie wanted, always gave her everything she wanted?"

"Yeah, Mike, they would; I know that ... but I don't want to stoop that low, and the publicity would hurt the girls."

"Okay, enough of that ... at least, you still have a good relationship with them. Are you looking forward to the movie? Will Rosemary and Alexandra be able to go to Mexico, be on location with you?"

"No, they won't be there, but Rosemary may be able to come down for a few days."

"That's good! I hear those Mexican girls are hot ... hate to think you may be sidelined," I joked.

"You don't have to worry about that ... never happen. I'll be working. By the end of the day's shooting, I'll probably be too damn tired ... just have a couple of drinks, a good shower and fall into bed," Dave said in earnest.

"I know, Dave ... don't you know when I'm kidding?"

"Yeah, I know, Mike ... but I'm like your German Shepherd; I'm a one-woman man." He chuckled.

"So I guess you and Rosemary will be getting married after your divorces become final. Believe me, send me an invitation. I'll fly out there just for your wedding," I said.

"Hey, hey, Mike! Don't rush things! Don't push me! Time will tell but I can tell you, right now, I'm not looking at getting married again ... to anyone ... anytime soon."

"Smart man. Give yourself and Rosemary time to really get to know each other. You've been together about a year now. Look ahead, say five, 10 years from now. Maybe you'll have your own kids," I said.

"Yeah, I will. I'd love to have my own kid, but then I think about the kid, being *my* son. What kind of life would he have ... growing up, I mean - with the publicity hounds, paparazzi? I'd hate to put any kid through that."

"Well, you managed to give Ellie's girls a good life; I don't recall seeing any news items where they were mentioned, or photographs for that matter. When you and Ellie invited me for dinner at your home, with Ms. Ball and her husband and Rock, I never saw the girls."

"We were careful to keep their privacy and we were lucky; they did not care about the film industry and they did not care about publicity. When we had dinner parties or such at home, they were either out with friends or they remained in their rooms. They are good girls," he said.

"Well, just be sure to let me know when you fly off to Mexico," I said.

"I will. Listen! You have a good Thanksgiving, if we don't speak before then."

"Thanks, Dave, and the same to you, Rosemary and Alexandra." I hung up my phone.

Thanksgiving would pass with no calls from Dave. I knew he was planning anther mini-vacation before starting his new film *Macho Callahan* so I was not concerned. There had not been any new gossip reported in the press so I assumed his lawyers and publicist had everything under control.

45

Dave called around noon, Sunday, December 7.

"Mike, it's Dave. How are you doing?"

"Great, Dave! Boy, it is good to hear from you! I was wondering if you were down in Mexico and they wouldn't let you come back," I said, joking.

"Not yet ... actually, I'm going down this coming week. We're ready to start filming the new film, *Macho Callahan*, so I'll be in Mexico for a couple of months.

"I'm sorry I haven't called but I've been pretty busy, with depositions and crap with my lawyers. We are making progress but it seems to be never ending."

"Has Ellie curtailed her slanderous gossip planting?" I asked.

"Hell, no! She's gotten worse ... a couple of friends have told me she claims Rosemary and I were screwing before we made *Where It's At*. Hell, I didn't even know Rosemary before we made the film. She's telling people I've been to bed with almost every actress I ever worked with, telling them she had suspected, but wanted to believe I would come back to her."

"Well, your lawyers and publicist must be doing a good job; I haven't seen anything in the New York press lately. So how close do your lawyers think you are to actually getting the divorce made final?"

"It's a few months off ... they were able to delay depositions and hearings so I could make this film. I hope when I get back, we can move the proceedings along at a faster pace."

"Have they any idea how much it's going to cost you ... not counting your lawyers' fees? Will you have to pay alimony for the rest of your life?"

"It will cost me a bundle; she is fighting to get half of everything I've worked my ass over the past 10 years to get. I've already sold the property in Palm Springs ... she's out to strip me bare, the bitch."

"That's a shame! After all you've done for her, all you have given her, why the hell couldn't she just take what you offered and be civil?"

"She is a jealous, insecure bitch and she knows she will never find anyone who will be as good to her as I've been - and put up with all her bullshit. She wants to drag this out as long as she can ... run up lawyer fees and make me sell property at a loss. I'm telling you, Mike, she is just being a rotten bitch about it."

"I can't believe her! She just doesn't want to let you go ... to let you be happy."

"I know, Mike, but I'm going to keep going and, no matter what it costs, when the divorce is final ... I'll be free!" Dave said in a strong voice.

"Do you think you'll give it some time before getting married ... to Rosemary?"

"Oh, yeah! I haven't discussed that with her yet, but I think she'll understand I need some time to clear my head, adjust to my situation," Dave said calmly.

"Yeah, but didn't you say she wanted to marry you the minute your divorce is final?"

"Yeah, she's been telling that to everyone. She can say anything she wants, but I like it just the way we have it. We share a home, we share our bed ... why screw things up?" he said with a slight chuckle.

"I sure hope it works out that way for you, Dave. I would hate to see you get burned again ... and so soon."

"Don't worry, Mike! I'm not a fool ... not anymore. Okay, listen ... you and Rose Marie have a nice holiday. If I can find the time I'll call you from Mexico, okay?"

"All right! You and Rosemary and the baby have a nice holiday, too, and keep in touch - but if you don't call from Mexico, I'll understand ... so take good care, Dave," I said and hung up the phone.

I certainly did not expect to hear from Dave until after the holidays. I knew he would be in Mexico filming and, on his return, he would be very busy with his lawyers as the divorce was set for trial.

I discovered that during the Christmas holiday season, everything to do with normal business seemed to shut down and it was all about shopping for gifts and office Christmas parties.

Rose Marie was all tied up with family for the holidays, so I would be on my own.

Christmas and New Year's Day passed and there was little in the news media about Dave and his divorce saga. As I had expected, I received no calls from him. I had no idea when he would finish with the shooting of *Macho Callahan* in Mexico but I was sure he would call when he had time.

46
~ 1970~

Dave telephoned me on Sunday afternoon, February 1, just before three o'clock; I was glad to hear from him.

"Mike, how are you doing?" he asked.

"Doing well, more important ... how are you? I haven't heard from you since early December ... is everything going well for you?"

"Yeah ... everything is fine. We finished the film. Rosemary and Alexandra are fine. We are about to start the trial to get rid of Ellie, once and for all," he informed.

"Yeah, I've read in *Photoplay, The New York Post* and *The Daily News* that you and Ellie have been trading shots during depositions with your lawyers. I see what you mean about Ellie but, damn, the lawyers, both yours and hers ... the media makes it sound like they hate each other as much as you hate Ellie."

"Yeah, I know ... I don't hate Ellie and I know she doesn't hate me but, as I told you a couple of years ago, I finally decided I would no longer allow her to control my life ... my every move. I want my freedom and the fact that Rosemary and I have fallen in love ... that's just my good fortune," he said with a little bit of a chuckle.

"Yeah, I know what you mean. You are a very lucky man. Rosemary is astonishingly beautiful and I see the way she looks at you. No doubt she wants you for her soul mate," I said.

"Yeah, Mike, I'm a very lucky guy. I may also be a very poor man after the divorce is final."

"What is this I read about you having to pay a casino over $44,000 ... is that true? I didn't think you gambled that much," I said.

"Hey, it's like I told you, Mike: sometimes you win and sometimes you lose ... it depends. Yeah, I had to pay the markers and Ellie wants half; she claims I gambled and lost 22,000 of HER dollars! Can you believe that?" Dave asked, raising his voice.

"Yeah, I can believe that. I also read where she is really pissed off about your buying a $3,000 dollar dress for Rosemary and over a grand a week on groceries. Man, you sure know how to eat," I said.

"Well, Mike, the gown was an accident; I didn't know it was that expensive ... and, yes, I like to eat well. You know that ... and imported caviar is expensive," he said before laughing out loud.

"So how long does your lawyer think the trial will last?" I asked.

"He isn't sure but, at least, two or three weeks. Ellie's lawyers have subpoenaed Rosemary to testify, as well as a bunch of other people," he said.

"That could take some time for each to testify ... but your lawyer can trip anyone of them up by what they said in their depositions when he cross examines them."

"Yeah, but I don't really give a damn. I just want this over, no matter what the cost."

"I don't blame you. Hey, you look all right in a full beard; they had a photo of you in the *Daily News*. I know that was for the movie ... are you going to keep it?" I asked.

"Yeah, Rosemary likes it. I'm going to keep it for a few more weeks; maybe I'll keep it during the trial ... Ellie hates beards."

"I bet Rosemary is happy that you are near the end. I read where she already has her divorce from her husband."

"Yeah ... but their separation and their divorce, which will become final this month, was very friendly. They didn't fight over money or property. Tolan has very liberal visitation with Alexandra so he's happy. Yeah, she's happy as hell ... I just hope she doesn't start pushing me for a wedding date. I just don't think I'm ready ... not for a while ... quite a while," Dave said.

"I think you are being wise there, but how long do you think Rosemary will stick around if you guys don't get married?"

"I don't have any way of knowing ... but if she pushes me and I'm not ready, and she decides to move out, then she's not the right woman for me anyway," he said in a determined and calm voice.

"I agree with you, Dave. If she is not willing to wait for you to be ready to make that big of a decision, then she is not the right woman for you."

"Time will tell but, so far, everything is great between us and I love Alexandra like she's my own. Rosemary is telling her I'm her daddy!"

"That is great! I'm sure you are the only real father-figure she's had. Didn't Rosemary split with Tolan right after falling for you ... while he was in New York? Did you know Tolan before you and Rosemary did *Where It's At*; had you ever worked with him?" I asked.

"Yeah, I knew him, but not well. We had no time to become friends. I think he is a talented actor and will do well. Everyone, even Rosemary, says he is a really nice guy."

"That's nice to hear ... too bad Ellie can't be as nice as him," I said. "So what are you doing on a nice Sunday ... relaxing, I hope?"

"Actually, I am. I'm playing golf today with some friends and then I'll take Rosemary to La Scala for a nice dinner. I'll be meeting with my lawyers tomorrow so I want to just relax this weekend."

"You deserve it. I'm doing the same, going to take Baron to Riverside Park for an hour or so and figure out where I'll go for dinner ... sure wish I could go to La Scala; I can still taste their food."

"Hell, Mike! Look around the city ... there has to be great Italian restaurants. You'll find one."

"I know, you're right ... but you mentioning La Scala put me in the mood for a nice Italian dinner."

"Well, Mike, my group has arrived so I'm off. You take care and I'll be in touch," Dave said.

"Thanks, Dave! You take it easy, too ... and good luck."

Dave hung up the phone.

I knew Dave enjoyed playing golf, a sport I could never figure out. I know when he first started playing he did so with friends and studio executives but, soon, Ellie wanted to take lessons and, as Dave said, it was just so he would not be out of her sight.

Dave said she was so bad and she did not have the patience to continue her lessons, so she gave up. However, she would go with him when he played and stay in the clubhouse talking to the women who may happen to be there. It seemed Rosemary let Dave have his space and time to do what he wanted to do.

47

I did not hear from Dave throughout February, but there was plenty of news about his battle with Ellie in the fan magazines and the New York papers. Dave had told me not to believe what I read in the fan magazines and newspapers; it would be "99 percent crap, not a scintilla of truth" in them.

Dave, finally, called me as I was going to bed on Sunday morning, March 8. It was just about one o'clock in Los Angeles and Dave sounded pretty drunk.

"Hey, Mike! It's Dave. You wanna meet for drinks? I'm at The Formosa. Come on over," he said, his speech very slurred.

"Hi, Dave ... you know I'd love to come over, but I don't think I could make it before they close. How the hell are you? It's been a while since I've heard from you; is everything okay?"

"Yeah ... actually, hell no! Everything is not okay. Everything is fucked up with this god damned bitch. Her son-of-a-bitch lawyers are making Rosemary out to be a whore, a home-wrecker and every other kind of low life I've never even heard of ... and, all the time, dragging this shit out so they can cheat me out of every dime they can. They're cheating me out of every dime ... she's a fucking bitch ..."

He was slurring his words, repeating himself and it was hard for me to understand his exact words. I just knew this was the first time I had ever heard him so angry and so drunk.

"So I take it you had a rough week in court? Is Rosemary with you?"

"Yeah, it was the worst fuckin' week of my life ... my entire fuckin' life."

"Is Rosemary with you now?" I asked again.

"No, we had an argument ... I left her ... I needed a drink ... wish you would've been here this week, Mike ... you could've been my post. I have to get ready for court in the morning - nine o'clock, sharp!"

"How did you get to The Formosa, Dave?"

"I drove ... I drove here ... why?"

"Dave, promise me you will have them call you a cab when you're ready to go."

"Yeah," he slurred.

"Dave ... promise me you will take a cab home ... get your car tomorrow. Will you promise me you will take a cab?"

"Yeah ... yeah ... I will. I'm too tired to drive ... okay ... I'll call you later," he said and the phone clicked.

I quickly called Los Angeles telephone information and got the number for The Formosa. I placed the call and the phone was answered by the bartender.

I explained I was a friend of Mr. Janssen's and he had just called me from their payphone and I believed he had too much to drink, and would they please make certain he was sent to his home in a cab.

The bartender knew David, of course, and he assured me they would make certain Dave would not be driving, even if the bartender had to take him home personally. I felt better.

After Dave's call, I was really worried the pressure of the divorce was getting the best of him. I was also concerned with the stability of his relationship with Rosemary; this was the second argument between them that Dave had told me about. He also said Rosemary has a hot temper.

In the almost five years I had known him, whether sharing drinks with him in person or in all of our telephone conversations, this was the first time I could tell he was really very, very drunk.

I decided I would break my self-imposed rule and call Dave the next evening, after his day in court, just to make certain he was okay and had made it through the day.

I made it a rule not to call Dave because I knew he was constantly busy and I did not want to take the chance of interrupting him. I also knew the trial was being held in Santa Monica and, at the end of each day's proceedings, Dave and Rosemary would rush past the media and go straight to their home. Rosemary would prepare them a good dinner and they would relax together without being the subject of public glare.

I called Dave at seven o'clock, Los Angeles time; he answered on the third ring.

"Dave, Mike ... am I interrupting you?"

"No ... not at all, Mike. This is a surprise!"

"I just wanted to see how you are ... that you got home last night and made it through the day."

"Yeah ... I took a cab home and fell asleep on the sofa. I'm doing fine."

"Well, I was just a little bit worried when you called last night. You were at The Formosa and you didn't sound too good," I said. "How did it go in court today?"

"They're still spreading my personal finances out for the entire world to see - the bastards! I'm keeping my mouth shut ... they haven't called me to the stand yet, but when they do ... I've got plenty to say!"

"How is Rosemary? Did she go to court with you today?" I asked.

"Yeah, she went with me. She's okay; she wants this bullshit over as much as I do so we can move on with our lives. We made up this morning, so all is good."

"Have your lawyers given any indication of how much longer it's going to take for the trial to be over?"

"It could be at least three or four more weeks. Her lawyers are calling store clerks, delivery people, many of MY friends - friends Ellie thought were on her side.

"She's finding out just whose friends they really are. Her lawyers are just dragging everything out, making a public spectacle ... really pisses me off."

"Is Ellie there every day, too?"

"Yeah ... the bitch is here with her girlfriends, putting on a big act - like I'm a real bastard of a husband, that I played around with every fucking woman I ever worked with ... a bunch of lies!"

"Have you spoken with her? Maybe she would stop her lawyers and just get it over with."

"When the trial first started, I was cordial with her. I was the perfect gentleman - but when her lawyers started all this bullshit ... lies about Rosemary ... lies about me ... I can't stand to even look at her."

"Well, Dave ... remember: one day at a time and this too shall pass."

"Yeah, I know ... I know. Thanks for being so concerned, Mike. Rosemary has dinner ready so we'll talk later, okay?"

"Yeah, Dave. Take it easy and stay in touch, okay?"

We ended the call and I felt much better, knowing that he had taken a cab from the bar the night before. I also felt better knowing that, whatever dispute he and Rosemary had had, had been resolved.

I slept late Sunday and, when I got up, Baron insisted we go to the park. I made a quick cup of coffee to take with me and we headed over to Riverside Park for his morning run.

On our way home, I stopped at the corner newsstand and bought the Sunday newspapers and *TV Guide, Photoplay, Modern Screen* and a couple of other magazines. I was sure there would be articles about Dave and Ellie's divorce saga.

There was an article in the fan magazines and one in the *New York Post*. The articles were basically the same, saying that Ellie's lawyers had uncovered evidence that Dave was squandering large sums of money on gambling in Las Vegas, expensive gowns and jewelry and food for Rosemary.

It had not been a secret that Dave and Rosemary were in love and Dave wanted his freedom from Ellie. Rosemary had gotten an amicable divorce from her husband and the gossip in the Hollywood media was Dave and Rosemary would be married the minute his divorce was final.

48

On Saturday, March 28, Dave called just after three o'clock in the morning, my time. He sounded sober and upbeat. "Mike, Dave ... how are you doing?"

"Good ... how is everything going with you? Is the trial about over?" I asked. "I saw in the *Post* that you had to give Ellie $10,000,000!"

"Yeah, thank God ... just waiting for the judge to make it official. Hell, I told you not to believe the tabloids; she did not get 10 million ... nowhere near it. Hell, I don't have anywhere near 10 million! Still it did cost me a God-damned fortune ... half of everything I have, of all I earned in the 10 years of marriage to that bitch! The worst is she was awarded half of my interest in *The Fugitive* and that will be bringing in a hell of a lot of money over the next few years."

"Maybe the reporter was calculating Ellie would get that much from the interest in *The Fugitive*. Still it cost you half of your money, your property. Hey, Dave, remember: you said you didn't care what it cost ... you just wanted your divorce," I reminded.

"I know, Mike ... it just hurts. She'll be living like a Queen on MY money ... and I still have to give her almost four grand a month alimony ... until she remarries or dies!"

"When will it be final; when will the judge sign the decree?" I asked.

"We don't know. Crowley told me it will take a few months for him to write the findings of facts and the law. It is final now; we just don't have the judge's signature yet. I'm not in any hurry to have the decree; there is nothing more Ellie can do to me ... or get from me."

"That is good to hear ... I'm happy for you. Look at it this way: it won't take you long and you'll make all Ellie has taken and more. You'll be working in movies and, surely, on television."

"I know, Mike. As long as I keep busy, I'll be happy. I have several projects lined up. I'll be doing a TV Movie of the Week in a couple of months and Abby has several film scripts for me to read ... I'll recover."

"I bet both you and Rosemary are happy ... now that it is over. No more court appearances, no more nasty stories in the tabloids..."

"You bet we are! It's been two years of absolute hell. Now we can relax and get on with our lives ... and I can go to work and not worry about sharing my hard earned money with the bitch."

"So how are you doing on cutting down on your alcohol intake? Remember, you told me you were going to cut way back."

"Well, it's like this, Mike: since you left, I had to find a good drinking buddy and, to my surprise, Rosemary likes her booze, too ... and, believe me, she can keep up with me. So, no, I haven't really cut back ... but I will."

"Yeah ... I hope you do, for your sake! You don't have Ellie as an excuse; I know she drove you to drink!"

"It wasn't just Ellie; it was my work and a lot of other things. Hell, I've always been a heavy drinker ... thanks to my mother - but I'm a happy drunk. I don't lose my temper."

"I'm not just talking about being a happy drunk or a mean drunk; I'm talking about your health ... your liver!" I exclaimed.

"Don't worry about it, Mike! I feel fine and I get a complete physical every year, sometimes more than one if the studio wants to insure me for a film. If anything shows up, the doctor will tell me."

"Okay, Dave ... don't pay any attention to me. Who the hell am I to lecture you?"

"I appreciate your concern, Mike, but don't worry ... I'll be fine ... and I've got Rosemary to help keep an eye on me, since you deserted me," Dave said with a laugh.

"I know, Dave. Sometimes I wish I had followed your advice and given myself more time to adjust to LA. I just could not get used to the smog and the freeways that it is so spread out. I love New York ... it is so compact, and so much more fun - at least to me."

"Well, I have to go now, but I'll be in touch," Dave said and ended the call.

I bought several of the fan magazines; almost all had photos of Dave and Ellie on the cover, with headlines that their divorce trial was over. There were also articles in *The New York Times, The New York*

Post and *The New York Daily News* all reporting that Dave was now a free man.

One of the fan magazines had an article saying that Dave and Rosemary were already making wedding plans. I knew this not to be true and had a little laugh over it.

Another article repeated the false insinuation that Ellie was awarded $10,000,000, which Dave and I had already shared a laugh over.

I came to the conclusion Dave must be busy as I did not hear from him until Sunday, June 27.

"Hey, Mike! It's Dave ... sorry I have been out of touch but I have been extremely busy. How are things going for you?"

"Everything here is going great ... how about you and Rosemary? How about your projects?"

"I'm busy ... I did a charity benefit with Bob Hope, Gregory Peck and others a few weeks ago at the Astrodome; then I did the shooting of a Movie of the Week for CBS. I haven't spoken with you in quite a while; I wanted to check in to make certain all is well with you."

"Thanks, Dave! I appreciate that. Now, I know it's none of my business, and I know you told me not to believe 99 percent of the crap written in the fan magazines, but they're all saying you and Rosemary are getting married. Don't forget my invitation."

"Mike, don't believe any of that shit! No, I am not getting married to Rosemary ... or anyone, anytime soon! It's all just the imagination of these idiotic writers, just to sell magazines."

"Well, another one says you are getting married because Rosemary is pregnant."

"Yeah, we've heard that one, too. She is not pregnant, doesn't look pregnant and, IF she is pregnant, it sure as hell isn't mine!" Dave said and let out a deep laugh.

"That's all good to hear. I mean ... don't get me wrong. Rosemary is a beautiful woman, very smart and nice. I just thought you may want some time to enjoy your freedom."

"You better believe it! I do! It doesn't matter, anyway. We live together and all is working out well ... why complicate things is my way of looking at it."

"I agree with you completely ... enjoy your freedom. So everything is still good with you and Rosemary? How is Alexandra? I bet she's getting big."

"Yeah, we're getting along fine and, yes, Alexandra is getting big - and she's smart as hell ... talks more than her mother."

"Hey, you said you made that Movie of the Week for CBS; I've been watching for it and I haven't seen anything."

"Oh, no! It hasn't aired yet. I think it will be in the new season, sometime in October or November. It's called *Night Chase*. I'll find out and let you know so you can keep watching for it in case I don't let you know in time. I think you will like it."

"What's it about? Sounds like a cop movie."

"Yeah, it is, in a way ... only I'm not the cop. I shot my wife's lover and I'm a fugitive ... on the run again."

"You have to be kidding me ... really?"

"I wouldn't kid you, Mike ... it is a good plot and good cast; trust me, you will like it."

"Okay, I'll be watching for it. So what else are you doing?"

"I'll be doing some guest appearances and, soon, another series; it will be produced by Jack Webb. Remember him? I'll be a U.S. Treasury Agent. I'll keep you advised. All right! We'll talk later," Dave said.

"Jack Webb! Of course, he's Sergeant Joe Friday. Okay ... from being a fugitive to being a cop ... good choice. Okay ... thanks for calling, Dave. Stay in touch."

49

Dave must have been very busy because I heard nothing from him until Saturday, July 18, at 4:40 in the morning.

"Good morning, Mike! It's Dave ... I didn't wake you, did I?"

"Actually, you didn't; I'm just brewing coffee and then I'm taking Baron to the park. How the heck are you? All I know is what I've been reading ... and you know I don't believe any of that crap."

"Yeah, I know. I don't believe any of it either. I've been busy ... need to work as much as I can ... make up all the money Ellie stole from me."

"Yeah, I can believe that. How are things with Rosemary?"

"It feels like we're an old married couple; the excitement has dissipated some."

"Uh ... that sounds a little like you're about ready to move on - bet you are damn glad you did not marry."

"You're right. Don't get me wrong! Things are okay between us; it is just that we are settled into our relationship ... living together ... but there are times when I want it, and she has a headache ... and times she wants it and I have a headache. Usually, I take two Excedrin and I'm ready," he said and laughed.

"Well, try and enjoy it as it is for as long as you can. Just keep your freedom until you know she's the one," I advised.

"Don't worry, Mike; I think I enjoy being a bachelor ... with benefits," he joked.

"So what has been going on with you? I haven't seen very much in the papers lately."

"I have been keeping busy. We are going over scripts for the pilot of Jack Webb's *Treasury Agent* and I have the lead role where I'm always at odds with my bosses in Washington."

"It sounds really interesting; do you like it? Do you think it will be as demanding on you, physically and mentally, as *The Fugitive*?

When will you actually start filming?" I asked.

"Sometime in September. I'll make sure you know. Demanding? Oh, yeah! It will be just as demanding in every aspect, possibly even more so. I'm ready for a new series. I've had a good three years off. On *Treasury Agent*, I like the writing; we have assembled a great crew and I'm sure we are all going to work well together. Who knows how long it will last as a series?"

"It's going to be on CBS, right? Did Mr. Webb give ABC a chance at it? I only ask that because you liked working with ABC."

"Yeah, he pitched it to all three networks. CBS is the only one who has shown an interest, so we'll see if they like the pilot; they're not committed yet."

"I remember watching Dragnet ... and, personally, I thought the dialogue was so far from the way real cops talk, and how they handle investigations. Don't tell him I said that ... but I know he wrote a lot of the scripts."

"Yeah ... well, he will be using other writers for *Treasury Agent* and I'm sure it will be a little more realistic ... more believable. I'm looking forward to it; I think it is just what I need to shake being remembered as *Dr. Richard Kimble* and to be appreciated for being a good actor playing a good cop," Dave said.

"I know what you mean ... *The Fugitive* ended three years ago; it has been off the air yet, all the articles I've read about you, they still call you *The Fugitive* and say little about your films ... *Green Berets*, *Shoes of the Fisherman*. I understand that because it was the series that made you famous."

"Yeah. Well get ready for it again ... they are starting the syndication run pretty soon."

"What do you mean?"

"It will be showing on television stations all over the world ... all 120 episodes."

"But that will interfere with your new series ... won't it?"

"Not really ... it will be mostly on independent stations. I don't think it will hurt the new series; it will show my fans I can play a cop just as well. Besides, it will give me a pretty good income ... and I need it now."

"Yeah, I see what you mean. I hope it will earn you back all you had to give Ellie, in short order. As for *Treasury Agent*, just make sure you have good dialogue ... believable dialogue."

"Don't worry, Mike! We will. Okay, Mike, I'll try and do better with staying in touch ... you take care and we'll talk later."

"Okay, Dave ... keep me informed about the new series."

I assumed Dave was at one of the country clubs and waiting to tee off for a day of golf. He sounded in a really good mood, very pleased with how his life was moving forward.

Based on what he said about his relationship with Rosemary, I was concerned they were not as happy as they had been initially. I wondered if Dave's being so much older than her may be playing a role in Rosemary's thinking. I was not concerned they would be breaking up anytime soon; usually the fan magazines plant that kind of news long before it actually happens. They had all done that three years before he actually left Ellie.

I recalled how, after reading *Secrets ... Trouble in Janssen's Marriage,* in 1966 and 1967, Dave's publicist arranged for a few select reporters from *Photoplay, Modern Screen, TV Guide* and a couple of others to visit Dave and Ellie in their home and do stories of how strong and happy their marriage was. Dave hated when Frank Liberman did this because he was so unhappy in his marriage even then and felt he was deceiving his fans.

He knew, however, Quinn Martin and ABC Television were very concerned with his public image. They felt a separation or divorce would have a tremendous effect on the series, on the ratings. Dave reluctantly played the game.

A month passed and all I knew about Dave was what the papers published. He called me on Thursday evening, August 27, at about nine o'clock.

"Hey, Mike! It's Dave. I got it! I am officially free of the bitch. Judge Wells signed the decree today so I am totally free of her ... except for the alimony!"

"CONGRATULATIONS, DAVE! I am really happy for you! You sound great and I'm sure that your decree is responsible for it."

"You are right! I haven't been this happy in years! Now I can plan my life and enjoy it ... and know what I earn will be mine."

"That is really good to hear, Dave ... I hope Rosemary doesn't start angling you to get married. If I were in your shoes, I would not even consider getting married again for, at least, a couple of years."

"I know, Mike ... I told you a few months ago, I am not going to get married to Rosemary, or anyone, in the foreseeable future."

"Yeah, like you said ... living with Rosemary, everything is great and there is no need to complicate things. But ... what will you do if she starts pushing for that kind of commitment?"

"I will assess my feelings for her at the time ... let her know I am NOT ready to get married again ... at least, not at the time ... and I'll just see what happens."

"You have a good plan, Dave ... now stick with it," I said, a hint of humor in my voice.

"I may be coming to Atlantic City for an Ice Capades program. If I do, maybe you could drive down from the city; it's only about an hour and a half drive and we could have lunch or something."

"That would be great. How long will you be there?"

"Just a couple of days ... I don't have all the details yet, but I'll call you when I do. Okay, I have to go. I'll call you later in the week."

"Okay, Dave ... thanks for the call."

50

Dave called me early Monday morning, September 7; it was Labor Day so our office was closed. I had planned on going to watch the parade on Fifth Avenue.

"Mike, it's me, Dave. I'm going to be in Atlantic City on the 10th and 11th of September, maybe even the 12th. Any chance you can go down there? That'll be next Thursday, Friday and Saturday."

I knew I couldn't go to Atlantic City on Thursday or Friday. I had previously scheduled appointments with the Personnel Director of Raytheon and the Human Rights Director for Bates Manufacturing; those appointments were hard to arrange and there was no way I could cancel either one. "I know I can't do it on Thursday and Friday; I have business meetings out of the office. Maybe I could do it Saturday morning, or even drive down on Friday night."

"I hope you can make it; it would be great to see you and have a couple of drinks together," Dave said.

"Is Rosemary coming with you?" I asked.

"No, I'll be solo. I'm doing a quick skit on the Ice Capades and then I'll shoot another Excedrin commercial. I don't know the exact times I'll be free but I'll call and let you know. If you can drive down Friday night, I'll get you a room at the hotel ... so let me know."

"I will, Dave ... that is kind of you. It has been a long time and it would be great seeing you again."

"Okay. I'll call you sometime Wednesday evening or Thursday morning," Dave said.

"That will be fine," I said and we ended the call.

I was hoping I could drive down on Friday evening and spend Saturday there and drive back to the city on Sunday morning. I would bring Baron with me.

Dave called me at my office on Wednesday at four o'clock. He told me he would be arriving in Philadelphia early on Thursday morning, be met at the airport by a driver and taken to his hotel in Atlantic City.

"That sounds good, Dave. I'm planning on going down there after I leave work Friday evening. I'll let you know for certain but don't get me a hotel room. I'll stay at a motel that allows Baron."

"All right ... so I'll give you a call on Friday afternoon in your office. Would that be okay?" Dave asked.

"Yeah, it would be perfect ... then we can coordinate where and when we can meet."

We concluded the call and I went back to work. I was hoping I could arrange to go down and meet him for drinks. It had been early March of '69 when I last saw him in New York, for location filming of his movie, *Generation*; he had hosted a dinner for Rosemary, Rose Marie and I at Joe Allen's Restaurant in the Theatre District. I was looking forward to going to Atlantic City.

Dave called me in my office Thursday afternoon.

"Change of plans, Mike. I may be able to go back to LA on the red eye flight tomorrow night. If I can't, I'll call you so we could still get together," Dave said.

"Okay, Dave ... it would be good to see you, but if you can get back to LA a day earlier than expected, go for it."

"Okay, I'll call you ... does it matter what time?" he asked.

"If it is before six o'clock call me here at the office; otherwise, call me at home."

Dave called me at my office Friday, just before one o'clock. He was able to work his schedule out so he would be catching the last flight from Philadelphia non-stop to Los Angeles. I could easily understand him. When I had to travel, it was always great to get home earlier than planned.

I was disappointed not being able to see Dave when he was so close to New York, but it was understandable. I was pleased to hear him so calm, happy and busy with many projects going on at once – and, seemingly, without a care in the world.

Based on what he had told me, though, I felt he would leave Rosemary if she pushed him too hard to marry her. He had been burned badly when the court split in half all he had worked so hard for and given it to Ellie as *community property*.

There was no doubt in my mind that Dave would remain a bachelor for several years. I knew he hated that he had to sign a check for almost $4,000 as an alimony payment to Ellie on a monthly basis.

I spent a lazy weekend at home and took Baron to Riverside Park, spending extra time for him to play and socialize with other neighborhood dogs.

On Friday, September 18, Dave called me at one minute past midnight. "Hey, Mike! Dave ... am I the first to wish you a Happy Birthday?"

"No, you're not; Baron beat you to it. He just gave me a big, wet kiss; I don't know how he knew it was my birthday."

"Okay ... well, Happy Birthday, anyway. How is everything in the city?"

"Good, busy ... always bustling ... hot as hell. I can't wait for the fall weather to get here. How are things on the West Coast?"

"They're good. I did a guest shot on Dinah Shore's show yesterday. I'll be filming the pilot for *O'Hara – U. S. Treasury* with Jack Webb starting sometime next week. Hey, listen! *The Fugitive* starts its syndication run tomorrow ... don't know what channel it will be on in New York, but it's your chance to catch the episodes you missed."

"I didn't know that ... I'll find it. I'm glad it will be on a Saturday night; that way I'll have nothing to keep me from watching. I'll make certain to send you my critique of each show." I laughed.

"You do that, Mike. At least I'll start getting some cash flow every quarter. I've had a lot of unexpected expenses lately," he said.

"Well, Dave, if you need a couple of hundred, I'll be happy to send it to you," I said, laughing again.

"No, Mike, I'm okay for now ... but if I do, I'll call you."

"How are Rosemary and Alexandra? Does Rosemary have any new projects I can watch for? I will take Rose Marie to see it."

"The film she did in Miami with Jackie Gleason will be released early next month. She's looking over a couple of scripts for new projects. I'll keep you informed when she commits to something. Alexandra is growing and showing signs she will be as beautiful as her mother."

"That's good to hear. Well, it has been a few months since your divorce became final ... any hints of getting married?" I asked, guardedly.

"Not yet ... and I don't expect any for at least a year and, even then, I'm not so sure I would be in the mood," Dave said.

"That's good. I'm glad to hear you are going to enjoy your freedom. You'll have plenty of time in a couple of years from now. If Rosemary is still with you, then maybe you will decide you were meant for each other."

"Yeah, Mike, but I seriously doubt we'll be together in a couple of years. I'm just enjoying the benefits of her being around ... and there are no legal binds and there's no pressure for anything."

"As I said, you have plenty of time; take it one day at a time. Hey, when will the pilot for your new series be aired?"

"It won't be until sometime next year, if CBS likes it and picks it up. Don't worry! I'll be sure to let you know the date in advance."

"So when will you get time to schedule another trip to New York? I'd like to take you, Rosemary and Rose Marie out for a nice dinner."

"It will be awhile. If CBS does not pick up the series, I will be out of work. Maybe I'll make a short trip there. I don't know if Rosemary will be with me; we'll see. I'll let you know. Okay ... I have to run so enjoy your birthday. Go out tonight and tie one on ... you deserve it, too. I'll be in touch," Dave said then ended our call.

51

It was Columbus Day, October 12, 1970. Business in New York City had come to a full stop. There was a large Italian population in the city and a big parade always walked down Fifth Avenue; I made plans to go and see it.

It was just after five o'clock in the morning. I was awake, having coffee and waiting for dawn's light to take Baron for his run in Riverside Park when the phone rang.

"Good morning ... uh ... Mike ... you ... uh ... uh ... awake?" Dave asked.

I could tell immediately he had been drinking, probably all evening. It was just after two o'clock in LA, so maybe he was just leaving a bar.

"Good morning, Dave ... how the hell are you?"

"I'm ... uh ... fine ... drunk. I'm ... uh ... waiting on a cab. I'm not ... uh ... stupid ... uh ... uh ... to drive," he said. His words were very slurred.

"Is Rosemary with you?" I asked.

"No ... I'm ... all ... uh ... by myself. You wanna come over?"

"You know I can't, Dave ... sure wish I could; I'd be there in a New York minute," I said. "Are you all right? Are you sure you're waiting for a cab?"

"Yeah ... I'm waiting ... uh ... on a cab. I'm okay, just a ... a little drunk. I didn't have anything else to do ... I'm going home ... goin' to sleep," he said and the phone went dead.

I was worried that he was really waiting for a cab. I did not know where he was and I did not want to call The Formosa, in case he was not there. I could not help but wonder how he remembered my number, as drunk as he obviously was.

I became more concerned about his relationship with Rosemary. That was the second time Dave had called me, very drunk; the first time he told me he and Rosemary had an argument that day.

I know Dave was paying all the bills and I was sure the house he was leasing in Coldwater Canyon was not cheap. I could not believe he was running out of money, as hinted by a couple of fan magazines, and under stress as a result of it.

I knew Dave was a monogamous guy, that he would give the woman he was involved with everything she wanted, and would do just about anything she wanted. He enjoyed giving her gifts - no reason required, he just enjoyed it. Dave was also a very big tipper at restaurants and bars, so his lifestyle was expensive.

He was not one who would easily give up on a relationship with a woman, especially one he had strong feelings for. I was worried that again he was having problems with Rosemary, and that was not good.

I decided I would call him in the evening at six o'clock Los Angeles time, just to make certain he was home safe, and ask if there was anything he wanted to talk with me about.

I had not seen anything in the New York papers about Dave and Rosemary. I had not picked up the fan magazines for a couple of months and that, as every fan knows, is where the gossip starts. The fan magazine gossip mills will report something about a star, his home life, his sex life - whatever is the most ridiculous rumor in the writer's mind – and, more often than not, a few months later, the rumor becomes the truth.

I knew Dave was relieved that his marriage and the contentious and protracted divorce proceedings had come to an end. He had seemed to be very happy with Rosemary. They had been together a while and, from our most recent conversations, they seemed to have settled down to a normal home life, as if they were a married couple with a toddler daughter.

Dave told me they had drastically curtailed their social life and were not going out to restaurants or *A* list parties as often as they had when they were first dating, even during the court proceedings.

I could not help but wonder if he and Rosemary were now having problems and wondered if they would be able to work things out. I certainly was glad he had not proposed to, and married, Rosemary - at least not so soon after his divorce as many tabloids had published that he would.

At nine o'clock, I called Dave's home number; he answered on the fourth ring as I was about to hang up.

"Dave, it's Mike ... how are you feeling this evening?"

"Hey, Mike ... actually I feel a little hung-over."

"Do you remember calling me around two o'clock, your time?"

"Yeah ... yeah, I know I did. Sorry if I woke you. I was leaving The Formosa; they were closing. I got a cab to take me to the studio. I slept in my Bullet."

"Dave, is everything okay with you? Is there something wrong? Are things okay between you and Rosemary?" I asked.

"Yeah ... everything is okay ... everyone argues every now and then. I just have to know that, when she is drinking, I cannot ... well, not as much as usual anyway."

"I know it is none of my business. I was just worried about you," I said. He must have gone home when he woke, I thought, because that's the number I called.

"No, Mike ... it's okay. I know I can always talk with you ... that's why I called, but I obviously had too much because I wasn't in any shape to call and talk with you ... or anyone. Everything is fine now. She's here; you want to talk to her?" Dave asked.

"No ... No ... No, that's okay ... you say everything is okay, that's all I need to hear."

"Okay, Mike ... I'll give you a call later in the week. We'll talk then, all right?"

"Yeah, Dave ... at least, I know you're okay. Talk with you later," I said and hung up the phone.

I was still concerned. Dave had always been a heavy drinker but he always maintained control over his faculties. When we had drinks together in person, I never heard Dave really slur his words as he had the night before.

I could not help but wonder if Rosemary was applying a little pressure on him to make their relationship legal by getting married. I knew Dave was nowhere near being in the frame of mind to even give serious consideration to getting married - not to her, not to any woman. It was much too soon after his divorce and his wounds were still fresh.

I also knew Dave was not working on a steady basis, as he and Jack Webb were awaiting a decision on *O'Hara, U.S. Treasury* and, when he was not working on a regular basis, he could be a little moody and anxious.

I never saw Dave lose his temper with anyone, and no one I have talked to had seen him lose control - the only exception being with Wayne during the filming of *The Green Berets*. He did allude to me there were occasions he got a little angry at Ellie but she had provoked him beyond his limit.

Even Ellie admitted to me they had numerous arguments during the last couple of years of their marriage, but Dave had seldom lost his temper and, when he did, it was her fault. He never struck her, threw things or put his fist through a wall.

I decided after speaking with Dave briefly that he was okay and, whatever he wanted to tell me, he would do so when he could call me and speak privately.

I went out for an early dinner and decided I would buy all the current fan magazines and peruse them for any articles about Dave and Rosemary.

I had a busy week ahead of me in the office so I put Dave and his troubles out of my mind, deciding I might learn more when he called again.

Dave called me in my office on Tuesday at 9:30 in the morning.

"Mike, Dave ... am I interrupting you?"

"No, Dave. How are you?" I responded.

"I'm okay. I appreciate you calling me last night, that you were concerned enough to do that. The problem I'm having with Rosemary is her drinking as much as I do, and then she presses me for a commitment ... and I'm not ready for that."

"I understand ... and if you called me and told me you were going to get married, I'd tell you to wait another year or two - not that you would take my advice, but I'd give it anyway."

"No, you are right and we already discussed this. No, I am not ready to get married ... to anyone ... not for a while."

"Okay, Dave. I was just concerned when you called the other night. You sounded like you were pretty drunk."

"Yeah ... you know what? I was. Okay, Mike, I won't keep you, but thanks," Dave said and the line went dead.

52

My conclusion of our conversation on Tuesday was that Dave was losing what he felt he had with Rosemary and was torn between wanting to stay with her and make things work, or to leave and try to adjust to bachelor life.

I could only surmise, based on what Dave had said, that Rosemary wanted a commitment from Dave. Since both of their divorces were final, she wanted to be married to him, as she felt he wanted from the beginning of their relationship.

I knew well that Dave's divorce had cost him dearly - not only emotionally; financially, it had cost him tremendously. He was not ready to enter into another marriage and risk the same hurt and financial cost in the event the marriage was to fail.

I could not help but wonder how much longer their relationship would last without Dave proposing marriage to Rosemary. I decided I would again start buying all of the Hollywood fan magazines as well as the New York newspapers so I could keep abreast of any rumors about Dave and Rosemary's relationship.

I knew Dave was, literally, a nervous wreck awaiting a decision from CBS on whether *O'Hara, U.S. Treasury* would be committed for a series production. I wondered if that was causing stress between he and Rosemary.

I would not hear from Dave again until Wednesday, November 11.

"Good morning, Mike! Happy Veteran's Day!" he greeted with a chuckle.

"Good morning, Dave, and the same and a salute to you, too," I said. "How the hell are you? It's been a while since we spoke and there hasn't been anything, good or bad, about you in the papers or tabloids of late ... what's happening?"

"Everything is falling into place. CBS exercised their option. We start production of *O'Hara* sometime in May. Jack and I are taking the pilot to DC to meet with John Connally, the Treasury Secretary, and see what they think and how much cooperation we can expect from them."

"Wow, Dave! Congratulations! That sounds really exciting! So you'll actually meet with the Secretary of the Treasury ... do you think he will provide you any help in your storylines, production?"

"Yeah, I think he will. You know, I met Connally back in '67 after we finished filming *Green Berets*; he was on that ABC American Sportsmen Safari we were on. I think he'll like the pilot and I think he'll be very helpful in our making the show very realistic. He and I hit it off well; he was a big *Fugitive* fan."

"That is fantastic; I'm really happy for you! I'm sure Mr. Webb is pleased you have that connection with Connally."

"Yeah, Jack was surprised when I told him Connally and I were old friends. He is really hyped up about the prospects for the show and I have to agree. It has a lot of potential ... a lot of promise. I'm just glad I'll be back to work."

"I bet you will! I guess it's been a while, aside from all the guest appearances you've been doing on the talk shows. Don't worry, Dave! It won't be long and you'll make up all the money you had to give Ellie. So how are things with you and Rosemary?"

"Tenuous ... at best. Not working all these months while she has been working almost non-stop - mostly guest parts on television series shows, but she's been busy; it has been driving me crazy."

"Is she still pushing you to get married?"

"Yeah ... but not as hard as she had been. Now it is a little more subtle ... and not as constant as it was. Mike, I'm still not ready and, having lived with her for well over a year, I'm not so sure she is the right gal for me."

"Wow ... that's a surprise! Does she know how you feel?"

"No, not yet. I am happy, sort of, the way things are now - but she likes to drink, almost as much as me ... and she has a temper hot enough for both of us."

"Damn, Dave! All I can say is ... proceed with caution. The last thing you need is to be married at this point."

"Yeah, Mike ... that's for damn sure. I think after I'm back to work on a steady basis, things will sort of smooth themselves out ... we'll see."

"Well ... just be careful! I'm sure you'll be happy when you are working and you won't be lying around the house so much ... maybe she will lighten up some, too."

"Yeah ... I hope you are right ... time will tell. Okay, Mike, I'll let you go and I'll be in touch soon."

We ended the call and I sat for a moment and reflected upon Dave's words and his demeanor.

He sounded very enthusiastic about the new series and going back to work on a steady basis. Still, I felt his situation with Rosemary was not evolving as he had felt it would.

Could it be that Rosemary wanted to marry him so badly that she could not see his point of view ... his reluctance, his reasoning to be cautious?

I felt certain Rosemary would understand Dave's feelings. After all, she was named as co-respondent in his divorce and she attended court with Dave almost every day.

I knew Rosemary had been very busy over the past few months when Dave had not been working steadily. She had appeared as a guest star on several television series so she was making money.

I could not help but think Dave was more than a little concerned about that. I knew Dave well enough to know he was old-fashioned when it came to women, that he would never allow a lady to pick up a tab.

Could his finances be so bad that he felt ashamed? Whatever it was, I hoped they could work things out between them and before they married, if in fact that was in their future. I would never ask Dave about his personal life, especially his finances. Still, I just could not believe he would be destitute.

I knew that when Dave was working, he really got inside the mind of his character; as the character's creator had envisioned him, Dave brought him to life. That is why Dave was such a great actor; his fans believed him to be the character he was portraying. After all, when Dave was in front of the camera's eye, David Janssen did not exist.

I would wait for Dave's next call and maybe everything would be working out well between him and Rosemary.

53

Dave called me on Wednesday, November 25.

"Hey, Mike ... just wanted to wish you a Happy Thanksgiving. What are your plans?"

"I was invited to Rose Marie's parents' but I really did not want to go so I'll just go out and pick up turkey dinner, with all the trimmings, for Baron and me. How about you? What are your plans?"

"Rosemary is preparing everything at home, so it will just be Rosemary, Alexandra and me. We've given the nanny and cook the day off. It will be a nice, quiet and thankful day here at home."

"That's good ... how are things with you and Rosemary?"

"Good ... calm. Since I've been putting in long hours on the pilot for *O'Hara*, I'm not home that much ... I'm so tired when I get home, I just collapse into bed. Before dawn, I'm back up and going to the studio."

"How do you like O'Hara's character so far?" I asked.

"I like it. O'Hara was a county sheriff in, of all places, a small town in Nebraska. His wife and child die in a house fire and he has nothing left. He decides to apply for a job with the Treasury and they hire him ...so he'll be bouncing all around the country. Writing is pretty good for the pilot.

"We are doing a lot of location shooting of exterior scenes for the pilot; it will be a two hour premier. Outside locations give a realistic feel to it and, of course, we have a great crew. Many I've worked with on *The Fugitive*."

"That is great, Dave! When will the premier be shown? Playing a Treasury Agent, I'm sure your fans will see there is no comparison to you as Dr. Kimble, of which I am watching every episode as they air on TV now," I admitted.

"First, we have to get the green light from CBS; we think it will be early spring. Yeah, I'm glad they have started the syndication of

Fugitive; I can use the money. I hope when people watch *O'Hara* they will see I can play a totally different character and be as good as I possibly can. I just wish Lieberman could get the media to stop making it sound like *Fugitive* is the only role I can be associated with."

"I understand that, Dave. Almost everything I read, it is still *David Janssen - The Fugitive* ... almost in the same breath. Does Mr. Webb have much to do with the weekly filming?"

"Oh, yeah! He's on the set every day. I like working with him. He's like me; he strives for perfection."

"Well, as long as you enjoy it, that is what matters ... but do you think you would do this for four or five years?"

"No, I don't think so ... two, maybe three ... that would be enough. Okay, Mike, I have to go so have a nice Thanksgiving and we'll talk soon." Dave ended the call.

Dave sounded good, sober and seemingly happy. He was still with Rosemary and still not married, so I took that to mean they were happy with their relationship the way it was.

Thanksgiving Day I stayed home and watched the Macy's Thanksgiving Day Parade on television. I went out just after four o'clock and bought a turkey dinner with all the trimmings and a whole pumpkin pie. I fixed Baron a good turkey dinner and we enjoyed our Thanksgiving together.

It would be several weeks before I heard from Dave again. He called me just after noon on Sunday, December 20.

"Mike, it's Dave ... how is everything with you?"

"Great, Dave! How are things with you, *O'Hara*, Rosemary and Alexandra?"

"Fine. We have a few bumps here and there but, for the most part, things are good. We've shot most of the premier for *O'Hara*. I'll tell you, Mike, I am glad to be back to work with something solid ... hopefully for a long run."

"When will the premier be shown?" I asked.

"We're talking about doing a two hour Movie of the Week as the premier and then it will air at its regular time slot, which CBS hasn't determined yet. It will be early spring when it airs. I'll let you know when I find out."

"Well, let me know because I haven't seen anything in the papers or fan magazines and I damn sure do not want to miss the premier.

"Maybe a good way to promote it a few weeks before the premier would be to get the fan magazines, maybe even *TV Guide,* to print some photos of you and some of your guest stars, maybe even an *At Home With David Janssen* like they did with you and Ellie. I bet Rosemary would really like that."

"Yeah, they're already working on stuff like that. A pain in my ass but you know me, Mike. I'm a company man and my own company has part ownership, so I want this to work," Dave said.

"Well, I know it will work ... keep the faith!"

"Okay, listen, you have a very nice Christmas. Are you going to your family's in Indiana or staying in the city?"

"I'm staying in the city; there is something sort of magical about New York at Christmas time and I want to experience it," I answered.

"I'm going to run now. We'll talk later. If I don't talk to you before, have a great Christmas," he said.

"All right, Dave ... the same to you, Rosemary and Alexandra. Are you still in touch with Ellie's daughters?"

"Yeah, I've already sent their gifts and a little personal card ... and, yes, Mike, to my mother, Gene, Teri and Jill ... my closest friends and people who work for me ... I've got it all covered," he said with a chuckle.

"Okay, Dave ... well, thanks for the call ... you have a good one," I said and hung up the phone.

I was happy knowing all was going well for Dave and Rosemary, especially during the holiday season. Now that Dave was working full time on his third television series, I was certain 1971 would be a good year for him and Rosemary. The only concern I held was if Rosemary could be happy with their relationship as it was and be patient with Dave where a marriage proposal was concerned.

The Christmas holidays in New York City, which carried through to January 2, were absolutely the most beautiful of any city I had ever seen. Of course, I am referring to Manhattan, but I am certain the other boroughs were just as festive.

I did not expect to hear from Dave until well after New Year's Day. I enjoyed spending Christmas alone with Baron. I had taken Rose Marie to our office party on Wednesday, December 23, and to a nice romantic dinner at the Top of the Sixes restaurant, which was a very nice five-star restaurant on the top floor of Six-Six-Six Park Avenue. She would be spending the holidays with her extended family and that was fine with me.

I would call my mother, brothers and sisters on Christmas Eve which would leave me free of obligations for the rest of the weekend. Norman had decided there would be no point in opening the office between Monday through Wednesday, the last days of December before New Year's Eve and we were all happy with that decision.

I would spend the time with Baron, with extra time for him in Riverside Park, and talk with people I had met there while our dogs played together.

54
~1971~

Just after four o'clock on Sunday, January 10, I had returned to my apartment with Baron, having spent an hour and a half in Riverside Park; the phone was ringing as we entered the apartment.

"Hello," I answered, a little out of breath having run to grab the phone.

"Mike, Dave ... did I get you at a bad time?"

"No, Dave, not at all ... just came in the door from the park. How is everything with you?"

"Good. We finished the pilot, just waiting for CBS to make their decision when to air it. How about you? Did you have a good New Year's celebration?"

"Oh, yeah! Kind of noisy, as you can imagine in Times Square, with zillions of yelling and screaming people," I replied with a slight laugh. "How is everything with Rosemary?"

"Rather cool at the moment. She is showing some signs of being less than happy. She hasn't pushed me for a commitment for several weeks now. I'm starting to feel maybe it's time for us to go our separate ways."

"Whoa ... you really feel that way? Has she cut you off in the bedroom?" I asked.

"Well, let's just say it is not as frequent or as good as it was last year. She is just ... it feels like she is putting some distance between us – which, actually, is a good thing for me especially now with the prospect of *O'Hara* going into production. I sure don't need to be in a situation like I was with Ellie."

"Damn, Dave! I was hoping everything would be working out for you two, that she would acquire a lot of patience and wait for you to propose marriage in a few years," I said.

"To be honest, Mike, I was hoping the same thing. I am just not ready to jump into another marriage; it can be very costly to get out of," Dave replied in a serious tone.

"One thing I had never even thought about before, Dave: what if Rosemary was to become pregnant? That would sure as hell force you to make a decision about marrying her," I said.

"Mike, believe me ... I thought about that when we first met. I've always been careful there."

"Yeah ... but you told me you would love to have your own kid ... boy or girl," I said.

"Yeah, but not yet. I have plenty of time. I want to make sure that, when I marry, it will be the last time in my life. There will be time for babies," he said with a chuckle.

"Okay, Dave ... I should have known you had already taken that into consideration and prepared for such eventuality. So maybe Rosemary is not the right woman for you ... do you think?"

"I don't really know yet ... I'm not ready to write her off, but I'm not ready to tie the knot yet either. If she can't be patient and she leaves me, then I'll know she is not the right one for me, won't I?"

"Yeah, you would. I just hope she loves you enough to wait for you ... as long as it takes."

"So do I, Mike. I love Alexandra as if she were my own and she is good at training me for fatherhood," he said with a sincere laugh.

"I hope you are right, Dave. I hope she is the right one for you. I remember meeting her at The Carlyle and thinking what a perfect couple you were ... how lucky you were."

"Well, time will tell, Mike. I'm just trying to keep things smooth and taking one day at a time," he said.

"That's the right way to look at it, Dave. So how does it look for *O'Hara*?" I asked.

"We don't have the final answer yet but Jack tells me his sources say things look good - very good - so I'm feeling pretty positive about it."

"Good ... any idea when you'll know for sure, when you would start filming?"

"Not yet, but I'll keep you informed. I'm going to be shooting another Excedrin commercial and Abby has me booked on a few talk shows, so I'm keeping busy ... a lot better than I have been over the last few months," Dave said.

"That's good to hear. I'm still watching *The Fugitive* re-runs ... very good ... now I see why you became so famous so fast," I said.

"Yeah, but I feel that role has me stereo-typed ... that the major film producers and directors don't feel I can make the transition to major films ... and that really pisses me off."

"I know why you think that ... but, hell, I saw you in *The Shoes of the Fisherman, The Green Berets* and *Where It's At* with Rosemary, as a matter of fact, and in no way did you come across as your Kimble character," I said in a serious voice.

"I know, Mike. It seems these idiots think they know everything and, if they have you stereotyped in their minds, nothing will change them. There is also the stupid comparison of me to Clark Gable."

"Personally, I thought you were damn good in the movies. Not once did I look at you and even think of *The Fugitive*; you were very believable in each role. I did think it was a strange your role in *Berets* was a journalist and then, again, in *Fisherman* you played a journalist. Talk about type-casting."

"Yeah, both roles were good. At least I enjoyed the characters in both films. Do you remember *Warning Shot*? I played a cop ... detective."

"Yeah, I do, as a matter of fact ... that was before *The Green Berets* and you were damn good in that one, too. You had a really good supporting cast: Keenan Wynn, Stefanie Powers, Ed Begley and the others," I said.

"Yeah, and it was one of my favorite roles, but it was not so big at the box office. All right, Mike, I have to go ... just take care of yourself and I'll be in touch."

"Okay, Dave ... be sure to let me know when the premier of *O'Hara* will be shown on TV and when you guys get the green light to start making the series. Thanks for calling ... now I know all is okay with you."

"Okay, Mike ... we'll talk soon," Dave said and hung up his phone.

55

I would not hear from Dave again until early March. I had not been concerned because he had appeared in several gossip columns and a couple of fan magazine articles, mostly with Rosemary at this or that restaurant and a few parties with other celebrities.

There was also an article saying CBS announced *O'Hara, U.S. Treasury* would be in their fall line up, citing Dave and Jack Webb had presented the pilot to Secretary of the Treasury, Connally, and had been assured full cooperation by the department. It made a one line mention that Dave and Connally had met in Africa back in 1967.

It was almost 9:30 on the evening of March 7 when my phone rang as I was making a batch of Brandy Alexanders for Rose Marie and a couple of other friends. Rose Marie and Sylvia had prepared a nice dinner for us in my apartment and I was making the after dinner drinks, which Rose Marie, Sylvia and Phil Landskroner had never tasted before. I made my Brandy Alexanders with vanilla ice cream in place of heavy cream. They were rich and creamy and, I am sure, a little fattening.

I answered on the fourth ring.

"Mike, it's Dave ... am I interrupting you?"

"No, Dave, I'm just making some Brandy Alexanders for Rose Marie and a couple of friends. We just finished a great dinner and are going to sit around a while and listen to music."

"Oh ... then I don't want to disturb you. I'll call again later in the week."

"No ... no, it's okay, Dave. I can talk. I see where CBS has bought O'Hara; that is great news. When do you start filming the episodes?"

"We don't have a set schedule yet, probably be the beginning of summer. That's one reason I was calling you. The pilot episode we filmed will be airing on April 2. It will be a two hour Movie of the Week on CBS."

"Man, I am happy to hear that! I've been waiting to see it. I've sort of been keeping tabs on you and Rosemary, through the gossip columns and a couple of articles in *Photo Play* and *Modern Screen,* which I am sure Liberman managed to place. They were nice articles ... says you and Rosemary are a very loving couple."

"Yeah ... again Mike, I caution you ... don't believe all that bullshit in the tabloids; it isn't always like they say it is. I'm glad we have *O'Hara* now. I can hardly wait to get back into the swing of things. You know, I was going to do a major film at Universal before starting on *O'Hara* but I had to drop out. They kept having delays in production and I would not have had time to do it before we began work on the series."

"That's a shame, Dave ... but the series will make you a lot more money, won't it?"

"Oh, yeah ... and, having been out of work for so long, I need it," Dave said in a lighthearted tone.

"I'm happy for you, Dave. I can't wait to see the pilot. I am sure it will be a hit and, before you know it, the media and your fans will look at YOU as a damn good actor, not just as Dr. Richard Kimble."

"That is one thing I'll be working my ass off to achieve, to get away from that damned stereo-type," Dave said.

"I'll be sure to write a good letter about YOU as *O'Hara* to CBS after the pilot airs ... make sure not to mention *The Fugitive* ... just you in the role of a cop ... a Fed," I said with a slight laugh.

"Hey, that would be great ... you'll do that?"

"Of course, I will! I'll send a copy to your office address, okay?"

"Thanks, Mike! Listen! I'll be going down to Florida in a couple of weeks ... maybe you can take some time off and meet me there."

"I wish I could, Dave, but I'm swamped here at the office. Since we have had so much time off over the holidays, we are just piled up with work. What are you going to be doing in Florida?"

"I'm going with Jimmy Farentino and a couple of other guys for some fishing. It will just be for four or five days ... just to have a little relaxation before starting the grind again," Dave said.

"Man, I wish I could join you, Dave. It sounds like a lot of fun, although I've only been fishing once in my life and, to be honest, I found it boring ... waste of time."

"Well, you must have done something wrong. It is a lot of fun, good clean fun and very relaxing. We'll do it sometime ... I'll show you," Dave said with a laugh.

"Okay, Dave, I'll hold you to that ... and I'll keep an open mind."

"All right, Mike! I better let you get back to your party ... I'll be in touch again soon."

"Okay. Thanks for calling, Dave," I said and hung up the phone.

I apologized to Rose Marie, Sylvia and Phil for the interruption and returned to the kitchen. While I was talking with Dave, apparently Rose Marie had told Sylvia and Phil to whom I was speaking.

"Mike, Rose Marie said that was David Janssen, the *fugitive*! How do you know him? Is he really a nice guy? I read about his divorce and it was pretty ugly, if everything they said was true," Sylvia said.

"Yes, Sylvia, that was David Janssen ... we are friends. I met him in Los Angeles in '65. Yeah, his divorce was ugly, but not on Dave's part. Rose Marie met him. Ask her if she thinks he's a nice guy," I responded.

"Oh, yes! He is really a nice guy ... a perfect gentleman ... and, yes, he is very handsome - more so in person than in the movies," Rose Marie chimed in, with smiles and gushes thrown in.

"How did you meet him?" Sylvia asked Rose Marie.

"He was here in New York with his girlfriend and Mike took me to meet him and then, a few nights later, we had dinner with him and his girlfriend," Rose Marie replied.

"Who is his girlfriend? Is it that same actress who broke up his marriage?" Sylvia looked to Rose Marie for the answer. What a couple of old lady type gossips; I smiled in my mind.

"Yes, it is Rosemary Forsyth. She had a baby and divorced her husband after meeting David and they did a couple of nude scenes in the movie, *Where It's At*. Mike took me to see the movie when it came out here; it was a good movie. You should see it," Rose Marie replied.

"Well, are they going to get married?" Sylvia asked, looking to Rose Marie and, then, to me.

"I seriously doubt it - at least, not anytime in the immediate future. Dave's divorce cost him millions; he is being pretty cautious about getting married again ... at least for a couple of years," I replied.

"We saw him in *The Green Berets* with John Wayne. It was a great movie. He was good, too. He was a journalist ... against the Viet Nam War. John Wayne was an Army colonel ... he did not like Janssen's character," Phil said.

"Well, to tell the truth, Dave really is against the war in Viet Nam and he does not like John Wayne ... in real life, as a person," I said.

"He doesn't like John Wayne as a person. What do you mean? How do you know?" Phil asked.

"Dave thinks Wayne is an extraordinary actor, very professional. As a person, he found him to be arrogant, a super egotistical personality who thinks his shit doesn't stink. He almost had a fist fight on *The Green Berets* set with Wayne.

"Wayne was giving this young Asian actor a really hard time because he screwed up a scene; Dave went to defend the kid and Wayne got really pissed off and started some shit with Dave. He was about to take him on when the director and several others stepped in to keep them from fighting.

"Anyway, that happened on a Friday morning ... that evening, Dave chartered a Boeing 737 and flew half the crew to Las Vegas for the whole weekend. The producer and director had to beg Dave to bring them back. They were delaying the production and that was costing a hell of a lot of money," I said.

I served the Brandy Alexanders and everyone was pleased with them. Each confirmed he and she were now hooked on Brandy Alexanders as an after dinner drink.

We sat around and talked for a couple of hours, then I took Rose Marie to her home. Phil and Sylvia left for theirs.

56

The Eleven O'clock News had just started on CBS Friday, April 2, when my phone rang.

"Mike, it's Dave ... did you see the show?"

"Of course, I did! I thought it was great. I really, honestly think you have another hit on your hands and, although your fans will still remember you as *Dr. Richard Kimble*, they will see you as *Special Agent, Jim O'Hara, U. S. Treasury Department* after a few episodes," I proclaimed exuberantly.

"I sure hope you're right. It feels good ... waiting for the morning editions to see what the critics say about it," Dave said.

"Have you talked with Mr. Webb yet? How does he feel about the potential success of the show?" I asked.

"Rosemary and I watched it together with Jack and his wife. The girls liked it ... felt it had an official feel to it ... even thought I was good as a Fed," Dave said with a slight laugh.

"I have to agree with them; you are very good ... very official. The plot was good. I have to admit I was kept in suspense all the way to the end."

"I really appreciate that, Mike. I know you are being objective, honest. I'll let you know what the critics say," Dave said.

"I'll let you know what the New York critics have to say. I'll clip anything I see about *O'Hara* and send them to you."

"Thanks, Mike! I appreciate that. I'll give you a call when I know what our shooting schedule will be like. I'm off to Florida now for a few days ... *fishing*!"

"Is Rosemary going with you?" I asked.

"Hell, no! This is for the guys ... no women allowed. Too bad you can't join us. I know you would like it."

"I believe I would and I wish I could get away; we have so many backlogs here in the office, there is just no way I could."

"Well, maybe next time. I'll give you a call when I'm back in LA. Take care, Mike," Dave said then ended the call.

I did not ask Dave where he was, but the background noise made me think he could be at The Formosa. If, indeed, he was, I doubted Rosemary was with him. I was glad to hear his positive thoughts about the prospects for *O'Hara* and his personal future. Since it had been almost five years since the end of *The Fugitive,* I felt his fans would be thrilled to see him in another weekly series. Time would tell.

The fact Dave called me soon after the premier of *O'Hara* asking my opinion made me feel good. I felt he valued my opinion.

Saturday morning, I bought all the newspapers on my way back to my apartment from Baron's run in the park. I would take the papers with me to my corner restaurant and peruse them over breakfast. I found reviews in *The New York Times, The New York Post* and *The New York Daily News.*

The reviews were not bad; for the most part, they were positive and very strong for Dave's performance. There was a hint in a couple that Jack Webb's *just the facts* way of making police procedural television shows was somewhat noticeable.

The ratings were not that good: third behind the established *The Partridge Family* on NBC and *Room 222* on ABC in this prime-time slot. I hoped the reviews in the west coast papers and trade papers would be more encouraging and to Dave's liking.

I would give Dave my opinion and the synopsis of the reviews the next time he called. I was sure he or his publicist had already obtained not only the New York papers but those of major television markets nationwide. My opinion was the show had great promise, conditioned on future scripts with a little more realism.

I saw Jack Webb's *just the facts* of the storyline and dialogue of his *Dragnet* television series - which drew from actual cases in the files of the Los Angeles Police Department.

I spent a leisurely Saturday around my apartment, completed some shopping and relaxed.

I clipped the reviews of *O'Hara* and mailed them to Dave, even though I was certain he would have them. I had hopes Dave would call either this evening or Sunday.

Dave did call me Sunday, April 4, before departing for Florida for his much deserved fishing trip.

"Hey, Mike! It's Dave. Just wanted you to know the reviews in the papers here are pretty damn positive ... I feel good about our prospects. We are up against more established shows on the other networks, but I'm sure CBS will keep a close eye on the ratings and maybe shift our time slot."

"Yeah, I saw in the New York papers that it came in third in the Nielsen ratings, but that's for the premier. Maybe CBS will change your time slot when the first real episode airs. Do you have any idea when the series will start airing?"

"Not yet ... we'll start production in a couple of months. I'll let you know. We're leaving for Florida this evening, may even go to the Bahamas or the Virgin Islands ... nothing set in stone ... depends on how the fish are biting," Dave said.

"I envy you, Dave ... just relax, have fun and put everything else out of your mind," I proffered.

"Yeah, that is exactly what I'm going to do ... clear my mind and not think of anything here in LA."

"Good ... by the way, how are things on your home front? Is Rosemary being a good girl?" I asked.

"Well ... that would be hard to say. Let me just say I am not about to make any wedding plans. To be honest, Mike, I think it may be coming to an end. She is 12 years younger than me and I think she is starting to feel the difference in our lifestyles."

"As I've always said to you ... just be careful. I don't want to see you get hurt ... or burned like you did with Ellie," I said.

"I know. Thanks, Mike! Funny thing ... Ellie was older than me but I never felt the age difference had any affect on our lifestyle. I'll tell you, though, there is no way I will be screwed again like I was," he said.

"Okay, Dave ... enjoy your fishing and let me know what you catch."

"I'll do that, although I usually throw them back in the water, unless I'm hungry for fish." He laughed.

The call ended and I made myself a scotch and water and sat down to reflect on how positive Dave sounded, yet I still felt concerned about his situation with Rosemary.

I knew Dave was very much in love with Alexandra, but he did not sound like he was willing to marry Rosemary for Alexandra. I could not help but wonder what reaction Rosemary would have, or what she would do, if and when Dave told her marriage was not in his plans.

57

I did not hear from Dave again until May 2. He did send me a postcard from Saint Thomas. Of course, I felt it was his way of making me jealous for failing to take him up on his invitation.

"Hey, Mike! Dave ... how is everything?"

"Great, Dave! I thought you had forgotten me; it's been a while," I said, joking.

"I sent you a postcard so you know I didn't forget you. Anyway, just wanted to let you know I am back. We will start production of *O'Hara* the first of next month so you know I'm going to be pretty damn busy."

"That is good to hear. How was your trip? Did you catch a lot of fish?"

"Yeah, actually, quite a few. We chartered a boat and went from Miami on down to the islands ... Saint Thomas. Everyone had a great time and it gave me some rejuvenation time I sorely needed."

"I'm happy for you. I did receive your postcard from there ... thought you were rubbing it in that I could not join you; you really know how to hurt a guy," I said.

"I was not rubbing it in ... although, you did miss out on a hell of a lot of fun; we all had a great time."

"Okay, I'll forgive you this time but, the next time, come hell or high water, count me in. I'll go ... no matter what," I said with a laugh. "So tell me ... are you glad to be home? Did Rosemary and Alexandra miss you?"

"Well, I feel Alexandra missed me. I really don't think Rosemary did ... but that's no big deal."

"That doesn't sound too good. I mean, you guys have been together almost two years. You have a lot invested there and I'm not talking about money. Do you have any plans? What are you going to do ... if I may ask?"

"I haven't really given it any serious thought but I feel like we are coming to a close. She has been pretty frigid since I got home, if you know what I mean."

"Dave, after what you went through with Ellie - remember, she named Rosemary as a co-respondent - I just hope Rosemary doesn't try and sue you ... a Breach of Promise suit ... maybe saying you promised to marry her if she divorced Tolan."

"I've been thinking about that. I really don't think she would do that, though. I've been good to her and Alexandra and I always made it clear to her, during and after the proceedings with Ellie, I was not going to even consider getting married for quite some time. I've never misled her. I don't think she would try and hurt me; I think she will just let me go."

"I sure as hell hope you're right. You know her, I don't; I just don't want to see you hurt, especially to be hurt in your bank account."

"I know, Mike. I appreciate that. I'm going to try to keep things sort of status quo for a while. Maybe things will get better once we start production."

"So you're admitting you do love her ... still," I said.

"Oh, yeah, Mike! I love her, but I have to admit it is not like it was the first year or so. People change ... things change ... you know that."

"I know, Dave, and it is much better to learn that - for both people to accept it and deal with it as adults, without all the acrimony, name calling, threats ... revenge," I said.

"You speak as a wise man, Mike ... I'll remember that," Dave said with a slight chuckle.

"Well, let's just hope and pray that, once you are back to a full work schedule, she will lighten up and realize you do love her and accept that she is better off with you and not married than to be not married and without you."

"I agree with you, Mike ... let's hope."

"It would probably be hard on Alexandra if you split. You're the only father she really knows."

"I know, in a way. Tolan still sees her when he can, but I'm the one she sees every day ... in our home ... so you're right. She probably looks at me as her daddy."

"Well, Dave, keep me informed. Don't let me read about a nasty split in the tabloids," I said.

"I'll keep you informed, Mike. I'll be in touch soon. You take care," Dave said, ending our call.

After the call, I was pleased to hear the positive attitude Dave expressed. He was happy to be getting back to work, even though he had never intended to do another series.

May 9, I watched the Emmys on television. I was surprised to see Dave and Suzanne Pleshette presenting an award. I was in awe! I knew Dave had really fallen for Suzanne when she appeared as a guest star on *The Fugitive* and, had he been able to obtain a divorce in a more timely fashion, I was certain they would have married.

As it was, Dave met Rosemary on the *Where It's At* film and they fell in love. Soon after he and Rosemary were publicly known to be a couple, Suzanne married. By all public reports, Suzanne was happily married to Thomas Gallagher.

As Dave and Suzanne waited for the winner to make it to the stage, I noticed they were exchanging whispers and loving smiles. I could not help but think that, had Dave married Suzanne, they would both have been very happy.

Dave had not told me about his being a presenter at the Emmys, let alone that he would be paired with his old flame, Suzanne. I made a mental note to ask about this the next time we spoke.

Dave called early on Sunday, June 6. I had just fallen into a deep sleep when the phone woke me. I looked at the clock on my nightstand; it was five minutes after five.

"Hello ... this better be Dave Janssen or I'm going to hang up."

"Mike, it's Dave. I guess I woke you ... sorry about that. Just wanted to touch base with you ... see how you're doing."

"Thanks, Dave! All is well here ... just working and working and working, not too much time for play."

"Well, you have to make time for yourself, Mike. We are in full production mode on the series ... feels good to be back working full time." He sounded very sober but a little depressed.

"How do you like it? How are the people you're working with; are you happy with them?" I asked.

"Oh, yeah! They put together a great crew ... everyone on the team are all pros ... good people."

"That's good to know ... helps make the show a success, doesn't it?"

"Oh, yeah! I feel really good with them and, when we go on location, most of them will go with us. I feel good about the show but I don't even want to think I'll still be doing it four years from now," Dave said with a laugh.

"You'll have to wait and see, Dave. Maybe your fans will be begging you for more, more, more," I said with a laugh, then asked, "So how are things on the home front? Has Rosemary adjusted to you working? Is she a little more loving?"

"Hell, no! I think it is over between us. I think I'm too old for her and I'll be damned if I'll let any woman try and control me again."

"So what are your plans? What are you going to do?"

"Well, as soon as she starts talking to me again, I think I'll just ask her what she wants to do. I mean, I'm not just going to kick her to the curb, but I want a strong relationship ... with real love."

"Yeah, I sure as hell know what you mean there. Have you guys been fighting? You said she's not talking to you. How in the hell do you communicate?"

"She's been giving me the cold shoulder for almost a month and that's going to end. I'm already hearing people – people who are supposed to be my friends - talking behind my back. Someone is saying I'm a fucking drunk ... and that pisses me off!"

"You don't think Rosemary is telling people you're a drunk, do you? I mean, she can match you drink for drink from what I've seen."

"No, I don't think she's saying it. It's just a bunch of backstabbers in this town; you can't trust anyone out here, especially in this business. I'm just fed up with the whole damn town."

"Well, you know, Dave ... my best advice has always been, take it one day at a time. You will work things out and you'll come out on top ... hell, you always do."

"Okay, I'll follow your advice, little brother. Go back to sleep. I'll call you later." Dave ended the call.

I went to the kitchen and turned on the coffee pot, then put fresh water in Baron's bowl. I decided I would have some coffee, watch the first part of the news and then take Baron to Riverside Park.

58

Dave called me Saturday evening, June 26, just before the six o'clock news on ABC.

"Hey, Mike! Dave ... how are things with you?"

"This is a surprise! It's only about three o'clock your time or is this a real surprise and you're at The Carlyle?"

"No, I'm in LA. I had to work today. We are on a lunch break so I thought I'd give you a call. Is everything good with you? How's Rose Marie?"

"Yeah, all is good with me. I'm picking Rose Marie up at eight for dinner and a movie. So how are things with Rosemary?"

"Glad to hear you're okay ... and Rose Marie. Things with Rosemary and me are all fucked up - and it is not just my drinking. She's pretty damn good at that; she just won't admit it, and she has one hell of a temper when she's had a few. It doesn't take much to set her off. She's not a happy drunk like me.

"Mike, I've tried to bring things back to where we were. I just don't see anything getting better. I'm trying to figure a way out - a nice way out, without hurting her or causing a scandal of any kind for either of us."

"I was kind of expecting that. If I was in your shoes, Dave, I would plan a nice dinner at home. After your cook serves, give her the rest of the night off. Make certain Alexandra is someplace else, out of the house. Then I'd say something like, 'Rosemary, I feel you aren't happy anymore. You aren't happy with me so I think, as two adults who care for each other, we should just go our separate ways.' That's what I would do.

"Of course, you should have nothing to drink before this - a bottle of good wine at dinner, okay or, for you, Dave, maybe one or two scotches before dinner. Oh, and I'd wait until near the end of dinner before you lay this on her."

"Damn, Mike! You amaze me! I would not have thought of that ... sounds like a good plan to me. Actually sounds like it will work. If she really is unhappy living with me, then it would be the easiest way for her to agree and then I could make plans to move out."

"I'm glad you agree with me, that it is a good plan. However, why should you be the one to move out? You're the one leasing the house. You like that house. You've been paying all the household expenses. Knowing you, you've probably been paying all the expenses, so why should you be the one to move?"

"Mike, I'm not about to kick her and Alexandra to the curb! What kind of guy do you think I am?" Dave asked sternly.

"Dave ... whoa! I don't think you're a bad guy! I was just saying that, since you leased the house and you have paid all the bills, maybe you would want to stay there and, of course, you would help Rosemary get a place for Alexandra and her."

"I know, but I'll be the one to move out. They are settled in and happy there. I can move ... easier for me. I'll pay a couple of months in advance for her and that will be it."

"You know what you're doing and I think you're being a perfect gentleman about it. I hope it works out for you. Let me ask you, though: do you think she is feeling there is too much of an age difference between you?"

"I don't really know, but I think there is. I just felt great when we started. There I was 12 years older, made me feel like I still had it - but I'll admit, Mike, it may be that plus our mutual love for booze. I don't know. I just know she's not happy and neither am I so we have to go our separate ways."

"You are right. I just hope it works out for both of you," I said. "Promise me you'll keep me informed, will you? I don't want to read about you and Rosemary in a scandal."

"Don't worry, Mike! I'll keep you informed. I'm not going to do it right away ... but I'll let you know."

"I thought you didn't work on weekends," I said.

"Usually, we don't, but sometimes we need certain weather conditions for outside shots; that's why we worked today. It doesn't bother me ... gives me a reason to be out of the house."

"So I guess there's still a little tension in the house?"

"On and off ... I never know when I wake up what kind of mood she'll be in. It changes from minute to minute."

"Well ... maybe you should think seriously about having that nice, quiet dinner at home ... just the two of you," I suggested.

"Yes, I'm sure that's what I'll do. I'm just waiting for the right time. I'll let you know before it happens."

"I really feel for you my friend. My wife and I went through a lot of mood changes ... and it was no fun ... no fun at all."

"Rosemary is really a great girl. I'm not the easiest guy to live with, especially when I'm not working and have so much time on my hands. I know it's not all her fault but I do think whatever love or feelings she did have for me have pretty much evaporated."

"Okay, Dave ... you know best how to handle it."

"Right, Mike ... hey, they're calling us back. We'll talk later," Dave said and hung up the phone.

I knew Dave was feeling very confident in himself, now that he had a new series and knew he had at least 22 shows to make. That would keep him busy for the rest of the year, and probably a good part of next year. I felt better for him but I knew his home life was causing him some undue stress which he did not need, especially starting a new series.

I was still buying *TV Guide, Photoplay* and *Modern Screen* magazines to make certain I did not miss any coverage of Dave's public activities. Lately there had been a few articles in the magazines hyping *O'Hara.*

Dave and Rosemary had appeared in photos taken of them in restaurants and, in some of the photos, it appeared that Rosemary was not happy being where she was, or being with Dave.

I wondered if the photographers noticed, or others would see the photos and pick up on the expressions on Rosemary's face.

Considering what Dave had told me, I had no doubt the end of their relationship was imminent. I only hoped Rosemary would agree and they could remain friends.

59

Dave had a hard life as a child growing up with a staunch stage mother. He traveled with her for a couple of years while she was employed with the road shows of the *Ziegfeld Follies*. Then, in 1940, soon after his ninth birthday, she placed him in the McKinley Home for Boys where he remained until he was almost 12.

Dave had discussed this only briefly when we compared our childhood experiences and our mothers. I got the feeling he did not like talking about that period of his life. Dave had been the target of bullying by a gang of older boys in McKinley and, although he learned to stand up for himself, he hated the time he was there.

His mother would tell him she would be there to take him home on weekends, but she would not show up. She would call and tell him she would visit him on Sunday and she would not show up or even call. It always embarrassed David because, when she did call, he was summoned to the office to receive the call; he knew everyone in the office would be listening.

It was clear he had not forgiven his mother for what he felt was her abandonment of him. I had no doubt in my mind that was the reason he insisted on bringing Ellie's daughters to live with them when they married and found a home. He hated the idea that Ellie had placed her daughters in exclusive boarding schools.

Personally, I think he held this against Ellie and it may have been the reason his mother and Ellie never got along. I think they each had that guilt on their conscience.

When his mother met, and was courted by, Eugene Janssen, Dave was paid a lot of attention by Mr. Janssen. When they were married, a bond developed between Mr. Janssen and Dave early on; Dave felt for the first time in his life he had a *real* father.

In December, 1942, Gene and his mother welcomed their first child, a daughter they named Teri. Dave was 12 and ecstatic about having a little sister. Three years later, they had another daughter, Jill; their family was complete. Dave was the epitome of the big brother.

As Dave enrolled in Fairfax High School, he assumed his step-father's name, becoming David Janssen for the rest of his life. He also began calling Gene *Dad*.

During his third year at Fairfax, Dave had developed a love for sports and was an outstanding player on the basketball team, as well as excelling in track and pole vaulting. His personal ambition was to play professional sports.

In 1945, he was picked for a small role in the RKO Studios film, *It's a Pleasure*. Dave enjoyed the action of movie making. He was cast as Johnny Weissmuller's little brother in the Paramount film *Swamp Fire*, released in 1946. He was looking at acting as just a way to make some money for college.

In his senior year at Fairfax, Dave had an accident as he was demonstrating his pole vaulting skills and seriously injured his left knee. This injury ended his dream of professional sports but opened the door for him to give serious thought to an acting career.

His knee injury would continue to cause him pain as he grew older. Over time, he had no less than four surgeries on his knee; still it was never perfect. When you see the limp *Harry O* had, that was not acting ... it was real.

Living through his mother's two divorces embedded in Dave's mind that divorce was absolute failure. His mother's divorce from Gene Janssen really bothered him. To Dave, he was an excellent father, a devoted husband and a good provider.

Dave maintained a close relationship with Gene after the divorce. I believe that was the reasoning behind Dave's desperate attempts to stay in his marriage with Ellie, especially the last three-plus years during which he was living in what he called *hell on earth*.

I knew darn well why Dave had not proposed marriage to Rosemary, knowing that is what she wanted. It appeared to me his life was again in turmoil. I felt it was only a matter of time and the end of his relationship with Rosemary would be front page news, not only in Hollywood, but around the world.

Dave was a very private man who kept his fears, insecurities and pain bottled up inside his mind. He drew on his skills as an actor in such a way to conceal his inner pain from the world. I feel certain that he shared his secrets not only with me but a few very close friends.

I know Dave considered Jimmy Farentino, James Garner, Paul Burke, Steve Lodge, Raymond Burr, Jackie Cooper, Rock Hudson, Milton Berle and Johnny Carson to be *true* friends in Hollywood, so I feel positive they may have known what he was going through. I know for a fact his closest friend, Paul Burke, knew as he told me so many years later.

To his legions of fans around the world, he was *David Janssen – The Fugitive*, a handsome man who had a beautiful wife, was rich and famous ... he had it all and, to his fans, he was always smiling and upbeat so all they saw was a happy man.

I enjoyed a few scotch and waters as a way to relax and unwind from a hard day's work. I believe Dave used alcohol as an escape from the pressures put on him by Ellie, now Rosemary, and the demands of his very public life.

I must admit watching Dave as he began drinking more and more worried me. I could tell by his voice when he would call me just how drunk he was at the time.

I was surprised when Dave called me on Sunday, July 4, as I had just awakened at six o'clock. I could tell he was drinking but he was far from being what one would call drunk.

"Good morning, Mike ... Happy Fourth of July!"

"Good morning, Dave, and the same to you. How the heck are you?"

"I'm good, Mike ... enjoying a nice long weekend."

"Well, let's see ... it's about three o'clock in the morning in LA so I know you're not playing golf. You must be at The Formosa ... am I right?"

"No, not this time. I'm in Palm Springs. I'm just leaving my favorite watering hole. I saw the time and thought you'd be up by now; if not, I'd wake you up."

"So I take it Rosemary isn't with you?"

"No ... I'm solo ... it's more relaxing this way. So how is everything in the city?"

"Going well ... a lot of festivities this weekend so I'm taking Rose Marie to Central Park to watch fireworks after dinner tonight. What are your plans? Anything special?"

"No, not for me ... nothing but total relaxation."

"Well, that's good ... you probably need a little *R and R*; you certainly deserve it. So how are things with Rosemary? I saw a photo last week in one of the fan magazines of you two at some black-tie affair and neither one of you looked too happy," I said.

"That's probably because neither one of us was happy. I don't know where we were, some damned party we had to go to. Anyway, I'm giving serious thought about having that dinner with her. I'm thinking of it as our farewell dinner. I would never hurt her intentionally but, since I've been ignoring the marriage subject, I know she has not been happy."

"By all accounts, and from all the press reports, I think not only Rosemary - but the whole world - expected you guys to get married before the ink was dry on your divorce decree."

"Yeah, I know, and I'm still peppered with questions about when I'm gonna do it ... and it pisses me off. I just have to smile and shake my head."

"Do you shake your head up and down or sideways?"

"Both ... to keep the idiots asking confused," Dave said with a big laugh.

"Well, tell me, what does Rosemary say ... lately, I mean? Does she flat-out ask you, does she hint at it ... has she told you she'll leave you if you don't marry her?"

"All of that; it's been going on before my divorce was final. She got an uncontested divorce from Tolan in Mexico. She didn't have any problem with him and she damn sure didn't lose half of all she'd worked for over the course of her marriage to him."

"Dave, I damn sure don't blame you for not wanting to get married again ... at least, so soon after your divorce – and, for Christ's sake, you have to be really, really in love with her and you have to know she loves you just as much!"

"I know, Mike, but you don't really know what I went through with Ellie. She turned out to be my worst nightmare and the cost was so damned unfair. No, Mike, I think it's going to be quite a while before I risk being burned again. I mean she should be happy. We've been together going on three years. I go to work, I come home, I pay the bills. I've never cheated on her. We live the same as if we were married. Why does she want to fuck that up? I just don't get it."

"Dave, from what you've been telling me these past few months, it sounds like neither one of you are happy living together anymore ... and if it's your refusal to make your relation legal, as they say, then I'd say the sooner you have that farewell dinner - as you call it - the better for both of you."

"I know, Mike, and I'm leaning towards doing just that; it's just a matter of the timing. I'll be sure to let you know when I do it. Okay, I'm heading back to the hotel to get some sleep. You get your ass out of your bed and take your dog out. I'll be in touch," Dave said with a slight laugh.

"Okay, Dave ... thanks for the call and have a good weekend," I said and hung up.

I thought about Dave's situation all weekend, even to the point Rose Marie noticed my mind was not on our activities. I could not talk to Rose Marie about Dave's private business so I put him out of my mind while I was with her.

As it turned out, we had a great July Fourth and, after the fireworks in Central Park, we stopped at the Oak Bar in The Plaza Hotel for a nightcap and then I drove Rose Marie home. I was home before midnight and took Baron for a quick run in Riverside Park.

60

I had renewed my daily and weekly purchases of the New York newspapers and the fan magazines, including my subscription to *TV Guide*. Considering my conversations with Dave over the past couple of months, I did not want to miss any articles about Dave and Rosemary.

There had been numerous photos of Dave and Rosemary in the fan magazines over the past few weeks taken at various social functions or popular LA restaurants.

Some of the photos showed them holding hands and smiling as they entered or left a restaurant. There were also a couple where their facial expressions showed tension between them. Still, I was relieved there were no earth-shattering rumors or allegations pertaining to their relationship.

Dave's next call came in the pre-dawn hours of Saturday, July 30. I could tell he was close to his limit of alcohol; his speech was very slurred and he sounded so tired and, I would say, depressed.

"Mike ... it's Dave. Are you okay ... awake?"

"Uh ... good morning, Dave ... yeah, I'm awake ... now. What's going on? Are you okay?"

"Ah ... yeah, I think so. I'm ahh ... going home. I wanted to give you a call and make sure you're okay. I haven't talked to you lately," Dave said.

"Yeah, Dave, I'm fine. Why wouldn't I be? My question is how the hell are you? You sound like you've had quite a bit to drink. You're not driving, are you?"

"Ah ... yeah ... I guess I have ... uh ... I don't ... no ... uh ... I'm not driving. You know me ... better than that ... just wanted to say hello ... and make sure you're okay."

I knew from his voice he was having real problems and I assumed it was with Rosemary. "So tell me Dave, what's going on? Is everything okay? Is everything okay with Rosemary?"

"No ... no, it's not okay with Rosemary; it's so messed up. She makes it sound like I am a real son-of-a-bitch 'cause I don't want to marry her. Hell, I just don't want to marry anyone at all ... plain and simple. Easy to understand, right? I just don't understand what she doesn't understand, why she doesn't understand."

"I know, Dave. After all this time, you would think she would understand - especially since she was there with you almost every day you were in court."

"I know ... I know ... you would think she could understand ... and accept it. Damn it! I've been good to her ... I've been damn good to her ... and to Alexandra. I can't give her what she wants ... she just don't understand."

"Well ... how is she acting now ... towards you? Is she being argumentative ... cold ... indifferent? I mean how is she treating you at home?"

"Sometimes ... sometimes she ... she acts like she did when we first ... met. Sometimes she is so cold ... she won't even talk to me ... for days. I'm ... I think it's really over ... I've gotta do something ... I can't live like this ... damn ... I'm damn glad I didn't marry her."

"Well, Dave, no one can say how she would be if you did marry her. Maybe everything would be okay. Maybe you would both be happy. You just don't know the answer to that."

"No ... no, Mike ... I think you're wrong ... I know her. She would be the same even if ... if we got married. I think it would be the same. She thinks I've been fucking this girl on my show. I didn't. I haven't ... I just had dinner with her one night ... after we worked late."

"Damn, Dave! Did you tell her you had dinner with another woman?"

"No ... hell, no! She heard it from someone ... hell, I don't even know how she heard about it, but it was nothing but a damned dinner."

"Yeah ... but I remember you telling me about telling Ellie the first time you had dinner with Suzanne, and you know what that started with Ellie," I said.

"Yeah, but it was the same. I just had a damned dinner ... that's all. What the hell! Can't I take someone to dinner without starting World War III?"

"Well, yeah ... you should be able to, but it sounds like she is just like Ellie. Now she thinks you're cheating on her and that's not good.

Dave, you have to get out of this mess ... for your sake! Why don't you have that dinner with her ... or do it any way you think is best ... but you have to get out of this situation! It's hurting you and I can tell - as you've said repeatedly - neither one of you is happy.

"You feel it's over; she probably does, too, but now she thinks you're cheating on her ... throwing it in her face, and that's not you. I know that, but you have to do something to end this. That's my opinion, Dave ... it's not good for you or Rosemary."

"Yeah, I know, Mike. You're not the only one that tells me that ... I'll do something ... soon ... uh . . . uh my cab is here ... call you later ... thanks for listening ... talk later." He hung up the phone.

I was wide awake and very worried about Dave. The way he sounded was really bad. He rarely goes over what he knows to be his limit of alcohol. He sounded very drunk and very depressed.

I had a fleeting thought of calling Rosemary and that's all, just a fleeting thought. I realized it was not my place to butt into their lives and Dave would probably be very angry if I did.

It was hard to be in my position as his friend – 3,000 miles away, not really knowing Rosemary well enough to even talk to her about their situation. I had it in my mind the age difference had become, or was now, a factor in her feelings toward Dave. I did not mention this to Dave because I did not want to anger him, but I felt he may have the same thoughts as me.

Dave had told me he was going home but I did not know if he was in LA and going to the home he shared with Rosemary and Alexandra, or if he was in Palm Springs and was going to his hotel.

I resolved in my mind there was nothing I could do and I would just hope to hear from him soon, just so I would know he made it home.

I would be in for a long wait.

During August of 1971, I scrutinized every newspaper and fan magazine looking for anything about Dave, or Rosemary and Dave. There was nothing at all relating to them and just a few articles about Dave and his *O'Hara* series.

Finally, on August 29, my phone jolted me awake. Clicking on my nightstand lamp, seeing the time - 4:15 in the morning - I knew it must be Dave. I certainly did not mind being awakened.

"Good morning, Dave. It's about time you called. I've been pretty concerned. Where are you? What is going on with you? Enquiring minds want to know!" I said before he said a word.

"How'd you know it's me?" he asked with a laugh.

"Dave, in the seven years I've known you, no one calls me after midnight or before six in the morning. I deduced it had to be you," I laughed. "So tell me, did you and Rosemary just get back from your honeymoon?"

"Hell, no! Are you crazy! It's over ... I moved out and it is really over and she knows it," he said in a firm voice.

"So you finally had that farewell dinner?"

"No...no! I wish we had ... no, we had a big fight a couple of weeks ago and it was nasty and very public. Embarrassed the hell out of me and that was the final straw," he said.

"How in the hell did that happen? Where were you? In a restaurant ... on the street?"

"We were at the race track with a couple of my friends ... and, of course, we all had a few drinks. I must have said something that didn't sit well with her and she just exploded! All hell broke loose ... and I blew up, too ... so the whole damn weekend went down the toilet!"

"What the hell did you do?"

"I don't know what the hell I did! I just said something she just didn't like; I don't even know what in the hell I said, but I'll never let her embarrass me again in front of my friends ... or anyone."

"So ... what did you do then?"

"We split there at the track. I went home and packed. I got the hell out of there. She's called me several times but I haven't talked to her yet."

"Where'd you go? Are you staying with friends or in a hotel?"

"No, I'm staying in my bungalow at the studio. I'll find an apartment soon, when I have time," he said.

"Well, I'm sorry to hear it ended that way - instead of a nice, quiet dinner, talking calmly as friends – but, if it had to happen that way, maybe it is for the best. At least, you know the love you felt for each other wasn't meant to last."

"I know, Mike. People fall in love and, just as quick and easy, they fall out of love. I know now I'll NEVER get married again!" Dave declared.

"Well, I'll tell you, Dave ... I am really glad you called. After our last talk, you sounded very drunk, very tired and very depressed. You said then you were going home but I didn't know whether you were in

LA and going home or if you were in Palm Springs and going to your hotel. Not hearing from you for a month really had me worried."

"I'm sorry. I know I had told you I would call you, but this happened so fast ... not my plan - and I've really been very busy. I'm really sorry I didn't call before now."

"That's okay. You called now so I can quit losing sleep over it. How do you feel about it, though? Are you glad it's over? What do you plan on doing? Do you think she'll sue you for Breach of Promise?" I asked.

"Are you kidding me? I NEVER promised her a damn thing - never made any promise to her that I did not keep!"

"I haven't seen anything in the media. Has Mr. Liberman been keeping a lid on it?" I asked.

"No, there have been a couple of small blurbs of bullshit in the rags here, but nothing big and no one knows any details. It's sure to hit the press soon, but Frank will handle it."

"Well, Dave, at least you can breathe now. I feel sorry for Alexandra but you said her father sees her quite often so she'll be all right. That part must be hard on you, though."

"Yeah ... that is the sad part but it's time to move on; things will work out. Okay, so now you know straight from me. You didn't read about it! I have to run, Mike. I promise I'll call you in a few days."

"Thanks, Dave! You take it easy ... be careful."

61

Dave was busy filming *O'Hara* and I assumed he was having his secretary seeking a suitable home or apartment for him. Not hearing from him for almost three weeks was not unusual, so I did not worry. I still had not seen in the printed media, or heard on TV or radio, anything about him and Rosemary's split. I was sure Dave's publicist Frank Liberman was keeping it out of the press.

The Hollywood press loved Dave and it was clear to me he loved them back. He always accommodated them when they asked for interviews, and he never said a bad word about the press, that I knew of.

Saturday, September 18, Dave called just as the sun was rising over New York City.

"Good morning, Mike! Happy Birthday!"

"Good morning, Dave ... thank you! I still don't know how you remember everyone's birthday. How are you? Have you found a home yet? How is the series going?"

"Mike, we both have good memories," Dave said with a laugh. "I'm doing good, still living in my bungalow, but Victor is looking to find a place for me. It's not so bad here: I am never late for work, I don't go out as much as I used to, I have a cook, I have a full bar ... so things are good. How about you?"

"Everything here is great. Rose Marie and I are still together ... no pressure for me to get a divorce ... at least, not yet," I said with a laugh.

"That's good to hear. Have you been watching the show?"

"Of course! Are you kidding me? I haven't missed a single episode! I like it ... sometimes I see a little of Jack Webb's *Dragnet* come through ... subtle ... but I can see it. How is it doing? Do you feel good about it?"

"Well, Mike, the ratings have been fluctuating a little too much in my opinion. I think we have good writers and every episode is based on an actual case handled by the Treasury department; that's encouraging.

"Yeah, I think maybe the writers slip some of *Dragnet* in to keep Jack happy. Still, we are up against established shows that have strong following by their fans. I'm not counting the show out; Jack is speaking to the network about a time change, so we shall see."

"Well, I like it ... I'm pretty sure it will pick up a lot of your fans from your movies and of course, *The Fugitive*. So has Rosemary been in touch with you? Are you two going to remain friends? Will you get to visit Alexandra?" I asked.

"No, I'm afraid our relationship is over ... completely over. She called several times when I first moved out. I did not talk to her and she found a place and moved a couple of months later. I haven't heard a word from her ... it's better this way."

"I still haven't seen anything in the media about it. Surely, they all know you moved out of the house. Has Mr. Liberman been keeping it quiet? I thought there would be a bunch of nasty rumors flying once the media found out about it."

"Frank's been doing his job ... no one is saying anything ... at least, to me. A couple of the columnists I am friendly with have asked; I told them the truth and they haven't printed anything ... yet. I really don't give a damn. It doesn't matter to me."

"You've got the right attitude, Dave. Everyone working on *The Fugitive* thought your divorce would hurt the show and your career so you continued to live in that oppressive situation. You waited a whole year before you ended it. I don't know how you did but it doesn't look like it hurt you professionally in any way, at least, not to me."

"Oh, I think it did hurt me, Mike ... at least a little. Abby said he had some resistance from the studios getting me good roles in major films, but Ellie and her lawyers made it sound like Rosemary was the reason for our break-up ... and you know Rosemary had nothing to do with it. Ellie made it sound like I was an adulterer ... that I was going after an impressionable girl who was much too young for me. Yeah, I think it hurt me a little."

"Okay, you know better than me, but I don't think it hurt you as far as your fans are concerned," I countered.

"Yeah, I think you are right there. I haven't seen any drop in fan mail so that's good; I'm very grateful for that."

"I'm glad to hear that. So are you just working and working and working? Don't you get out at all? There has to be some beautiful gal out there that could make you feel better ... help you relax after work," I said.

"Plenty of time for that, Mike. Now I just want to relax and concentrate on the show. I need a break from being tied down, Mike."

"Okay ... just be careful with the next girl you fall for. Make sure she knows you're not going to be ready for marriage ... for a while ... until YOU are ready."

"Don't worry, Mike! I'll make that damn clear ... no misinterpretations ... no problems. You know what? It's funny. This is the first time I've lived alone in at least 14 years. I kind of like it ... nice and quiet ... no daily obligations to anyone ... no one to come home to ... not that bad."

"I know what you mean, Dave. I would love to have Rose Marie move in with me but she is too Catholic; her parents would be horrified and, in a way, I like my freedom. I come home and Baron is happy. He doesn't hammer me with questions, he's not jealous ... he doesn't require much to keep him happy."

"Maybe I should get a dog ... no ... it wouldn't be fair to the dog," Dave said.

"Well, maybe if you got a Saint Bernard, he could go everywhere with you and carry a flask for you," I said, laughing.

"Yeah, now that's an idea. I'll have to think about that," he said with a deep laugh. "All right, Mike! I had better get some sleep so you have a great birthday and we'll talk soon."

"Okay, thanks again, Dave, for calling."

We ended the call.

In the almost seven years I had known Dave, we never missed sending birthday greetings to each other.

I knew from press reports that Dave was earning $30,000 per episode for *O'Hara* so I calculated for all 24 episodes he would be earning a gross of $720,000.

I did not calculate that he owned a good percentage of the show, so adding that unknown factor, even at a minimal, the series would make Dave a good portion of what his divorce from Ellie had cost him. No wonder he sounded so upbeat.

I could not help but think that Dave, indeed, had it all. Just on this one series, he was earning in one week almost twice my annual income. However, knowing what I knew of his private life, I would not want to be in his shoes.

Although I never asked and did not know of Dave's personal financial affairs, other than what was made public by Ellie's allegations in their divorce action, I knew Dave to be very generous at tipping waiters and waitresses and parking valets. I had asked him once why he left such large tips, sometimes much larger than the actual bill.

He said, "Mike, I earn a good living. I do not tip to impress anyone. If I receive good service, and I always do, I know the person serving me deserves to be appreciated so I tip above the norm to make up for the assholes who don't tip enough, or the real assholes who don't tip at all ... and, here in LA, even the most successful people in this business, you'd be surprised at the cheapskates I know." His answer on tipping made me think, and I adapted his style for my own.

Hearing the way Dave spoke, the sincerity in his voice, was the first time I realized what a sensitive and compassionate man he really was.

I had known for quite some time that he really cared about people in general, especially single mothers. I knew for example, he had seen a television report of a house fire which left a single mother and her two young children homeless. The report had mentioned she was struggling to keep her family together. Dave sent a check to provide a home and groceries for her; he did this anonymously.

I found out years later when talking with Ellie that Dave had done this on numerous occasions during their marriage, giving away sums running into the thousands of dollars. He was also very charitable to families in need during the Christmas holidays. He did this without Ellie's knowing and I detected she did not at all like his little acts of charity.

62

The third of October was a beautiful Sunday in Manhattan with a magnificent sunrise gleaming off the skyscrapers and warming the city. I was enjoying a fresh cup of coffee on the balcony with Baron when the phone rang just after 7:30.

"Mike, are you awake?"

"Of course, Dave ... having my second cup of coffee watching the sunrise. I guess you're just about to go to bed ... or are you just waking up?"

"Yeah, going to bed ... it's been a long day but I wanted to check in with you. How is everything with you?"

"All is well here ... and with you? Have you found a place to live?"

"No, not yet. Actually, I'm at the Gene Autry Hotel here in Palm Springs - looking for a place here and I'll stay at my bungalow on the studio lot while filming. I like it here and it is away from the party circuit in LA. I'm giving myself a break. I'm thinking of building a house here; I have some land Ellie didn't get."

"That sounds like a good plan ... you really deserve a break. Will you live there and commute to Los Angeles? Any news on *O'Hara;* are your ratings sky-rocketing?"

"No, I'll still get a place in LA. This will be my little retreat; I'll stay in LA while working. As for the ratings, they're holding steady ... nothing to be excited about. We start filming again next week. I just got back from a mini-vacation."

"Oh, yeah! Where'd you go?"

"I took Dani on a little boat trip down to Mexico. It was a lot of fun; we really enjoyed it."

"Dani?" I asked.

"Yeah, Dani Greco. We've known each other since the beginning; we were sort of classmates at Universal Studios about 20 years ago.

She and her husband, Buddy, were our neighbors in the Sierra Towers."

"Oh, yeah! I know ... they hosted your anniversary party, the night you told Ellie your marriage was over."

"Yeah ... you remember. We've been like best friends and, now that she has filed for divorce, we've re-discovered each other," he said with a sly chuckle.

"Wow, Dave! That sounds interesting - will I be getting a wedding invitation?" I asked with a laugh.

"Hey, Mike! Don't rush me; she isn't even divorced yet. She's a lot of fun and we have a lot in common. She is a terrific cook, a great lady all around ... a fantastic hostess. She knows everybody and everyone loves her. I'm still not ready for any commitments yet ... to anyone."

"At least you are remaining cautious ... that is good, but don't let it stand in the way of true love. Just make certain it is real love on both sides before you give in," I advised.

"You don't have to worry about that. Believe me! I will not make the same mistake again - too damned expensive!"

"Well, I haven't faced that yet but, then, I don't have nearly as much to lose as you did - but I don't want to experience, even on the smallest scale, what you did."

"As the old adage says, 'Time heals all wounds,' and I don't know if I'll have enough time left to fully heal," Dave said with a serious laugh.

"So, tell me, Dave ... do you have anything lined up for when you go on hiatus from *O'Hara*?"

"No, not yet. Abby is working on some prospects. I may just take a little time off and decompress; I've had a hectic schedule for the past few months."

"Well, I think you have the right idea there. You need to take care of yourself ... unwind and take some time to smell the roses."

"I know, Mike ... and I agree. I need that, especially now. You know we talked about this before. I am thankful for the work but doing a series is a hell of a lot harder than shooting a feature film ... demanding, hectic schedule. I didn't think I'd do another but Jack sort of twisted my arm. Of course, he sweetened the deal ... no way I could turn it down, but I'm not really into this show at all."

"I'm sorry to hear that ... I like it. You know, one of my mother's brothers was a Secret Service agent. He chased counterfeiters ... died at his desk of a heart attack. I don't really remember him but my mother always spoke highly of him. You know it's not easy to get into the Secret Service."

"Yeah, Mike, but even though the plots are all based on actual cases, I just don't feel good about the writing and Jack is exerting such tight controls. I'm sure the actual cases were not as boring as they come across on the pages of our scripts. Truthfully, I hope we're not picked up for next season."

"Are you serious? Do you think *The Fugitive* has hurt this show, that your fans still look at you as Dr. Kimble?"

"Yeah, actually, I do think that. Everywhere I go, the *Fugitive* fans always yell out to me, calling me *Dr. Kimble*. Yeah, I still like it; it's flattering in a way but, damn it! That's not who I am; I want them to look at me for what I am doing now ... you understand?"

"Of course, and I agree with you, but you have to appreciate how people were affected by *The Fugitive*. A lot of your fans, including me, wanted YOU to keep on running," I said with a slight laugh.

"Yeah, Mike, you have a point. Still, the fact is I don't like *O'Hara* but I'll keep trying to make him better, in spite of Jack."

"Hey, I think I told you once, police incident reports are pretty damned boring. Now court transcripts - criminal court's, that is - are far more interesting, suspenseful ... even exciting in some cases."

"On that point, you are right. Look at Ray Burr as *Perry Mason* ... excellent scripts ... great acting all around."

"Definitely, but do you think he could do another series and people would accept him? I don't think so; I know I'd still look at him as *Perry Mason*."

"Yes, I agree with you. I think it's the same with Jim Arness and his *Gunsmoke*. It proves my point. Hollywood, especially the television side of it, is so damned close-minded. They keep recycling the same damn stories and they put an actor into a stereotype role and do everything to keep him there."

"I don't know about that, Dave. Personally, I think if the show is good and the actor ... the star ... delivers in such a way as the fans believe he or she IS that character, then it proves the actor's talent is extraordinary - and YOU of all people have to agree that YOU were *Richard Kimble*," I said with sincerity.

"All right, Mike! I cannot disagree with you ... and thanks for the compliment," he said with a laugh.

"After all, Dave, with *The Fugitive* being shown in re-runs, you - I mean, *O'Hara* - is competing with you." I laughed.

"Point taken. Hell, I don't know why I'm bitching about this. I'm working, the money is coming in ... what the hell! I'll just keep playing along," he said with a deep laugh.

"Right! That's the right way to look at it but, in the unlikely event you're not picked up for next season, you should really take some time off. Do what you want to do ... play golf, tennis ... go fishing. Enjoy yourself. Enjoy your freedom, at least, for a while, then when you are fully refreshed, you can do some feature films - whatever Abby can line up, whatever YOU want to do," I suggested.

"Best advice I've heard all day. I think I'll do it," Dave said with a laugh.

"Hell, Dave ... who am I to even try to give you advice? You know the business better than anyone and you know yourself better than me ... or anyone, so just do what you want. I have a feeling you'll do just fine for yourself."

"All right, Mike! Thanks for the career counselling. I feel better already. Now it's time for me to hit the sack ... I'll be in touch," Dave said.

"Okay, Dave. Keep me informed ... and don't forget to smell the roses."

This was the first time Dave let me know he was not as full of confidence in *O'Hara* as he was when he first told me about the project. I did enjoy the show, mainly because of Dave's portrayal of *Agent Jim O'Hara*.

Still, I had to agree with him: the plots and the scripts had the hum-drum marks of Jack Webb's, *Dragnet*. Yeah, to be honest, most of the episodes so far were dull.

Dave did not sound depressed in this conversation. He did sound frustrated and his frustration was with the scripts and, perhaps, a little with Jack Webb's exertion of his control over the show. In the episodes I had seen, Dave's portrayal of his character was solid, at least in my opinion.

63

I would next hear from Dave on Saturday, October 23, in an early morning call.

"Mike, Dave ... did I wake you?"

"No, Dave, I was actually waiting for your call," I answered, glancing at my clock radio; it was 3:20. "Of course, you woke me ... but I'll forgive you this time."

Dave laughed. "Hell, you should thank me; it's almost time for you to get up, anyway. How is everything with you?"

"Good ... everything is good, Dave ... how about you? How's my friend Jim O'Hara?"

"Good ... very good. I've decided I'll build a house here in Palm Springs. It will be my main house where I can come to really unwind from the hustle and bustle and craziness of LA."

"That sounds great! Where will you build ... have you found the land?"

"Oh, yeah! I still have a nice lot Ellie didn't get; it's high on a hill, great views ... secluded. It will be my little piece of heaven on earth. You'll have to come out for my housewarming. Of course, that won't be for about a year."

"I'll make damn sure I do; it will be nice to see a real bachelor pad - just make sure you have a bottle of scotch for me," I said with a chuckle.

"You know better; there will be enough scotch for both of us. I'm really looking forward to it. Now I can afford to build, and the show is getting better, so I'm looking forward to having my own permanent place. Everything is coming together nicely."

"You damn well deserve it. Have you heard anything on the show being renewed for next season?" I asked.

"Not yet, but I'm not worried about it. My residuals from the *Fugitive* syndication are coming in so money will not be an issue."

"That's good to hear. Ellie took a hell of a bite out of you but, like you said, you can always make more money, and now you're doing it with peace of mind. You deserve it and I'm happy for you, Dave."

"Thanks, Mike! I'll let you know when we break ground. It'll take about six to eight months before it's completed and, of course, the decorators will come in and do their thing. You will definitely come out for the housewarming party. I'll send you a ticket, so no excuses ... okay?"

"Okay, Dave, whatever you say. I'll really look forward to it. Maybe you could get Ellie to do the decorating ... bet she'd do it for free," I said with a laugh.

"You better be kidding! I don't want her near the property ... let alone the house," he said, letting out a chuckle.

"You'll have to send me some photos as it progresses. I'd love to see it as it goes from your architect's plans to reality."

"I'll do that, Mike. I will be keeping a close eye on the builders, so I'll be taking plenty of pictures."

"So will you take an apartment for when you're working in LA?"

"Yeah, Victor is scouting around for me now. Staying at the studio is getting a little bit boring; it's time I get something more permanent."

"So how is your love life? Anything going on with Dani Greco?" I asked.

"Well ... we are dating ... and she comes by and cooks for me. She is a marvelous cook but I don't really see anything coming. She's a fun girl to date; let's just leave it at that. How about you ... have you moved toward a divorce ... is Rose Marie still hanging in there with you?"

"Okay ... as long as you are having some fun, with someone who makes you have fun. I haven't done anything as far as filing for a divorce, neither has Joanne - as far as I know – and, yes, Rose Marie and I are still having fun."

"Well, you're going to have to do something; don't let it go as long as I did. You are sort of trapped until you either reconcile or cut the ties and, from what you've told me, a reconciliation doesn't seem to be in the cards. What the hell would you do if Rose Marie told you she really loves you and wants to be your wife? You'd be stuck!"

"Yeah, Dave, you've got a point there. I guess I've just been fooling myself ... hoping against hope. I guess I had better look into it ... maybe I'll call Joanne and ask her if she wants a divorce ... just to make sure."

"You better do it soon ... before you are really making big money. As long as you are married, she can really hurt you, financially. Trust me! I KNOW!"

"Yeah, I know! I know you're right and I will follow your advice ... soon. However, Dave, I don't think it is very likely I'll ever be making the kind of money you do."

"You never know, Mike. Don't limit yourself. You've got a good head on your shoulders. Okay, Mike ... time for me to grab some shut-eye. Now you can get out of bed, have your coffee and take your dog to his park. I'll be in touch."

"All right, Dave! Thanks for the call; it's always good to talk with you."

Dave was right. Even though I would normally sleep until about six o'clock on the weekends, Baron was now wide awake and he followed me to the kitchen. I turned on the coffee maker and gave him his morning treat. I would take him to Riverside Park at dawn.

Dave had sounded pretty sober and in really good spirits. His decision to build a permanent home in Palm Springs was an indication to me that he was finally moving on after his divorce from Ellie and his three year relationship with Rosemary.

I was convinced he would be cautious in contemplating marriage anytime soon. Even so, in the ensuing months, I would read in the media he and Dani were becoming an *item*.

At the time I knew very little about Dani Greco. Dave had told me she and her husband, Buddy, had lived two floors above Dave and Ellie in the Sierra Towers apartments and they had hosted the fateful Tenth Wedding Anniversary party, where Dave announced to Ellie their marriage was over.

Sunday morning, November 7, I had just returned from the park with Baron. My phone was ringing.

"Hello."

"Mike, it's Dave ... don't tell me I woke you. I've been trying to call you for 15 minutes."

"No, Dave, you didn't wake me. Baron and I just came back from the park. Is everything all right with you?"

"Yeah, of course. Just wanted to give you a call, see if you or your wife has filed for a divorce yet?"

"Actually, I spoke with Joanne's mother last Monday, after we had talked. Seems Joanne has a new boyfriend; her mother says she does want a divorce. I tried to tell her I was giving up being a cop, working in executive recruiting here ... that doesn't seem to matter to Joanne. So, my friend, I guess I had better take your advice. I guess her love just wasn't really there for me."

"Mike, I can't say I feel sorry for you. It is better to know your situation before things drag on and it ends up hurting you more and costing you a lot of your hard earned cash. Do you have any idea if she is going to make demands on you?"

"No, her mom told me to just file and she would not contest it. She doesn't want anything from me."

"Well, you are fortunate there. My advice to you would be to get a lawyer and file for it right away. Women are always changing their minds; it could hurt you, especially to be blindsided."

"Yeah, I will do as you say. How about you? How are things with you and Dani Greco? I've seen in the magazines where you two are hitting the town, one party after another. Are things getting serious?"

"No, we're just friends ... friends with benefits, and I am the one reaping all the benefits. She hasn't gotten her divorce from Buddy yet so we're just having a lot of fun, as friends do. There is nothing serious ... at least, not yet."

"Okay ... at least, you're having fun ... that's good. How about your house in Palm Springs; are you making any progress?"

"The architect is having a scale model built for me. I'll send you some photos; it's really neat. I can take the roof off and see the interior layout ... I'm really anxious to break ground."

"I'll look forward to seeing the photos. How many rooms? How many square feet will it be?"

"It will be 75,000 square feet, not including the garage. There will be the master bedroom, four guest rooms, five and a half baths, living room, dining room, library, office, kitchen, maid's quarters and laundry room. There will be a four car garage attached. Oh, a pool and maybe a tennis court."

"Damn, Dave! That sounds like a mansion ... so many rooms for a bachelor ... sounds like you could get lost in it."

"Hey, it's in Palm Springs. I have to have room for guests and, who knows? I may have a live-in girlfriend every now and then," he said with a laugh.

"How many cars do you have?" I asked.

"I only have the Rolls convertible now, but I'm going to get another to keep there. I'll fly back and forth from LA."

"Okay, now I understand; it makes sense," I said. "I keep forgetting a man in your position needs a lot of room to entertain."

"Yeah, I guess so ... not that I'll be doing that much entertaining. I just like a lot of room, even when I'm alone."

"Hey, you've worked hard for it ... you've earned it."

"Do you still have your car ... the T-Bird?" he asked.

"No, I traded the one I had when we met for a '67, first year they made a four-door ... suicide doors. Then I traded that one for a '68 Lincoln Continental ... still have that."

"Why in the hell do you need a car in Manhattan?"

"It's my security blanket. If I want to get up and go, I can go ... anywhere! When I first relocated to the city, I had to ride the subway back and forth to work. I could not stand the noise and the filth. I swore to myself I would get rich enough to never have to ride the subway again ... and now I can afford to drive back and forth to work.

"The funny thing is, they have this alternate side of the street parking thing, for street cleaning. I didn't know about it and my car was towed twice in the same week ... cost me $15 for the parking ticket and $25 a pop for the impound ... learned my lesson," I said.

"Hell, Mike, when I lived in Manhattan, I couldn't afford a car. I took the subway every day ... several times a day. It's expensive having a car there, isn't it?"

"A little. I pay $140 to park my car in the apartment garage and $100 to park in a lot near my office but, to me, it's worth it, knowing I have my means of escape and I don't put up with the subways."

"I guess you have a point there. I just don't think I would keep a car there ... too much traffic for me to put up with," Dave said.

"Dave ... you can afford to have a limousine when you're here," I said with a laugh.

"I damn sure could not afford a cab, let alone a limousine, when I lived there," he replied with a deep laugh. "Now when I'm in the city, the studio provides me a limo and driver ... usually," he said with a laugh. "All right, Mike! I'm going to grab some much needed sleep. You take care and we'll talk soon."

"Thanks, Dave! Don't forget to send me the photos," I said.

"Don't worry! I will ... may be a few weeks, but I will," Dave said then hung up the phone.

64

Dave called me just after one o'clock Sunday morning, November 14.

"Hey, Mike! Dave ... thought I'd give you a call before you went to bed. How the hell are you?"

"Fine, Dave ... how about you?"

"I didn't wake you, did I?"

"No, actually Rose Marie and I just got home. I'll take Baron out for a quick run ... very quick, and it's about 25 degrees here."

"Too damn cold for me ... has Rose Marie moved in with you?"

"No ... I wish ... her parents would not approve. We just saw *Jesus Christ Superstar* on Broadway and then had dinner. I wanted to stop and take Baron out, and then take Rose Marie home."

"Sounds good. How did you like the play?"

"It was actually better than I expected ... no famous stars, but there were some damn good actors and actresses. How are things with you? How is the house building coming along?"

"Everything is good. I'm still working on *O'Hara*, very busy. The house building is on hold ... actually, haven't broken ground yet. I'm holding off on it for now."

"Well ... have you found anything more permanent in LA? I mean, outside the *Silver Bullet*? You have to find a real home to hang your clothes ... lay your head. I know the Bullet cannot have enough room for your wardrobe," I said with a laugh.

"Yeah, Victor has found a couple of places. I'll be checking them out later in the week. I've been busy ... no time for much of anything."

"How is Dani? Is everything going well with you guys?"

"Oh, yeah! Going great ... she's beautiful, of course you know that. She's a lot of fun, a great cook and she makes a mean Martini," he said with a chuckle.

"So how is your drinking; are you still controlling it or has it taken control of you?"

"I'm good ... pretty much under control. You know me; I know when to slow down. Dani has helped me a lot there. I have to watch my weight ... so don't worry about me."

"I'm not really worried about you, Dave, but I do care. I just don't want to read that you've been busted for driving under the influence. I'd feel guilty I'm not there to drive you home," I said with a slight chuckle.

"That will never happen. I'll either have a driver or take a cab. I won't risk making you feel guilty," he said and laughed.

"Do you know anything about your series ... will we see you next year?"

"I really can't tell you, Mike. We haven't heard anything from CBS. I think the scripts have improved a hell of a lot. We have good writers, good directors, great supporting actors ... established stars ... but it's all up in the air right now. As for me, personally, I still don't like the way it comes out as a finished product but, if we are picked up for next season, you can bet I'll be there."

"Personally, I hope you get a new season. I have seen improvements in the storylines. I find myself liking it more each episode."

"Thanks, Mike! I appreciate that. It has potential. I'm just not sure what the honchos in New York think. We'll just have to wait and see."

"Do you have anything lined up for when you go on hiatus or in case the series is not renewed?"

"Not yet. We are sort of in a holding pattern, waiting on word from New York. Abby will get something to keep me working, at least during part of our hiatus. I will take some time off to rejuvenate myself."

"That's good ... just make sure you let me know so I don't miss anything you're doing."

"I'll keep you informed, don't worry. How are things going with Rose Marie? How's Baron?"

"They're both good. Rose Marie asked me about my filing for a divorce and I told her you were giving me good advice, and I was giving it serious consideration ... and I am."

"You really should, Mike. It appears, from what you've told me, there's not a chance for you to get back together. Don't wait until things get nasty for you. Think of her; maybe she will want to marry someone else."

"You're right, Dave, I'm going to do it but, then again, like you, I don't think I'll be in the frame of mind to jump out of the frying pan and into the fire," I said with a forced laugh.

"Rose Marie isn't pushing you, is she?"

"No, not at all. I think she is concerned about what her parents think. They know I'm still married and they're Catholic; you know how they think."

"Yes, I do ... well, I'm sure you can handle it ... just be careful."

"I will ... I'm not stupid," I said, laughing.

"I know you're not stupid. I don't want to see you get hurt ... more than you have been. True love is not easy to get away from; it hurts ... I know, I've been through it," Dave said.

"I know what you mean, but since I've been with Rose Marie, my feelings - my love for Joanne - has been ... how can I say this ... dying? I have come to realize it would never work - our marriage - and I realize that she must not have loved me as much as I, or she, may have felt in the beginning. I guess I am getting over it ... time to move on."

"That's good and, although I never met your wife, I think Rose Marie is a great little gal. She seems happy with you and you seem comfortable with her ... just take it slow and easy."

"Sounds like good advice, Dave. Is that how you're doing it with Dani?"

"Oh, not really! Our situation is totally different. We've been friends since we first met years ago and we both went through marriages that ended for one reason or another. We are not rushing things ... just having fun, at this stage."

"I understand what you're saying; I know you won't make the same mistake twice."

"Hey, don't get me wrong! The first half of my marriage was great; it was the last half that had me living in hell on earth - her insecurities, jealousy, health problems (which she blamed on me) ...you bet I won't make the same mistake again. IF, and when, I get married again ... to Dani or whomever ... it will last the rest of my life," he said in a serious tone. I knew he meant it.

"You sure have the right attitude, Dave. I hope neither one of us rushes into anything without our eyes wide open."

"All you have to do, Mike, is step back and look at your situation and then look to the future ... is it right for you? Then you ask yourself IF SHE is the one you want to grow old with. We are all going to grow old and it would be nice to have someone you want to grow old with. Okay, Mike ... I'll let you get back to Rose Marie and Baron. I'll keep in touch."

"Thanks, Dave ... oh, Rose Marie says hello ... and Baron sends a bark," I said, as Baron barked.

"Yeah, okay ... my regards to them both. Talk later."

I hung up the phone. Rose Marie stayed in the warmth of the apartment as I took Baron for a quick walk.

65

The day before Thanksgiving, November 24, Dave called me at my office just before three o'clock in the afternoon.

"Mike, Dave ... am I interrupting you?"

"No, Dave ... this is a surprise! What's up with you?"

"We're breaking for lunch and I wanted to wish you a Happy Thanksgiving. What are your plans for tomorrow?"

"I'm having dinner at Rose Marie's parents' home and we will go to a movie after the dinner. How about you and Dani?"

"We have a long weekend, so we may go to Palm Springs, relax. Dani will be cooking our turkey so I plan on just unwinding. What movie are you going to see?" he asked.

"It's been out for about a month, *The French Connection*, with Gene Hackman. Have you seen it?"

"No, not yet. Gene is a good actor, so we will see it. It was filmed mostly there in New York so I'm sure you will enjoy it. Does Rose Marie like cop movies?"

"Oh, yeah! She picked this one ... she likes cop shows, comedies, romance films ... not too keen on westerns or war movies, though."

"You have to let me know if you like it. I'm going to run so you have a great day tomorrow. Make sure Baron has a good Thanksgiving dinner. I'll call you later."

"Thanks, Dave ... the same for you and Dani," I said.

Dave sounded sober and happy. I was glad his series was moving ahead and the ratings had been improving. My honest opinion, at the time, was I had seen great improvements in the storylines and I had a feeling Dave may have had some talks with the script writers.

Thanksgiving Day passed and I enjoyed a four day weekend from work. The weather was moving towards winter but Indian summer was still in the air so it was nice to take Baron to Riverside Park for extended periods of time.

Dave called on Saturday, December 4, just after six o'clock in the morning.

"Good morning, Mike ... had your coffee yet?"

"Good morning, Dave. As a matter of fact, I'm on my second cup ... waiting for the rain to let up so I can take Baron to the park. How are things with you? Are you getting up or just going to bed?"

"I'm getting up; we have a shooting schedule in a couple of hours."

"So are you in San Diego or Los Angeles?"

"San Diego. I'll be going home tonight and then we may go to Palm Springs. So how was your turkey day? Did Baron have a good dinner?"

"It was a good day; actually, the whole extended weekend. Baron always eats well, you know that. So how was yours and Dani's day?"

"It was great ... excellent dinner! We had a few friends over and, after dinner, everyone cleared out. We just relaxed."

"That's nice. Have you heard any news about your series being renewed?"

"No ... not a word, but the ratings are improving - that's a good sign. I'll tell you, Mike; this is not my kind of show. If the U.S. Treasury Agents really work cases like this, it's a wonder they ever make arrests and get convictions. I'm just kidding. I just don't like the scripts ... some are better than most, but it's not my kind of show."

"I think it has been getting better with every episode ... maybe I'm biased, but you look like a good federal agent," I said with a slight laugh. "If I were to be judging just your performance, I'd have to say it looks like you are giving it your best."

"Thanks, Mike! I always try to give my best, whether I like the script or not, but sometimes I can feel my heart just isn't there to make it better."

"That's understandable, Dave. Still, each show looks good to me; it is just some of the dialogue I can't believe, even when it is your dialogue," I said.

"That's what I mean! See! Even you notice it is not realistic, as it should be."

"Maybe you should hire a real ex-Treasury agent to write the dialogue," I suggested.

"Couldn't do that ... the writer's union would raise hell," Dave responded, then laughed. "Well, I have to run but I'll give you a call and let you know what's going on."

"Thanks for calling. Take it easy and keep me informed."

The rain had stopped so I took Baron to Riverside Park before going out for breakfast.

Dave had sounded good over the phone and I just had the inner feeling he had been cutting back on his drinking, and gave credit to Dani Greco for helping him do it. That was really good because I could see how it had been affecting him.

Dave's next call to me came on Sunday, December 19.

"Good morning, Mike ... you awake?"

"Of course, I am! Are you going to bed or getting up?"

"Just going to bed. We had a party and it lasted a little longer than we had planned. It was good, though - good friends, good spirits. How are things going with you?"

"Everything is fine, but it is getting too damn cold here. I guess I forgot what winter is like in the northeast."

"Well, it is a nice, balmy night here in Los Angeles, but you made the choice, so live with it. I bet Baron enjoys it, though. Have you had any snow yet?" Dave laughed.

"No snow yet and, yeah, Baron loves it; he was born into it and he loves to run in the park and doesn't want to come back home until he is ready. It doesn't matter to him if I'm freezing."

"Like I said, you made the choice. I just wanted to let you know it's not looking good for *O'Hara* to be picked up for another season ... so I'll probably be out of work again."

"How do you know it's not looking good? Has anyone said that to you or Mr. Webb?"

"No, not yet. We only have a few more episodes to film and, usually, we would know something by now. It doesn't really matter to me. I don't have my heart into this one so I'm sure Abby will get me into something, more in the major films. I want out of the gruelling schedule of a series."

"Well ... I, along with millions of your fans, will be sorry that you won't be on television each week so you'll have to tell your agent he has to work hard and get you into as many movies as he can. You don't want your TV fans to forget you," I said, then laughed.

"Oh, I'll still be on TV ... the talk shows, variety shows ... maybe even a made-for-TV movie or two."

"Oh ... okay ... that's good to hear, but there's still a chance you'll be renewed, right?"

"Yeah, a slim chance I would say ... but, actually, I am hoping we're not picked up," Dave said.

"All right, then; if that's what you want, I'll go along with it. You can always file for unemployment, can't you?" I joked.

"Yeah, right ... I don't think I'll have to do that, but you never know," he said with a laugh.

"Please, keep me informed when you have the official word, good or bad. How are things with you and Dani Greco?"

"Good ... getting better. We're going out a lot together, having fun. I stay mostly sober, which is good. We're going to the Hollywood premier of the film *Nicholas and Alexandra* next week, then to an after party and that will be a fun night."

"I've seen the ads for that movie in the papers here; I don't think it's the kind of movie I'd like. You'll have to let me know if you liked it and then I'll think about seeing it, taking Rose Marie to it."

"Speaking of ... have you gotten off your ass and filed for a divorce yet? I'd hate to see you lose Rose Marie; she seems like a really nice girl."

"No, I haven't filed yet. I'm thinking of going to Connecticut; that's where we got married so I figure that would be the right, and easiest place, to file."

"Then just do it, but don't rush into anything with Rose Marie. Give yourself some time ... like I am doing."

"I will follow your advice, Dave. I know it is good ... and don't you worry! I won't be in any hurry to get married again. I'll make damn sure she is the right one," I said.

"All right, Mike! I'll be in touch ... stay warm. If we don't speak before, you have a great Christmas," Dave said.

"Thanks, Dave! I hope you and Dani will have a very Merry Christmas, too, and a great New Year. Take care."

Dave sounded really good ... better than he had for several months following his divorce from Ellie. Maybe Dani Greco was really good for him; if so, that would be great.

66

Dave called Thursday, December 30, just after five o'clock in the morning.

"Hey, Mike! It's Dave ... didn't wake you, did I?"

"No, Dave, I'm usually up by four ... that way I can be in my office before the rush hour starts. How is everything with you?"

"Good ... everything is going well. I just wanted to give you a call and wish you a Happy New Year. What are your plans?"

"I'm taking Rose Marie to the Rainbow Room ... dinner, dancing and to see the fireworks over the East River. It sure as hell isn't cheap but I wanted to do something special for Rose Marie. I'm sure it will be a lot of fun. What will you and Dani be doing?"

"We're invited to several parties. Knowing Dani, we will probably go to every one of them. She's in charge of our social calendar, but I'm sure we'll have a lot of fun. I've been to the Rainbow Room, very romantic ... have you been there before?"

"No, but I've heard from my boss that it is the best and that's what I want to show Rose Marie."

"I'm sure she will enjoy it; you both will. You're right! It is expensive but, in my opinion, well worth it. The food is excellent."

"I'm really looking forward to it. How are the views from there, 65 floors up?"

"Views are excellent but you can only see slivers of the East River ... it's not that large, so I hope you are prepared to tip the Maître D' for a good table, and get there early. If you've already made your reservation, call them back and make it an hour earlier."

"Good advice. I've made the reservation, but I'll update the time. What do you recommend I tip the Maître D'?"

"On any other night, I'd say a 20 but, for New Year's Eve, you better make it a 50. Tell the Maître D' I sent you."

"Ouch! That's steep ... I'm in the wrong business. I'll do it, but I'll be eating at McDonald's for the next month," I said with a laugh.

"Well, Mike, all I can say is when you're enjoying your Big Mac with fries, think of the memories of that night; it'll make the Big Mac taste better." He laughed, then added, "Okay, Mike, you asked me to keep you informed, so here it is: *O'Hara* is history. We weren't picked-up for a second season and, to be honest, I am relieved."

"Damn! To be honest, I'm sad about it. I would think a second season would show great improvement with the scripts and building your ratings. So what will you do when the filming is over?"

"First thing I'll do is take a break ... take Dani and run off to an island somewhere ... a place with no televisions, radios or telephones ... just a nice long break. After I get tired of that, I'll climb all over Abby to get me some work. I'm not even going to concern myself with it; I damn sure don't want another series," Dave said firmly.

"Still, I'll miss seeing you in it every week. What did Mr. Webb say when he got the news?"

"He was pissed off. Of course, he would be! He's already shopping it around to the other networks. I just kept quiet and let him rant and rave. I don't think he'll have any luck getting it onto another network; even if he does, I'm through with it."

"Dave, if he does get another network and you won't do it, he'll have to kill *O'Hara* and bring in a new agent," I laughed. "Have you told Dani? What did she have to say about it?"

"Yeah, I told her immediately. She's as happy and relieved as I am. I'm not an easy guy to live with when I'm not happy at work," he said with a mischievous laugh.

"I bet she's looking forward to going away with you ... alone ... isn't she?"

"Oh, yeah! We are both eager to get away."

"How long do you think you'll be gone? Where are you going?" I asked.

"We'll be gone as long as it takes to make us tired of being wherever we are ... and where we are going? Who the hell knows! I've left that to Dani; it will be a place neither of us have ever been, so that should be interesting."

"All I can say is that you deserve it, Dave. If anyone deserves it, it's you! Doing it your way will be nice, give you and Dani a lot of quality time. Maybe you'll come back as 'Mr. and Mrs.' ... I'm sure that would make Dani happy."

"Hey, Mike! Don't even think that; it isn't going to happen! Not for a long, long time ... if ever!" Dave said.

"Yeah, I know that's what you say - that you want to enjoy your bachelor life but, hell! You spend all your time with Dani; you must be pretty sure she's the one," I said in earnest.

"I'm not sure of anything. I'm not rushing anything. I'm not going to get married until I am damned good and ready and, if the woman isn't ready, I'll move on. I'm not about to be trapped; by the same token, I'm not out to trap anyone, either."

"I wasn't implying any of that, Dave. I know you're not going to make any move like that until you are ready. It just seems like the fan magazines ... the Hollywood media ... practically has you two married."

"Mike, you know better than to believe that garbage. Believe me! They make all this crap up! Just because they see us out together, they plant gossip ... garbage. I promise ... when I am ready to get married, I'll call you and send you an invitation myself!"

"That's good to hear. Thanks, Dave! I won't believe anything I read, unless I hear it straight from you."

"Good ... I appreciate that. So, when does your divorce become final; when are you and Rose Marie getting married?"

"Touché, Dave! You really know how to hurt a guy, don't you?" I laughed.

"Well, I won't push you any more about that, but I better get an invitation to your wedding," Dave said, laughing.

"Don't worry, Dave! You'll get an invitation; you may be old and grey before that happens, though."

"All right, Mike! I'm going to go now but I'll stay in touch. You take care and you and Rose Marie have a great time at the Rainbow Room, and both of you have a great 1972."

"Okay, thanks, Dave but, if you can, give me a call before you take off. Let me know where you're going for vacation."

"I will, Mike. Take it easy," Dave said, then ended the call.

I was sad to hear about the imminent demise of *O'Hara* but I knew that is exactly what Dave wanted. In this call he sounded really great and happy. I also felt he was very secure in his relationship with Dani Greco.

I knew she was not yet divorced from Buddy Greco, but she seemed to make Dave happy and, judging from the articles I had read recently and the photos of Dani and Dave together, it appeared she was extremely happy, too.

I made a point to scour the television and entertainment sections of the newspapers and to continue buying the TV and movie fan magazines for any public announcements about *O'Hara's* demise, but could find nothing in the weeks following my conversation with Dave.

I was also watching each new episode to see if I could see any real improvement in the scripts and acting. Looking more closely, I could tell Dave was not really doing his best; I hoped that would not leave a bad taste with his fans.

New Year's Eve in New York is like no other place on the earth. People of all ages, races, nationalities, native New Yorkers and tourists alike come together in a mass at Times Square to watch the giant crystal ball drop down in sync with time to welcome a new year.

This evening was special for me. I hired a limousine and picked Rose Marie up at 6:30 and went directly to Rockefeller Center and to the Rainbow Room. I did as Dave suggested and dropped his name with the Maître D'. We were ushered to a nice window table for two near the dance floor. I tipped him a crisp 50 dollar bill. There was a big band and the Rainbow Room was decorated for the festivities.

Our evening was outstanding. We enjoyed a fabulous dinner, a lot of dancing and romantic talk. I told Rose Marie that Dave and Dani were attending several parties in Beverly Hills and I was certain they were not having any more fun than we were. She said she would like to see the glamorous Hollywood parties with all the stars but said she was perfectly happy spending New Year's Eve with me at the Rainbow Room.

I could not help but think 1972 would be a great year for Dave. With his series ending, he would be able to again have his agent concentrate on starring roles in major films, which is what Dave yearned for. He had told me several times the difference between a television series and a major film: series work was a gruelling 14-16 hours a day, sometimes seven days a week. A major film would take three to four months to produce and he was not required to be on set for every scene, every day. After a major film wrapped, he would have a couple of months of down time.

67
~1972~

I did not hear from Dave until Saturday, January 8. I was sitting on my terrace with Baron, having my coffee watching the sun rise, struggling to peek through the dark grey sky. The holidays long over, it had been a busy week in my office. New York was getting back to business.

"Good morning, Mike. It's Dave. How are you?"

"Great, Dave ... and you? How is everything going with Mr. Webb and *O'Hara*?"

"Everything is going well. As I expected, Jack has had no luck getting anyone to pick up the show. For that, I feel my prayers have been answered," he said with a chuckle.

"How are things with you and Dani?"

"Couldn't be better ... first time in a long time, I can honestly say I'm happy - happy with everything in my life right now."

"That is really good to hear! It's good to know you, finally, have someone who makes you happy. Any idea yet as to your vacation?"

"No, we will be filming the last episodes of the show for the rest of this month. Dani is checking out travel brochures ... trying to decide where she wants us to go, so I'll be surprised when she makes a decision."

"Make sure you call me so I can envy you as you guys lie on the beach with Pina Coladas and I'm freezing my ass off here."

"Don't worry! I'll let you know! I'll even drink a couple of Pina Coladas as a toast for you. So tell me, how was your New Year's Eve at the Rainbow Room?"

"It was absolutely outstanding! I did as you suggested and told the Maître D' *you* recommended the place; he escorted us to a great window table on the east side of the room. I grimaced as I discretely palmed a 50 dollar bill into his hand, and he smiled.

"The evening could not have been better; we will definitely return there. After the midnight hour, we were going to go to Times Square but it was impossible with traffic and too damn cold for us to walk. I had Rose Marie home by a little after 1:30. She really enjoyed the evening, and so did I."

"I'm glad to hear that. It is one of my favorite places in New York, great food and excellent service ... and people respect your privacy."

"I totally agree with you. Although, not being a celebrity like you, we had no concern about privacy. I paid the photo girl for some nice photos, sort of a memory token for Rose Marie; she loved it! At least, her parents will see I treat her right ... and I am a gentleman," I said with a little laugh. "So how was your New Year's Eve with Dani?"

"It was one of the best New Year's Eves of my life! We went to three or four parties. I held back on my alcohol intake and really enjoyed myself. Being with Dani was more fun than I've had in years. We watched the sun rise and then went to bed. I slept until about three."

"You really made a night of it, didn't you? Good to know Dani makes you so happy."

"She does, Mike ... and to think we have known each other so many years. I feel like I wasted all those years with Ellie, but I can't change the past. I'm damn sure enjoying the present and looking forward ... never look back."

"You sure have the right attitude, Dave ... just took you a while to get it." I laughed.

"Yeah, you're right ... now I have to make the best of it and, with Dani, it's a hell of a lot more fun."

"You're a lucky man, Dave ... a lucky man, indeed."

"You know it ... and so do I, but I've paid my dues. I've paid dearly."

"I know, Dave ... I saw what you went through. Now it's your time to be happy ... you earned it ... you deserve it."

"Thanks, Mike. I am and I'm rolling in it. Okay, Mike, I have to go so you take it easy and we'll talk soon."

"Good, Dave. You take care, too, and have fun." The call ended.

It felt good to hear from Dave and to hear him so happy and focused. He was actually relieved *O'Hara* was ending. He did not feel at fault for its failure. I personally did not feel his lack of enthusiasm for the show contributed to the failure.

Dave called me on Sunday, January 23, just before noon.

"Good morning, Mike. How are you doing?"

"Great, Dave! How about you and Dani?"

"We're good. Dani is looking for a place for us to move to; things are a little awkward with our current living arrangements. How are Rose Marie and Baron?"

"They are both great ... so you and Dani are going to move in together? That's really good. I mean, you seem happy together; now you'll find out if you can live together - accept each others idiosyncrasies," I said with a chuckle.

"Yeah, you have a point there, but I think we both pretty much know each others' likes and dislikes. She is one hell of a cook and she is a stickler for making healthy food. She hates processed foods; she does everything from scratch, many of her own recipes. She's really helping my body; I feel better than I have in years."

"That's good to hear ... sounds like she just may be the right one for you, Dave. I haven't seen anything in the papers or magazines about *O'Hara* being cancelled; have they changed their minds?"

"No, they haven't changed their minds and Jack isn't having any success in selling it to anyone. They will let the public know when they announce their new fall season but you already know it, so don't waste your time looking for any announcement."

"Yes, I can say I heard it straight from the top man, although I haven't even told Rose Marie. I don't talk about it with anyone."

"That's okay ... you can tell her; does she watch the show?"

"Yeah, actually, she likes it; we watch it together most weeks. She's not really familiar with law enforcement or cop-speak so I don't say anything negative. I just let her enjoy it."

"That's nice of you, Mike. You must get a laugh out of some of the dialogue, though."

"Yeah, I do, Dave. As I said, a lot of Jack Webb's *Dragnet;* I'm sure glad you don't walk like him."

We both laughed.

"So have you ... or Dani, decided where you are going for vacation when the series ends?" I asked.

"No ... she's looking at places but we haven't really made a plan yet."

"How about new projects for you? Have you given Mr. Greshler the green light to put you out there for casting directors?"

"Hell, no! I want to relax for a while. I'll let him know when I'm ready, but I won't be in any rush."

"That's good, Dave. Don't stay away too long, though."

"Don't worry, Mike! I won't. You know me; I get restless if I don't have something working."

"Have Mr. Greshler get you into a good detective or mystery film. You come across as a good cop, one who can turn mean in a heartbeat," I said.

"Yeah, I like the genre and I like that kind of role. I don't want to play the bad guy - you know, the criminal."

"I agree with you ... after all, you were wrongly convicted and on the run for four years - but everyone knew you were innocent ... so Dave, bottom line is you have to always be the good guy and you play the detective role with strong realism."

"Well, thanks, Mike ... I have to run, but I'll be in touch soon. Take care of yourself."

"Okay, Dave ... thanks for the call."

68

I had not heard from Dave for almost a month so I assumed he was very busy with filming the final episodes of *O'Hara*. I had seen a couple of photos of him and Dani at Hollywood parties so I knew he was okay.

Dave called me on Monday, February 21, as I was making my morning coffee.

"Good morning, Mike. It's Dave. Sorry I've been out of touch ... been really busy. How are things with you?"

"I presumed as much. Everything here is fine. Baron is getting really big. Rose Marie and I are doing well. Have you finished *O'Hara*?"

"Yes, and I am very happy that bomb is over and done with. I'm in Palm Springs - relaxing, playing tennis and golf, topped off with cocktail hours," Dave said.

"Sounds like you are finally enjoying yourself. Is Dani with you?"

"No, she's in LA. She is scouting around for a place for us to live. I'm at the Gene Autry Hotel here. I go back and forth to LA, meetings with Abby ... parties with Dani ... but I am really enjoying my time here. Bob and Delores Hope are here and Bob is teaching me how to improve my golf game."

"That sounds like a lot of fun. Does Mr. Hope make jokes watching your swing?"

"Hope makes jokes about how the clouds move ... nothing gets past him so, yeah, he makes jokes about me. Even I have to laugh ... but my swing is getting better, so he must be a good teacher."

"It could be you are a good student; have you thought about it that way?" I asked with a laugh.

"No, but I do agree with you. I'll let Bob know that when we're out on the course next."

"I thought you told me you and Dani were going to take a long vacation. Someplace without TVs, phones - so where are you going? When are you going?"

"We haven't made any plans to go anywhere. I'm happy here and Dani comes down, too, so we may not go anywhere. Hey, Mike! Don't forget! I'm out of a job. I don't have any money for a vacation," Dave said with a good laugh.

"Yeah, Dave ... I forgot. I feel so sorry for you and Dani. If she stands by you in this dark period of unemployment, then you will know she is the right gal for you," I responded, laughing.

"Hell, Mike! I already know that! She has been outstanding, makes me feel 10 years younger. Yes, I think she is the ONE, but I like my freedom so don't even mention my getting married," he said.

"You damn sure do not have to worry about that. I would be the last man on earth to suggest you get married; I know you are capable of making that decision all by yourself."

"Okay ... thanks, Mike! I don't think I'll be making that kind of decision any time soon. So everything is good with you?"

"Yeah ... I'll be glad when spring gets here. I've had enough winter. I can't stay out with Baron for more than half an hour. He doesn't want to come home; I tell him I don't have a fur coat like him."

"You can always come back to LA. I bet Baron would love it out here ... the beach, the ocean ... good weather year 'round."

"No, Dave ... he might like all of that, but he would not like the smog, the traffic. I wouldn't do that to him. He's fine here. So tell me, has Mr. Greshler found any projects for you that you would, at least, consider?"

"Yeah, he has some things he wants me to look at, but I have time. I'm not going to rush into anything."

"Yeah, Dave, but you've been out of work for quite a while now. Aren't you restless?"

"Not quite ... I'm having too much fun. Of course, I could use the money but I still have some time to enjoy."

"Well, Dave, I have a couple of thousand in my savings account so, if you run short, I can send you enough to cover your bar tabs," I said in a joking manner.

"Thanks, Mike! That's really nice of you. Don't worry! If I get that low on cash, I'll call you," he said, letting out a big laugh.

I certainly knew Dave was not in need of money. I also knew his lifestyle was expensive, especially now that he and Dani were a couple. I knew Dave always picked up the check and would never let a lady pay for anything.

"Okay, Dave, I'll keep it available. It will be a while before *O'Hara's* final episode is shown so your fans won't forget you, right?"

"Yeah, it'll run through the summer so I have time to relax. Mike, I really do need this down time, both physically and mentally."

"Speaking of physically, how is your knee?"

"I feel major improvement. So far I have no pain, even when it is cold outside."

"That's good! You may have found the right orthopedic surgeon. Does that mean you'll be running and jumping when the script demands it?"

"Not really. I'll do what I can but the studio insurance won't allow me to do a lot of the stunts - have to have a 'double'. I'm going to run; I'll give you a call later."

"Okay ... thanks, Dave. Do me a favor and let me know when you're going back to work and what you'll be appearing in."

"Don't worry! You'll be among the first to know. Take care and we'll talk soon."

"Thanks, Dave."

In the seven years I had known Dave, I think this was the first time I had known him to not be working on something or another. Even if he was not doing a series, he was either starring in a movie or a Movie of the Week for TV, or having guest appearances on the various talk or variety shows. He sounded better than he had in months.

On Friday, March 3, Dave called me in my office just past five o'clock.

"Hey, Mike! Am I interrupting you?"

"No, not at all. I was just getting ready to leave the office, go downstairs for a couple of drinks before going home. How the heck are you?"

"Doing great! I found a house here in Palm Springs to lease; Dani and I have leased an apartment in Century City. We'll be staying here for a while; Dani is having renovations done on the apartment."

"Good ... have you decided when you'll go back to work?"

"Not yet ... I am looking at a few things that look interesting, but I have some time before anything is scheduled for production. Don't worry! I told you I'll let you know when I've committed to something."

"I know ... I know. I'm just not used to not seeing you in something - on television or in the theatres."

"I'll get into something soon. I'll let you know. I just called to see if you can send me five grand?"

"Uhh ... uhh ... sure, Dave. I have close to three in my savings account. I'm sure I can get an advance from work."

Dave burst into laughter ... sustained laughter that lasted at least two minutes. "I'm just kidding you, Mike. I don't need any money. I just wanted to see what you'd say." He was still laughing.

"Okay ... okay. All right ... you got me good!" I said.

"Yeah ... but, at least, I know I have a real friend, Mike. That means a lot to me," he said, seriously.

"Well, Dave ... if you did need it, I would send it!"

"I know, Mike, and I appreciate that. Now, the same goes for you. If you ever need my help, just call me ... I'll be there."

"Thanks, Dave ... that's good to know."

"All right, Mike. I'll give you a call in a few weeks. I am sure I'll commit to some project by then. You take it easy."

"Thanks, Dave ... call me."

69

Sunday morning, March 19, my phone jolted me awake at 3:20; I had just gone to bed at two o'clock.

"Mike, Dave ... did I wake you? Of course, I did, but it's Sunday so you can sleep late. How are you?"

"Fine, Dave. I just went to bed about an hour ago ... and, no, I can't sleep late. Baron won't let me. What's up with you?"

"Just got home from a party ... thought I'd give you a call, see what you are up to."

"That's nice of you Dave. Is Dani with you?"

"No, she's in LA. I just spoke with her."

"You woke her up, too?"

"Yeah, but she knows if I'm away, she sleeps with one ear open. How are things with Rose Marie? How's Baron? How's your weather there?"

"Rose Marie is fine; we went out last night which is why I just got to bed. Baron is fine - 84 pounds and growing. Spring is almost here ... weather has been pretty decent ... not quite spring, but almost. Now, what about you? Are you and Dani going on that vacation you've been wanting?"

"No vacation ... at least, not for the foreseeable future. I'm really enjoying myself here in Palm Springs. Dani comes down most weekends. I go back and forth to LA, meet with Abby, Fred ... I'm looking at some projects."

"That all sounds great, Dave ... so I can count on seeing you on the silver screen or television sometime soon?"

"Well not real soon, but soon. I'm sure something I've done is on television, re-runs ... you just have to look," he said, with a chuckle.

"Do you have any plans to come here in the near future?"

"Not yet ... when I do, I'll be sure to give you a call. I may take a few more weeks to really relax, then I'll be anxious to do something ...

maybe by the end of next month. I'll let you know."

"So how is everything with Dani? Any hints of a wedding?"

"Everything is good. We're living together ... we have all the benefits of being married, without any of the financial risks ... and that suits me just fine. No, she hasn't pressed the issue. I'm not ready for it anyway; she knows that. She still doesn't have her divorce from Buddy so we don't even discuss a marriage."

"Just checking, Dave. I need some advance warning to make plans to fly out for your wedding ... sure don't want to miss that," I said with a slight laugh.

"Yeah ... right!" He laughed.

"Just make sure I know when you will be here so we can at least have a few drinks ... maybe I'll have the honor of meeting Dani in person."

"That's a good possibility. I'll let you know. Okay, Mike, good talking with you. Now we can both get some sleep. I'll be in touch."

"Thanks, Dave! You take it easy."

Hanging up my phone, I went back to sleep instantly. I awoke to Baron licking my face and hitting me with his huge paw; my clock-radio showed six o'clock - time to go to the park. I fixed a cup of coffee in my travel mug and took Baron for his run in Riverside Park.

Thinking back over our early morning conversation, I concluded everything in Dave's life was going very well and he was extremely happy. He sounded sober, happy and rested. I was anxious to hear what his next movie would be.

Over the next three weeks, I saw nothing in the New York newspapers or the Hollywood fan magazines about Dave.

I would not hear from Dave until Sunday morning, April 16, at 4:45.

"Good morning, Mike. It's Dave. How the hell are you?"

"Wait until I wake up and I'll figure it out. How are you doing?"

"Good ... really, really good. Did you hear Rosemary got married?"

"Rosemary Forsyth? No, I haven't seen anything in the papers here. Who did she marry?"

"Some millionaire businessman ... I hear he's about 10 years older than her. Maybe I was wrong to think the difference in our ages would make such a difference if we got married."

"Well, Dave, you aren't having regrets about breaking up with her, are you? Look at it this way! She must not have really been in love with you; it hasn't been that long since you broke up and she's already found an older man to marry ... and a rich older man at that."

"No ... no regrets about breaking it off. I am much happier with Dani and, you're right. It sure as hell didn't take her long to latch onto another rich old guy," Dave said, then laughed.

"When did she get married?" I asked.

"Thursday or Friday ... I just heard about it last night from a mutual friend."

"So I guess you weren't invited to the wedding."

"No ... I would have gone if I had been invited."

"I bet you would have. Well, you sure dodged the bullet there. I remember not long ago the Hollywood media had you guys practically married."

"Yeah, I know ... and you're right. It is a good thing I didn't fall into that trap; I'd probably be in divorce court again now."

"Well ... at least, you are happy with Dani. She's close to your age, isn't she?" I asked.

"Yeah, I think I'm about four or five years older ... not that it really matters."

"Yeah, that's not bad. Thinking of that though, you were about 12 years younger than Ellie and about 12 years older than Rosemary. Believe me! I think you're better off with a gal like Dani."

"You are 100 percent correct, Mike - and not only is Dani gorgeous, a fine actress, a great hostess ... but she's a really damn good cook, too," Dave said.

"There you have it then ... she's the one you should stay with - just don't rush down the aisle anytime soon."

"Don't worry about that, Mike! It'll be a long time before I do that again and when, and if, I do - it will be for the last time."

"Well, I guess we should just wish Rosemary and her new husband many happy years together," I said.

"Yes, I wish them happiness."

"Have you given any thought to doing any films or television?"

"Actually, that's why I called you. I'm pretty sure I'm going to be doing a movie about a girl who was kidnapped and held in a coffin, buried ... until her father paid the ransom. It happened somewhere in Florida or Georgia. It was based on a real incident."

"Yeah! I remember that. I think it was the Mackie case; he's a home builder in Florida, luxury homes ... his daughter was kidnapped and buried in a box. She almost died. Her dad paid the ransom and the FBI captured the kidnappers and rescued her. It was all over the TV news and papers, a real big story. I think it happened four or five years ago."

"I think you are right, Mike. Someone wrote a book about it and now they're making it, based on the book, into a Movie of the Week for TV."

"Oh, I thought it would be a major film, but I think it will be a good TV movie. Are you a good guy or bad guy?"

"I'll be playing the girl's father ... that is if, and when, Abby gets the details worked out."

"When will you know?" I asked.

"In a few weeks ... I'll let you know."

"Will it be filmed in Florida, Georgia or in LA?"

"Here ... plenty of locations here to match the scenery of both Georgia and Florida."

"Who else will be in the movie?" I asked.

"I have no idea yet who they will be casting. I'll keep you informed. I'm anxious to get back to work and this is the most interesting project that Abby has brought me."

"Well, I am glad you're going back to work. The re-runs of all your films are running out; it will be good for all your fans to see you in something new."

"Yeah, I guess you have a point there, Mike ... and I'm ready for some new challenge."

"Promise me you'll call me the minute everything is confirmed ... what network and when it will be shown."

"I will, Mike; you'll be among the first to know. Okay, get up and take Baron to the park. I'll be in touch later."

"I will ... you take it easy and be sure to call me when you know something firm." The call ended.

70

I was excited to know that Dave was getting back to work. He had not done anything since *O'Hara* ended.

He mentioned this new project would be a TV Movie of the Week and, even though I knew he wanted to do something for the big screen, at least he would be doing something for himself and for his fans.

Dave called me on Saturday morning, April 29, just before eight o'clock. Baron and I had just walked in the door from the park.

"Good morning, Mike. It's Dave. How are you?"

"Doing good, Dave, and you? Don't tell me you are just going to bed."

"No, actually I got up about an hour ago. I'm flying up to LA in a couple of hours. I'm meeting with Abby about the Movie of the Week I told you about and then Dani and I will, finally, be moving into the condo."

"That's nice ... so will you be staying in LA?" I asked.

"Yeah, I'll be there for a few weeks. We will be doing a lot of decorating, things Dani wants to buy to finish off the condo, and I'll be working with Abby on the contract for the movie. I plan on staying there for a few months. I'm keeping the house here so Dani and I will have a place to unwind."

"Good ... I'm glad to hear you are ready to get back to work. Honestly, Dave, to me, you sound better than you have in months. Dani must really be good for your mind and everything else."

"Thanks, Mike! That is good to hear. You're right! I feel better than I have in over a year and I give all the credit to Dani. I'm happy *O'Hara* is over and I took the time to relax and enjoy life. Now, I am ready to work."

"That's great! I'm sure millions of your fans will be happy to see you back ... in any role. I know I will."

"Thanks, Mike! How is Baron ... Rose Marie?"

"They are both well. I can't believe how fast Baron is growing; you would not recognize him. His ears stand up perfectly and he carries his tail just right. Rose Marie and I are still having fun together ... no pressures, and that's good."

"Okay, I just wanted to touch base with you and let you know the Movie of the Week is a solid deal, so the next time we talk I'll be able to tell you all about it. Take it easy and I'll give you a call soon."

"All right! Thanks, Dave! I'll be looking forward to it."

Dave did, indeed, sound better in our last few calls than he had in over a year. I was convinced his relationship with Dani had a lot to do with, not only his happiness, but Dave considerably cutting back on his drinking. I compared how he sounded now, to when he first started living with Rosemary, and I was positive he was happier, more secure and confident.

May 14, 1972, was a beautiful Sunday in New York City. Baron and I were enjoying my coffee on the terrace and the spring-like temperatures climbing into the sixties. Dave called around noon.

"Good morning, Mike ... Dave. How are you doing?"

"Just fine ... just fine, thanks. How is everything with you and Dani?"

"Good, really good. We are settled into our condo, having a great time. Just wanted to let you know we start filming *The Longest Night* this week. It'll be a Movie of the Week for ABC."

"That is really good news, Dave. Do you know who your co-stars will be?"

"Yes! As you know, I'm the father of the kidnapped girl; Sallie Shockley plays her; Phyllis Thaxter plays my wife, Norma. I recommended Jimmy Farentino to play the main kidnapper, John Danbury. Richard Anderson, Mike Farrell and several others are cast. I think you'll like it."

"I'm sure I will. I know Richard Anderson and Phyllis Thaxter guest starred with you in *The Fugitive.* I've heard of Mike Farrell but I've never heard of Sallie Shockley."

"She's a new, young actress; I haven't met her yet. I've worked well with Phyllis, Jimmie and Rick ... so I'm really looking forward to doing it. It has a solid script, based on the book ... so it should be pretty interesting."

"It sounds like it will be. I remember reading about the real kidnapping a couple of years ago. It was a big story on the national TV news when the girl was rescued and the kidnappers were finally caught. So when will we see it on TV?"

"I have no idea. As you know, there will be a lot of post production work before ABC puts it on their broadcast schedule. Maybe just a few months ... I'll give you a call when I know the date for sure."

"Thanks, Dave! I will be certain not to miss it! You have to let me know when you've finished filming it. Give me your objective opinion, okay?"

"Yeah, Mike, I will. In the meantime, watch my re-runs." Dave laughed.

"I do ... I am ... but I want to see something new ... something I haven't already seen over and over," I joked.

"Mike, I'm back in the swing of things. I've told Abby to pile the scripts on me; I want to keep as busy as possible. I need the money," he said, with a big laugh.

"Well, whether you need the money or not, I know you're a lot happier when you have something to do ... so I hope Abby gets you a lot of offers."

"Okay, Mike. I have to run but I'll give you a call and let you know how we are doing on the filming."

"Oh, do you know if you're going to go to Georgia or Florida to film it?" I asked.

"Hell, no, Mike! We'll be doing it right here ... actually, in Thousand Oaks; it's a suburb of LA. I'll be home every night."

"That should make Dani happy."

"Yeah, it will make us both happy. I'll give you a call soon, so take care."

"Thanks, Dave." I hung up the phone.

This Movie of the Week would be Dave's first work since he finished *O'Hara* at the beginning of February and he sounded very excited and anxious to get back to work. He also sounded very well rested and extremely happy with his personal life.

Over the next few weeks, I would see photos of Dave and Dani at various Los Angeles restaurants or going to, or coming from, *A* list parties. He looked great and Dani was absolutely gorgeous.

I could not help but wonder how his life would have been had he pursued Dani and married her instead of Ellie. Would he be as happy after 13 plus years of marriage to Dani? In my mind, I thought he would be. One thing is certain; he would be a lot richer.

Several weeks passed without a word from Dave; I assumed he was very busy with filming the movie. I knew he would call me when he had the chance.

Dave called on Sunday afternoon, June 18, just after one o'clock.

"Mike, it's Dave. How are things with you?"

"Good, Dave. Everything is good. Have you finished the movie yet?"

"Yes, we wrapped it up on Friday. I still don't know when it will air, so don't ask." He laughed. "Everyone connected with it is happy and, from watching the dailies, I am very pleased. I think it will garner some pretty good ratings for ABC."

"Are you pleased with your work in it?" I asked.

"Yeah ... I really am. I feel I felt what the real father felt - his reactions, his fighting to remain calm and focused. I think everyone did outstanding work."

"I'm happy for you, Dave. I can't wait to see it! Please, promise me you'll call me the minute you know the date it will be on; I sure don't want to miss it!"

"Okay, Mike ... I promise I'll give you a call."

"How are things with you and Dani? I've seen some photos in last month's *Photoplay* of you two going into some restaurant, looking like newlyweds," I said in a joking manner.

"Stop that, Mike! You know better than that! Looking happy, okay - but don't assume anything else." He laughed.

"I was just kidding. I know you wouldn't forget to send me an invitation if you set a wedding date."

"I know you were just kidding ... and I will send you an invitation; you may be old and grey by then. I'm going to some town in Louisiana. Abby has me doing a film called *Moon of the Wolf*. We'll be doing it on location so I'll be out of touch for a while."

"Damn! You really are keeping busy, aren't you? What's this movie about? Is it for the big screen?"

"It's about a string of gruesome murders in this small Louisiana town. I'm the sheriff and it doesn't take me long to figure out I'm dealing with a werewolf. It's a horror movie and, no, it's not big screen; it's another ABC Movie of the Week for TV."

"I don't see you tangling with werewolves ... do you like the script? Who will be your co-stars?"

"It's not really my kind of thing, but it is a good script. Barbara Rush and Brad Dillman will be in it; I like working with both of them. I think it may turn out pretty good."

"If you say so, Dave. I'll watch it and let you know my honest opinion."

"We are going on location, a small little Louisiana Bayou town. I like Louisiana; I'm looking forward to it. All right, Mike! I'll run for now and call you in a few weeks."

"Okay, Dave ... thanks for calling and letting me know about the movie. You take it easy."

71

I did not hear from Dave again until Friday night, June 30. My phone rang just after seven, as I was getting ready to go pick Rose Marie up for dinner.

"Hey, Mike! It's Dave. How is everything in the big city?"

"It's going great, Dave ... a little warm but a good start to summer in New York. We had a really bad storm last week ... a hurricane! Can you believe it? I thought they only happened in Florida. Not too much damage here in the city, just a lot of rain. Still I think it's a lot better than what I see you have in LA, with fires and the smog. How are things with you? Have you done the movie in Louisiana or are you still there?"

"Just got back to LA a few days ago. The film is in the can and I'm relaxing for a while. The fires are nowhere near me; they have not threatened any homes, thank God ... and the smog is not as bad as you say. If you lived here long enough, you'd get used to it," he said with a laugh. "How are things with Rose Marie?"

"Good. We are going out to dinner tonight and then to a movie. How is Dani? I meant to ask you the last time we spoke: did you take her to Louisiana with you?"

"She is fine and, no, she stayed home. I was only there a little over seven weeks."

"Did she miss you? Did you miss her?"

"Hell, yes, on both sides, but that is good. As they say, 'absence makes the heart grow fonder.' Anyway, it's good to be home."

"So, tell me, honestly ... did you like the movie? Do you think it is a movie your fans will like you in? Do you know when the film will be aired?"

"Yes, actually, I like the finished product and I hope everyone who sees it will like it. I don't know yet when it will be aired, but I'll give you a call when I do."

"What is next? Do you have anything planned?"

"Not yet ... Abby is looking at a few things I may be interested in doing. I'll let you know but, for now, I'm just going to relax, play some golf, tennis ... and Dani will have us partying some. I can count on that," he said and, again, let out a laugh. "Okay, Mike, I have to run. I just wanted to check in with you, see how you're doing. Take care ... we'll talk soon."

"Good, Dave! Thanks for calling. Be sure to let me know when the movie will be on TV, please."

"I will, Mike ... take care."

I was glad to know Dave was finished with his latest project and was back home with plans to relax. He sounded good, and happy. I did not ask but I did wonder if he and Dani were giving any serious consideration to marriage.

The only thing I missed about living in Los Angeles was being able to see Dave and have drinks or lunch or dinner with him. I appreciated and valued his friendship. The fact that he would take time to give me a call every few weeks showed me that he valued me as a friend, too.

The weeks passed and I found nothing in the media about Dave or the movie, or Dave and Dani for that matter. I knew he was not out of mind for his loyal fans.

Dave called me on Sunday, July 9, just after two o'clock in the morning.

"Hey, Mike! It's me ... are you awake?" Dave asked.

"Yeah, I was just going to bed but, if you're in New York, I'll be happy to meet you for a drink or two."

"Well, I wish I was. It would be good to have some drinks with an old friend. I'm just getting home from a party; hadn't a chance to call you lately, so decided now would be a good time. How are things with you?"

"Everything is good, Dave. How is everything with you ... and Dani?"

"Good, all is going smoothly ... I'm still relaxing ... looking at some prospects Abby has sent me."

"Have you heard when the movie you did in Louisiana will be on TV?" I asked.

"Not firm yet, but it may be sometime in September. I'll let you know so you won't miss it. How are Rose Marie and Baron?"

"Both are doing well, thanks. You would not recognize Baron. When he stands on his hind legs, with his front paws on my shoulders, he is almost as tall as me."

"Really, how much does he weigh now?"

"He is about 98 pounds now. He is beautiful."

"Remember when I met him; he was what ... just a few months old? I looked at the size of his paws and told you he was going to be a big dog," Dave reminded.

"Yes, I remember and you were right. His father weighed over 120 pounds; Baron looks exactly like his father."

"I'm glad for you, that you have him. I wish I could have a dog but, with my schedule, it wouldn't be fair to the dog."

"Well, Dave ... maybe when you retire, you can have a ranch someplace and have a whole pack of dogs," I said with a chuckle.

"Yeah, Mike ... I'll put that on my list of the first things to do ... buy a ranch somewhere and then adopt a whole bunch of dogs from the Humane Society," he said with a laugh. "Hey, though ... don't rush me! I'm nowhere near retirement age!"

"Believe me, Dave! I'm not rushing you into retirement. You're still a young guy and, even when you get 'old and grey,' they will still need 'old men' like you in the movies," I said with a chuckle.

Dave laughed.

"So you haven't decided on any new movies ... television shows?" I asked.

"No ... I'll be doing some guest appearances on talk shows, but no major projects yet. Don't worry; I'll let you know when I do."

"Okay. How is Dani doing? Any word yet on her divorce?"

"No ... it is still in the works, but we are in no rush. Everything is going good for us. I'm going to go, grab some shut-eye. You take it easy; I'll give you a call soon."

"All right, Dave! Thanks for the call ... you take it easy, too."

I was glad to hear from Dave and it was nice he called before three or four o'clock in the morning. I fell asleep immediately after our call ended.

Dave called on Thursday, July 20, at 4:30 in the morning.

"Mike, it's Dave ... how are you?"

"Good, Dave ... and you?"

"Doing well ... I'm going to be in Baltimore for a telethon with Bob Hope for that hurricane you had up there ... Hurricane Agnes. I guess it really did a lot of damage in and around Baltimore. Bob is doing a relief telethon to raise money to help the victims. He asked me to go and I jumped at the chance."

"That is really nice of you, Dave. Will it be telecast live?"

"Yes, it will. I'm not sure which network; I'll let you know."

"Yeah, please let me know ... and will it be broadcast nationwide ... here in New York?" I asked.

"Yes, it will be nationwide. I'll be doing a little comedy skit with Bob, so it will be fun," Dave said.

"That is good. I like it when you do comedy; I think everyone does ... and, with Bob Hope, it has to be funny," I said, then added, "Baltimore isn't too far from here. I wish I could come down and see it ... see you. Will there be a studio audience?"

"I'm not sure. I don't really know ... I'll find out and let you know. Yes, it would be great if you could come down ... maybe you could take the train ... be a lot faster than driving."

"I'll see. I would love to be there. When will it be; do you have a schedule yet?"

"Yeah ... the telethon will run for 24 hours, starting the evening of the 22nd. I'll get the details and call you back; you can let me know if you can make it."

"The 22nd - that's a Saturday! I could make it! I'll have to get someone to take care of Baron but that won't be a problem. Maybe I can get Rose Marie to stay at my apartment; I'll find out and let you know."

"Good. I'll give you a call sometime tomorrow. Take care and we'll talk then."

"Thanks, Dave! I'll look forward to it."

After our call I gave a lot of thought to making the trip to Baltimore and wasn't sure I could really do it. I decided to wait and make a decision when I spoke with Dave the next day.

Dave called me at my office on Friday just before noon.

"Mike, it's me, Dave. We're at the airport waiting to board. There won't be a studio audience; all of us will be manning the telephone banks in between doing skits with Bob. I don't know how long it's going to take, but it looks like we will be flying back to LA as soon as it ends."

"Well, I must say I'm disappointed, but I'll be sure to watch it. Hell, when I see you manning the phone, I'll call in and make a donation."

"That would be good ... do it! I'll give you a call when I'm there."

"Okay, Dave ... thanks! I'll talk with you soon."

72

The Bob Hope Relief Telethon was aired nationwide and I was able to see Dave as he appeared with Bob Hope and then as he was sitting at the dais manning a phone, taking donations. I called and made a donation of $100 but Dave did not answer my call. I would let him know when he called me.

Dave did not call me while he was attending the telethon so I just assumed he was very busy and tired.

He did call me the following week, Sunday afternoon, July 30, around one o'clock.

"Mike, Dave ... sorry I missed calling you last week. It was a very fast moving and busy telethon. Did you call in?"

"That's okay, Dave; I could see you were all busy. Yes, I called in and made a donation. The girl who took my call said she could not transfer me to you and she said a lot of people were asking to be transferred to you. I said you must have a lot of fans; she agreed. From the reports in the New York newspapers, you guys raised a ton of money ... that was really good to hear. Are you back in LA?"

"No, I'm in Palm Springs ... relaxing, playing some golf. How are things with you?"

"Good, everything is going well. One of our client companies offered me a job. The company, Bates Manufacturing, is out of Maine, but their executive offices are here in New York. Anyway, they are diversifying and want me to head up an executive recruiting subsidiary. It is very interesting and offers a good compensation package."

"That is great ... are you going to take the offer?"

"I'm leaning towards it. Norman has been good to me and I don't want to leave him in a lurch. I'll discuss it with him tomorrow; I just got the offer Friday evening. It sounds like a great opportunity. I would be President and Chief Operating Officer ... I'll most likely accept it."

"It sounds too good to pass up. Let me know what you decide ... I certainly wish you good luck."

"Thanks, Dave! So how is everything with you ... Dani? Is she with you there?"

"Everything is fine. She stayed in Los Angeles - had some parties over the weekend she was committed to. That's fine with me; I don't feel like going to parties. I just wanted to relax this weekend."

"I understand that. Does she go to the parties alone or do you trust her with someone to escort her?"

"She does what she pleases; I don't give it a thought. I do what pleases me, so that's the way it is," he said, then laughed.

"Okay, Dave ... that makes sense," I said, trying to convince myself that it did.

I had the gut feeling that he and Dani may be having some bumps in their relationship, but I wasn't sure and I knew, if that were the case, Dave would tell me IF, and when, he wanted.

"I think Dani and I will be taking a vacation to Italy ... not certain yet, but I want to get away and she hasn't been to Europe, so it will be a fun trip."

"That's great. When are you going? How long do you plan on being gone?"

"Oh, if we go, it will be in a week or so. I haven't made any reservations yet. If we go, it will only be for a couple of weeks or so."

"I bet Dani will love it IF you go. You've been there a couple of times. I'm sure you know all the best places to go ... show her a good time."

"Yeah, it will be fun. I want to do this now before I start another project. When we get back, I'll be ready for work. I'll make this my last vacation for a while ... a long while."

"I bet Dani will be impressed to see that you have a lot of fans there, too."

"That doesn't mean anything to her. She knows *The Fugitive* was shown all around the world, and I made *Shoes of the Fisherman* there. We will still have more privacy there than we do here in LA."

"Yeah, I guess you're right. Well, let me know when you decide to go and when you plan on being back home. I don't want to worry, not hearing from you."

Dave laughed. "All right, Mike! I'll make sure to let you know. Don't worry! I'm going to run, but I'll give you a call soon. Take care."

"Thanks, Dave ... I'll be here ... waiting for your call."

Dave sounded good, in good spirits, completely sober. I could easily understand his wanting to take a trip, to take Dani to Europe. I was sure they would both enjoy the trip and the time alone.

On Monday, August 7, I arrived home to find a message from Dave on my answering machine: "Mike, Dave ... we're off to Europe. I'll call you when we're back."

I was sorry I missed his call, but I was glad he decided to take the trip. I would be anxious to see if he would remember to send me a postcard, as he had when he and Ellie were in Italy for the filming of *The Shoes of the Fisherman*.

Saturday morning, September 2, I was awakened at 4:05.

"Hey, Mike! It's time to wake up ... take Baron to his park."

After shaking myself awake, I could tell Dave had been drinking. It was a little past one o'clock in Los Angeles.

"Yeah ... Dave ... thanks for the wake-up call ... and Baron thanks you. So, are you back in the States?"

"Yeah, we've been back a few days. Had a hell of a good trip ... Dani loved it all, especially the food. She collected a lot of recipes so I think I'll be eating a lot of Italian food for months to come."

"Hey, I'm pissed off at you! I didn't get even a postcard!"

"Aww ... sorry, Mike! I don't think we sent a single postcard ... to anyone ... so don't feel bad. How are things with you? Did you take that job?"

"Yes, and I love it! It's very challenging, far more complex than what I was used to. I hired my own people and everything is going great. I have an office three times larger than I had with MSI; I think I made the right move. Norm had no ill feelings; he agreed it was a great opportunity for me."

"That's good to hear. Glad to know you are enjoying it. How are Rose Marie and Baron?"

"They are both doing well. As you can hear, Baron is saying hello to you," I said, as Baron let out a couple of deep barks in the background loud enough for Dave to hear. "So tell me, did you spend all your time in Italy?"

"Mostly ... we did go to Paris so Dani could do some shopping."

"That was nice of you. Do you have any money left? Were you mobbed by millions of your fans?"

"Yeah, I have a few dollars and, yes, I signed a few autographs and, yes, Dani was impressed," he said with a laugh.

"That's good. So what's next? Are you ready to work? What is going to be on your work schedule?"

"Abby sent me over a pile of scripts so I'll be doing a lot of reading over the next few weeks. I don't know yet what I'll be doing but I'll call and let you know when I've committed to something."

"Please don't forget to call me! I don't want to miss seeing your next project."

"Don't worry, Mike! I'll call ... I'll call," Dave said as he laughed.

"Do you know if you'll be doing a feature film or something for television?"

"I have a stack of scripts ... both feature films and TV. I have to see the subject before I decide. I'll let you know."

"What about casting ... will you know who will be in the film before you commit?"

"Some of the projects, yeah, I'll know; others haven't been cast as yet. It does matter to me who I'll be working with ... so relax; I'll give you a call when I know."

"Okay ... okay, Dave! I just want to make sure it will be something I want to see you in. By the way, I haven't seen any ads for *Moon of the Wolf* yet ... do you know when it will be broadcast?"

"Yes. Actually, I just opened my mail and it will be on ABC on the 26th ... prime time ... so watch it. Don't miss it ... and that's an order!" he said, then chuckled.

"Yes, Sheriff! I won't miss it! I promise."

"Okay, Mike, I just got home so I'm going to bed. You take it easy. We'll talk soon."

"You got home early ... get some sleep. Thanks for the call."

73

Dave called me on Sunday afternoon at 1:45, September 17. It was a beautiful afternoon. I had the terrace doors open as I was cleaning my apartment. Baron was relaxing on the terrace.

"Mike, it's me, Dave. How are you doing?"

"Good, Dave, and how are you doing?"

"Good ... very good. I've signed on to do another Movie of the Week ... looks good, I like the script. I'll be going to Salt Lake City; we'll be shooting most of the film there. I think you'll like it, too.

"I play an ex-army pilot, now a radio station traffic reporter, flying a helicopter and reporting on the morning traffic rush hour. I spot a gang of bank robbers leaving with a hostage, a female. I alert the station to contact the cops and I follow the get-away car; they transfer to a helicopter and the fun begins. What do you think so far?"

"Hey, Dave, I like it! When the gang transfers to a helicopter, what the hell do you do, chase them?"

"Of course ... and, later, I'm joined by a police helicopter and it is becomes a pretty dramatic, fast-paced chase."

"Do you catch them ... save the girl; no doubt she's a beauty, right?"

"You'll have to see it. I'm not going to tell you the whole plot ... how it ends," Dave said and laughed.

"Oh ... just like the end of *The Fugitive* ... you keep me in suspense. I get it! All right, Dave! You have to tell me the title and when it will be on TV. How long will you be in Salt Lake?"

"I'm not sure yet, probably a week, 10 days. The producer is Alan Armer who did a lot of *The Fugitive* episodes. Billy Graham will be directing; we worked together on *The Fugitive,* too. I like them both."

"I know you like to fly ... do you know how to fly a helicopter?"

"Hell, no! I won't really be doing the flying, but it will look like I am. I'll let you know after we've finished."

"When are you going? Can you take Dani?"

"Probably the end of this month. Dani won't be going; she has commitments here."

"Well, that's nice ... as you say, 'absence makes the heart grow fonder'. I'm sure you'll find a good, neighborhood bar to spend your relaxing time. Salt Lake City, that's the seat of the Mormon Church, isn't it?"

"Yeah ... it is, but I don't plan on going to church while I'm there," he said and let out a little laugh.

"I didn't think you would. Do you know who your co-stars will be?"

"Ralph Meeker is the main guy, everyone else is new ... no one you would recognize."

"That's good ... nice to know they are giving some of the unknown actors a chance. Working with you may be a big boost to their careers. I hope none of them will be too intimidated by you."

"I'm sure they won't be intimidated by me. I always get to know the cast, break down any inhibitions anyone may have ... as long as they know their lines, and are prepared, that's good with me."

"It really sounds like it's going to be a good movie; you have to tell me more when you are finished with it."

"I'll give you a few more teasers, but you will have to wait until it's aired."

"Which network will it be on? What is the title?"

"CBS ... good people there ... I think we'll get some good ratings from them. Right now, it's called *Birds of Prey* but that could change."

"Okay ... I'll be patient. How is everything with you and Dani?"

"Good ... we're doing well. She's been trying out her Italian recipes ... we have a few friends in for dinner; she puts on a real feast every time. We follow dinner with a little poker. Every one of our guests enjoy a good dinner and a fun, relaxing evening."

"I'm glad to hear you are relaxing and enjoying yourselves, Dave. You both deserve it. Will you make sure to call me when you finish in Salt Lake, let me know what you think of the finished movie? Do you have anything else lined up?"

"Of course, I will! I'm trying to decide on a few interesting scripts - action and crime plots. I'd really like a comedy but I guess no one thinks I'm funny," Dave said with a laugh.

"You don't really believe that ... I think you're funny, when you want to be. Anyone who has seen you with Bob Hope, or your Hollywood Palace skits, knows you're funny."

"Yeah ... a little bit, maybe. I think television really stereo-typed me starting with *Richard Diamond* though and, especially, *The Fugitive*. Then you have to consider the major films: *The Green Berets, The Shoes of the Fisherman, Marooned* ... almost all of them, my roles have been serious, dramatic characters."

"Yeah, Dave, but you are so good in those kind of roles ... maybe you should ask Mr. Greshler to flat-out promote you to the studios or casting directors for a good comedy script," I suggested, interrupting him.

"You have a good point there, Mike. To be honest, I've never asked him to do that ... but I will."

"Yeah, Dave ... look at Doris Day, Rock Hudson and Tony Randall in the *Pillow Talk* movie, which led to *Send Me No Flowers*, which was basically on the same theme as *Pillow Talk*. Rock Hudson, Doris Day and Tony Randall are hilarious in both of them. You know them; why don't you talk to them? Maybe they can even help you get a comedic role in a big screen movie. Listen to me! An idiot who knows nothing about the movie or television business giving YOU advice on how to get a role," I said and let out a sincere laugh.

"Actually, Mike, I would never call you an idiot, that you are not. You just gave me some good advice. I had never thought to even suggest to Abby to promote me for comedy roles. I agree with you, too; Doris, Rock and Tony are great in those movies. They were so long ago. How do you remember them?"

"Our oldest sister, Judy, took my sister and I to see both of them; she had a crush on Rock Hudson ... and you. I really liked them. As you know, I met Rock Hudson in Indianapolis when he did the promotion for *Battle Hymn;* it is the true story of Air Force Colonel Dean Hess ... "

"Yeah, I know. I remember it ... Rock was outstanding!"

"Yeah, he was. It was through my Air Force club. The Air Force Recruiting Officers took me and some of the other boys to the premier and we met the real Colonel Hess and Rock Hudson. Colonel Hess gave me a pair of his colonel's eagles."

"That's interesting; do you still have the eagles?"

"I gave them to my little brother when I joined the Air Force. My point, though, is that Hudson was hilarious in *Pillow Talk* and his role in *Battle Hymn* was a serious, dramatic role," I said.

"Yeah, I know ... I agree with you."

"What I'm saying, Dave - and I am not being biased - but I think you are just as good of an actor as, maybe somewhat better than, Rock Hudson ... and I think you can play a comedic role just as good as he does."

"Thanks, Mike! I'm going to talk this over with Abby ... see what he can do. Let me ask you, though ... how do you think I would be looked at by fans that have me stereo-typed as *Richard Kimble*, then see me doing a comedy like *Pillow Talk*?"

"Dave, your fans love you! Of course, they became your fans, mainly through *The Fugitive*, but that ended in 1967. You have done so many other films and television appearances, I think IF Mr. Greshler could get you a good comedic role, your fans would see your funny side and love you even more."

"Okay, Mike ... I'll take your word ... your unbiased opinion ... and push for a good *Pillow Talk* type role."

"Good ... let me know when you get one. I definitely won't miss seeing you in the role."

"You'll be the first to know ... well, maybe the third or fourth to know, but you know I'll call you. Okay, I'm going to run, so we'll talk later."

"All right, Dave ... keep me informed. Thanks for calling."

This was one of our deepest conversations regarding Dave's career. It was the first conversation where I gleaned his inner desire to do comedic roles and where he more fully disclosed his inner thoughts that Hollywood's studios and casting people had actually stereo-typed him. If my point of view and sage advice would prove beneficial for him, I would really feel great.

74

Dave called next on Sunday, October 22, just after nine o'clock in the morning.

"Good morning, Mike. It's me. How are things going with you?"

"Well ... very well ... are you back from Salt Lake City?"

"Yeah, I've been back a few days. We finished the film here in the studio. Now I'll be heading to Jerusalem, Israel, for a film titled *Sabra Command*. It's a pretty good script ... I'm a colonel in the U.S. Air Force - a weapons expert, supposed to be on vacation in Israel. The U.S. Air Force accidentally drops a nuclear warhead in the desert and I am called in by the CIA to find and disarm it before the terrorists get a hold of it."

"Hey, Dave! That sounds like a great plot and very timely, too, with all the unrest over there. However, being ex-Air Force, I hate to tell you OUR Air Force would never be so incompetent, especially with a nuclear warhead," I said with a chuckle.

"Well ... be that as it may, that's what the script says, and it sounds good to me, so I'm gonna do the film," he said, then laughed.

"Okay, I'll watch it just because you're the star. Who else will be in it?"

"No one you would recognize. They're mostly foreign actors. It's not a big budget, major studio film. It's an independent film company, but the script is interesting to me and the pay is good."

"It sounds like it will be a hit. How long will you be over there? Can you take Dani with you?"

"We may be there anywhere from four to six weeks and, definitely, I am taking Dani."

"That's good. I bet she is excited. Have you ever been there before?"

"Dani is excited and no, neither of us have been to the Middle East, or Israel. It will be interesting to see that part of the world."

"Well, when you get back, please give me a call and let me know all about it, and your experiences there. I have a lot of Jewish friends here in New York, mostly business acquaintances, but really good people. I hope they have good security for you; that part of the world is very volatile, especially with the Palestinians."

"Yeah, I know. Things have quieted down since the Israelis kicked the Palestinians' ass in the seven-day war back in '67. The Israeli military and police forces are among the very best. I don't think we'll have to worry about our safety."

"Dave, just be careful anyway. Do you know anything about when *Birds of Prey* will be broadcast?"

"No, haven't heard anything on it yet. When I do I'll be sure to call you. Okay, Mike, I have to go now, but I'll be in touch before we leave for Israel."

"Okay, Dave. Let me know if you have to fly through New York. I'd love to come out and meet you at the airport, meet Dani and maybe have a drink or two between planes. I don't care what time it would be."

"I don't know our flight arrangements but, if that's a possibility, I'll be sure to call you. You take it easy. We'll talk soon."

"Thanks for calling, Dave."

It was obvious to me that Dave was back, throwing himself into work. This new movie came almost immediately after he finished the Movie of the Week, *Birds of Prey*. He sounded good on the phone - sober, happy and interested in his new project.

I did not hear from Dave until Friday morning, November 3, at 5:15.

"Mike, I hope I didn't wake you. We're taking off for Israel but we're not going to have time between planes in New York for you to meet us. Perhaps when we come back, we will have the time. Sorry to disappoint you."

"You didn't wake me, Dave, and that's okay. I understand. Just make sure you and Dani are careful over there. I'm sure the Palestinian terrorists would love to take you prisoner."

"Don't worry about that at all, Mike! We'll be fine ... and we'll also be careful. I'll touch base with you when we get back. Hopefully, I can call you from JFK and we could meet there for some drinks."

"That would be great, Dave. I'd like it if we could; it's been a long time since we had a drink together."

"Yeah, it has ... I'll give you a call when we're back. You take it easy."

"I will, Dave ... thanks for calling." The call ended.

I was certain Dave was anxious to get this project underway.

I knew he would get a little nervous just before they started filming but, after the first day of action, he would be fully immersed in his character and everything would go smoothly for him.

I would continue scanning the fan magazines as well as the New York newspapers to see if there were any articles or photos regarding Dave, his projects or he and Dani and their relationship before wasting my money and buying them. The remainder of November yielded nothing in the media about Dave.

Dave called me just after noon, at 12:10, on Sunday, December 10. He was calling from Los Angeles, not JFK Airport.

"Mike, it's Dave ... we're home ... in LA. We did not even have time to give you a call when we changed planes in New York. It was very late and we had to go through customs and rush to the gate for the flight to LA."

"That's okay, Dave, no problem. It would have been nice to see you and have the chance to meet Dani, but I certainly understand. So, how was your trip? How was the film ... do you like it?"

"Mike, it was a disaster! I have never worked with people who are supposed to be professional, know the business - but couldn't get it together! These assholes are the worst bunch of incompetents I've ever dealt with. They didn't have locations arranged for ... paid for in advance; they didn't even have all the permits required, which caused one delay after another. Most of the crew were inept at the simplest task ... even some of the actors kept flubbing their lines. The director ... what an amateur! I hated every minute!"

"Wow, Dave! I've never heard you so angry! I can't believe you had so many problems! Had you ever worked with any of the actors?"

"No ... and I never will again. Most of the crew were Israelis and they know next to nothing about making a movie. Mike, it was the worst experience I've ever had in this business."

"Was there anything you did like - the scenery, the people, the food?"

"Israel is beautiful; the people are nice, friendly. The food is good. However, lucky for me, I had Dani and Dani can really cook! Greg Peck and his wife were there doing a film so we had them over for dinner several times. Only problem: where we were staying, the electrical wiring was lousy and Dani kept blowing fuses, which was really funny. Lucy's son, Desi, is working on Greg's film and he joined us a couple of times. Being with Dani and away from the set was the only happy times I had."

"So I guess it need not be said you are happy to be home!"

"You can say that again; I don't plan on going back there again."

"What about the movie? Before you went over you told me it was a good script. What about now that you've done it; do you think it will do well at the box office? When will it be released?"

"No, I don't think it will do well. I'm just glad it's over and I can move on. Who the hell knows when it'll be released? We'll see."

"You don't blame Mr. Greshler for getting you into it, do you?"

"Hell, no! I got myself into it ... no one to blame but myself. So Mike, how are things in New York with you?"

"They're good ... I'm settled into my new job, things are going very well."

"How are Rose Marie and Baron?"

"Both of them are doing well, Baron says 'hi' to his Uncle Dave. So what will you be doing next?"

"We are going to just relax ... enjoy Christmas. We may go to Palm Springs for a while ... no definite plans. Are you staying in New York or going to visit your family in Indiana?"

"I am staying here; it doesn't look like there will be good weather for driving. I'll stay here, relax and maybe celebrate with Rose Marie. What kind of film is Gregory Peck doing?"

"He's doing a western ... says he likes it."

"A western in Israel? What the hell is wrong with California, New Mexico ... Nevada? I've never heard of a film, a western being done by Hollywood actors in Israel," I said with a little laugh.

"It's not unusual ... done all the time. A lot are done in Italy ... we call them 'Spaghetti Westerns,'" Dave said as he laughed.

"Okay, I guess it is as you always tell me: 'things are not always what they seem to be.'"

"Yeah. Well, Mike ... I have to run so we'll talk soon. If we don't talk beforehand, have a Merry Christmas and the same for Rose Marie and Baron."

"Thanks, Dave, and the same to you and Dani. Talk later."

***

To read the remainder of the story, be sure to look for *David Janssen – Our Conversations, The Final Years* at Amazon.

40791287R00203

Made in the USA
Charleston, SC
16 April 2015